Old Ironsides

Old Ironsides

THE MILITARY BIOGRAPHY OF
OLIVER CROMWELL

Frank Kitson

WEIDENFELD & NICOLSON

Weidenfeld & Nicolson

The Orion Publishing Group Ltd
Orion House, 5 Upper Saint Martin's Lane, London WC2H 9EA

British Library Cataloguing-in-Publication Data
A catalogue record for this book is available from the British Library

ISBN 0-297-84688-4

Distributed in the United States by
Sterling Publishing Co Inc., 387 Park Avenue South, New York
NY 10016-8810

Printed and bound in Great Britain by
Butler & Tanner Ltd, Frome and London

Contents

List of Maps

Foreword by Julian Thompson

In a commemorative publication issued by *The Times* in 1992 to mark the 350th anniversary of the Civil War, in a section headed 'Fighting for Parliament', Oliver Cromwell rates over four times the column inches given to the Earl of Manchester, the Earl of Essex, Sir Thomas Fairfax and Sir William Waller. This is a reflection of the widespread belief that he was the chief military opponent of King Charles I. As Frank Kitson points out in this book, those who believe that, ignore the fact that it was Essex, Waller, Manchester and Fairfax who commanded Parliament's armies against Charles I, and not by any stretch of the imagination Oliver Cromwell. So why does a man who in 1642, at the age of 43, had never commanded any troops, started with no military knowledge whatsoever, and fought his last battle nine years later, rate as a great commander? Frank Kitson makes this clear in his soldier's study of Oliver Cromwell.

At the outbreak of the Civil War in England in 1642, there was no standing army. The only formed bodies of troops were the trained bands in the major cities, and county militias. These were mostly poorly trained and indifferently led, and their terms of service limited them to employment in the defence of their city or county. There was, however, a substantial body of English and Scottish officers who had gained much experience fighting as mercenaries on the continent of Europe during the Thirty Years War. Nearly all the senior commanders on both sides in the Civil War had served in the Dutch, Swedish, Russian, Imperial (Habsburg) and various German armies. For example, Prince Rupert, who became the Royalist cavalry commander, and his brother Prince Maurice came to England with over 100 professional officers from the Dutch and German armies. Other commanders who had fought in the European wars included Sir William Verney, Sir John Meldrum, Philip Skippon, Sir Charles Lucas, Sir Charles Wheeler, Sir Jacob Astley, Edward and Richard Feilding, the Earl of Oxford, the Earl of Essex, George Goring, John Byron, Sir William Balfour, Sir James Ramsey and Thomas Fairfax.[1] Oliver Cromwell had yet to see service. To assist the professionals in training their troops, and provide guidance to all officers, there were a number of what we would now call training pamphlets available, such as John Cruso's *Militarie Instructions for the Cavallrie*, based on the practices in the Dutch army, but easily changed to suit the circumstances of the Civil War in England.

Cromwell, as MP for Huntingdon, began his military career as the commander of a troop of horse, around 60 horses and men. It is not clear what, if any, part Cromwell played in Edgehill, the first battle of the Civil War. But it marked the beginning of his military education, for as Frank Kitson points out, he quickly concluded, as Rupert had before him, that cavalry must maintain their momentum in the charge, rather than slow to a walk to discharge their pistols, before increasing speed over the last few yards – the favoured practice at the time. To be effective, troopers had to be able to use their weapons while controlling their horses; hence the necessity for thorough training. He was also convinced that only men of spirit, who believed in the cause for which they fought, would be any use on the battlefield.

He was soon given his chance to put his ideas into practice, when commissioned as a colonel to raise a regiment of horse, to become famous as the 'Ironsides'. He also learned much from Meldrum and Fairfax. The latter was a charismatic man, described by Kitson as 'usually a silent and mild man, but he became a whirlwind of skilfully directed ferocity whenever the enemy appeared. He was tall, with black hair and very dark eyes, and was generally known as Black Tom. He was hugely admired and even loved by his men. He had started his military career at the age of seventeen . . . he was still only 31 years old.' Fairfax was responsible for raising the New Model Army, something else for which Cromwell is often, wrongly, credited.

Cromwell was a fine horse-trainer and strict disciplinarian, who exercised his men hard, ensuring they had the best mounts obtainable. In 1644, after taking part in a number of engagements, he was appointed lieutenant general of horse under the Earl of Manchester. That year, at Marston Moor, Cromwell commanded the left wing of the combined Scottish Parliamentary army, in the largest battle ever fought on English soil, with more than 40,000 troops engaged. This gave him experience in commanding what modern soldiers call a force of all arms: in his case cavalry, infantry and artillery. The right wing, by custom in those days the senior command, was under Fairfax. The battle was a Parliament victory thanks to Cromwell, who took his cavalry round to the rear of the Royalist line under the cover of darkness – albeit at the suggestion of Fairfax. But a successful night move and attack in darkness by a large body of cavalry, notwithstanding a bright moon, can be carried out only by well-trained and well-commanded troops. If any proof of Cromwell's genius as a trainer and growing ability as a commander is required, Marston Moor provides it.

The following year, Cromwell was second-in-command to Fairfax at the crushing defeat of the Royalist army at Naseby. Although Cromwell played a key role at Naseby, the credit for the victory goes to Fairfax. Cromwell's first independent command came in what is sometimes called the second Civil War, which began in 1648 when Charles persuaded the Scots to invade England. In 1648 Cromwell defeated the Scots at Preston.

The following year saw the trial of King Charles, in which Cromwell played a leading role. His famous sense of humour was at its most loutish when he flicked ink at the other commissioners as he bullied them into signing the King's death warrant. Fairfax had been made a commissioner but refused to take part. In what Frank Kitson rightly calls an act of judicial murder, Charles I was beheaded on 30 January 1649.

Now began Cromwell's most impressive period of command. He was appointed commander-in-chief and Lord Lieutenant in Ireland, where the Catholic Anglo-Irish gentry and some Protestants were continuing a campaign of rebellion which had begun in 1641. Cromwell's campaign was faultless, tactically speaking. The fighting was not particularly bloody, and on every occasion bar two when he took a town he allowed the inhabitants and garrison to depart unharmed. But he is remembered for the two exceptions: Drogheda and Wexford. For these his name is execrated in Ireland for the massacre of Irish Catholics; as so often, especially in that country, myth gets confused with fact. Most of the dead at Drogheda were English Royalists, or Irish Protestants fighting on the Royalist side. At Wexford, the killing was done in spite of Cromwell's orders to the contrary. Far more damaging to future Anglo–Irish relations and worthy of Irish abhorrence was Cromwell's settlement, which resulted in mass evictions, so that by 1656, two-thirds of the land in Ireland was in the hands of new owners.

On his return from Ireland, Cromwell was appointed Lord General for the campaign against the Scots. The young Charles II had landed in Scotland and another invasion of England looked imminent. With George Monk as his lieutenant general of the ordnance, the campaign that followed showed Cromwell at his most brilliant. He inflicted a crushing defeat on the Scots at Dunbar, after a night approach march and dawn attack. In one of the touches of wry humour that are found throughout this book, Frank Kitson in describing the English horse pursuing the Scots for a good distance adds that, before doing so, 'they halted to sing Psalm 117, which would have delayed them no longer than it takes to tighten a girth'. Kitson, as a rider to hounds, should know.

The following year, the Scots invaded England more or less down the route of the present-day M6. Cromwell, then in Edinburgh, marched south at the astonishing, for those days, rate of twenty miles a day, covering 300 miles in three weeks. At Worcester he caught up and inflicted another comprehensive defeat on the Scots. The survivors fled north, to find Monk in total control of the country, which was governed from England until the Restoration nine years later. Cromwell remained Lord General but his soldiering days were over.

The author does not attempt to assess the next phase of Cromwell's life, as head of state. But he does observe that republican efforts to present Cromwell as the 'purveyor of freedom and even as the founder of our democratic institutions' are somewhat overdone, given his record of ruling the country through the army; dissolving Parliament; and enforcing heavy taxation and repressive laws, including abolishing Christmas, horse racing and football.

Cromwell was certainly no egalitarian or social reformer. Although his way of talking to soldiers, his practical jokes and humour, and his love of horses, endeared him to his men, he brooked no ill discipline. Some men and officers who mutinied were shot. It is fashionable in some circles to portray the Civil War as a conflict fought by the nobility and gentry against the common people. This is a distortion. The divide was between those who supported the King and those who backed Parliament, and between Catholics and Anglicans on the one hand and Presbyterians and 'Independents', of whom Cromwell was one, on the other. Like most civil wars before and since, it divided families: brother fought against brother, and father against son. For Cromwell his overriding concern was wholehearted support for Parliament; until, that is, it thwarted him.

Frank Kitson's summary of Cromwell's talents makes it clear that he deserves the title of great commander. He learned fast; he was energetic; he had a good eye for ground; he had both physical and moral courage; he was a good operational and logistic planner; he was bold and innovative; like Napoleon, he understood the principle of concentrating his force against part of the enemy army and defeating that, before turning on the remnants; he could delegate and did not allow himself to become immersed in one part of the battle to the detriment of his control of the whole. Perhaps above all, he was a great trainer.

In this last attribute, as Frank Kitson points out, he should perhaps be remembered as the 'father' of the British army, since many of his principles were adopted by Charles II's army at the Restoration. Although only one of Cromwell's regiments remains intact to this day: the Coldstream Guards (Monk's Regiment of foot), the Household Cavalry Regiment includes the Blues, or Royal Horse Guards, formed from Colonel Unton Croke's Parliamentary regiment of horse. But Cromwell's spirit marches on in the British army's dedication to its duty, its humour, its professionalism, and above all its willingness to close with the enemy.

Julian Thompson

1 · Cromwell's World

Oliver Cromwell is sometimes regarded as a politician who took to soldiering. More frequently he is seen as a general who took advantage of his position as the commander-in-chief to overturn the political institutions of the day and establish himself as the ruler of the country. Although both of these contentions are superficially correct, they miss the point. Cromwell was in fact an intensely religious man who used both soldiering and politics, often at the same time, to achieve his underlying aim of leading the people to God.

Oliver Cromwell was born in 1599 and lived until 1658. Surprisingly for one who became so proficient as a soldier, he had no military experience whatsoever until he was 43 years old and the period during which he was active in this field was limited to the ten years between 1642 and 1652. The purpose of this book is to examine his performance as a military commander in the widest sense. To do this, it will be necessary to show how he forged the instrument that he later used and also to show how his gradually increasing political influence assisted in promoting his military position. Before this can be done, it is necessary to take a brief look at the world in which he lived and at the main events that occurred in his life before he embarked on his career as a soldier.

THE MOST INFLUENTIAL event of the sixteenth century was without doubt the Reformation, which started in Germany and spread throughout Europe in different ways and for different reasons. Although in Europe as a whole the Reformation involved a great deal of theological debate and doctrinal rearrangement, in England it took hold as a by-product of Henry VIII's dynastic and matrimonial requirements, and was conducted in such a way as to avoid excessive dogmatic excitement by continuing systems of worship along roughly the same lines as before. The aim was not so much to reshape theology as to remove the Pope's influence from the running of the Church and to transfer the material assets of the monasteries to the King. In putting this arrangement into effect, no one was more committed and effective than the King's great minister and Lord Chancellor, Thomas Cromwell, Earl of Essex, who ultimately fell out of favour and was executed for treason in 1540.

Thomas Cromwell had a sister whose son, Richard Williams, he employed. Richard amassed a vast fortune while working for his uncle and changed his name to Cromwell. He died in 1546 leaving a son, Henry Cromwell, who lived in a grand house built by extending the former Hinchingbrooke nunnery just to the west of Huntingdon. Henry, who was knighted in the reign of Queen Elizabeth, had six sons and five daughters. The oldest son, Oliver, inherited Hinchingbrooke when his father died in 1604. Like his father, Oliver was knighted. Both father and son played leading roles in the county such as representing it in Parliament and acting as High Sheriff. Both were highly regarded for their generosity and geniality.

Sir Oliver had five brothers and five sisters. One of these brothers, Robert Cromwell, was the father of Oliver, the subject of this book. Young Oliver was named after his rich uncle at Hinchingbrooke, who was also his godfather. He was thus the great-grandson of the Richard Cromwell who started life as Williams and laid the foundations of the family fortune. Oliver and his five sisters were brought up by his father Robert in a house in Huntingdon, itself an extension of a former small monastery. As a result of having so many uncles and aunts, the young Oliver found himself blessed with a large number of cousins. In order to get a general idea of the family within which he grew up, it is worth looking briefly at some of his relations.

His uncle Sir Oliver of Hinchingbrooke was a lifelong Royalist who in his old age gave extensive financial support to the King in the Civil War. His son Henry fought for the King throughout and would have had his estates sequestered but for the intervention of his cousin Oliver. Another uncle married the daughter of the Chief Justice of Chester and was himself knighted. One of Oliver's aunts married Sir Francis Barrington; their grand-daughter married the prominent Parliamentarian and lawyer Oliver St John, who was therefore Oliver's first cousin once removed. Another aunt married John Hampden, whose son of the same name was another prominent supporter of Parliament. This son and Viscount Saye and Sele were represented by St John in the famous ship money case. A third aunt married Richard Whalley. Her son became one of Cromwell's closest supporters in the army. Both Robert Cromwell and his son Oliver were offered and declined knighthoods, presumably because they did not feel that they were rich enough to undertake the duties involved: they paid the statutory fine instead.

AFTER KING HENRY VIII's death the English version of the Protestant religion was refined and consolidated by Archbishop Cranmer during the reign of King Edward VI. It was then overturned, to the accompaniment of much burning of martyrs, by the Roman Catholic Queen Mary. When Elizabeth came to the throne in 1558 she restored it, complete with a full ecclesiastical hierarchy of priests and bishops, together with Cranmer's incomparable Prayer Book. In the early part of her reign, she pursued a policy of moderation towards her Roman Catholic subjects, but this became more difficult with the passage of time, because Roman Catholic plots, backed by Spain, increased. Gradually the whole country united behind the Queen to fend off the Spanish menace, and a general hatred of both Spain and Roman Catholicism ensued.

Long before Elizabeth died the Scots had settled down with a Presbyterian form of the Protestant religion based on the teachings of

Calvin. In its purest form there were no bishops within the Presbyterian Church, but James VI, son of Mary Queen of Scots, reintroduced them for purely administrative purposes. He succeeded to the throne of England as King James I in 1603; on his way from Scotland to London he stayed with the Cromwells at Hinchingbrooke. In order to avoid the expense of war he strove to avoid conflict with Spain, thereby causing offence to many of his subjects who still regarded Spain as the great enemy. He caused even greater offence by leaving much of the running of the government to young favourites such as the Duke of Buckingham. In matters of religion he was more successful, continuing to back the Church of England as established by his predecessor, whilst at the same time remaining a Calvinist himself and ensuring that those of his subjects who held similar views were not inconvenienced in the exercise of their religion. To this end, he appointed few High Church bishops.

The Thirty Years War broke out in 1618 when James's son-in-law the Elector Palatine, who was regarded as the Protestant champion of Europe, accepted the throne of Bohemia, contrary to the wishes of the Habsburg Holy Roman Emperor. At this time James's unpopularity increased because of his refusal to back the Elector, which he could not do without alienating the King of Spain, also a Habsburg. On the other hand, James did allow a privately raised and financed band of Englishmen under the command of Sir Horace Vere to go and fight under his son-in-law's banner. Many of those who took part in the English Civil War 24 years later got their first taste of military service in this way.

In 1625 James I died and was succeeded by his son King Charles, who continued his father's dependence on Buckingham. Buckingham became even more unpopular in 1628 after leading an unsuccessful expedition to relieve the Huguenots (French Calvinists) at La Rochelle. When Parliament assembled in March, it refused to vote the money needed to continue the campaign until the King had given assurances on a number of matters connected with the raising of money without the consent of Parliament and imprisoning men without trial. These points were incorporated into a Petition of Rights, which the King accepted, albeit with certain mental reservations, in order to get the money needed for the prosecution of the war. After several more stormy exchanges between the King and Parliament, he dismissed both houses, hoping that there would be some successes against the French to report by the time that Parliament next assembled. In August Buckingham was murdered in Portsmouth, just as he was about to set off on another expedition to relieve La Rochelle.

Parliament reassembled early in 1629, by which time the Huguenots had surrendered, much to the distress of the many English Protestants who had Presbyterian leanings. If the King thought that he would become more popular as a result of Buckingham's death, he was quickly disillusioned. Parliament now turned its attention towards religion, which was a tricky subject, because the King was not only married to a French Roman Catholic but was supporting a High Church Protestant group known as the Arminians who were considered more tolerant towards Roman Catholics than the law permitted. The Commons therefore put forward a resolution that whoever furthered either Popery or Arminianism, or collected, or even paid, certain taxes, was to be regarded as a public enemy. Following the death of Buckingham, Parliament turned its hatred against the Lord Treasurer, whom they accused of raising taxes illegally and of being a Roman Catholic. When members tried to carry a Remonstrance, the King announced an adjournment, which was followed by violent scenes in the House as several members held the Speaker in his chair while the Remonstrance was carried. Parliament then dispersed and did not meet again for eleven years.

CROMWELL WAS EDUCATED at the Grammar School in Huntingdon, after which he spent one year at Sidney Sussex College, Cambridge. His studies there were cut short by the death of his father in 1617, which obliged him to return home to help his mother. Three years later he married Elizabeth Bourchier, the daughter of a London merchant. Having reached the age of 21 a few months earlier, he was able to take possession of his father's estates, consisting of the house in Huntingdon and various bits of farmland and urban property, which he continued to look after for the next eleven years. Little is known of him during this period. He was basically a gentleman farmer who enjoyed such pursuits as hunting and hawking. Later in his life he was well known for having an eye for a horse and also for his skill in horse management, an aptitude that he must have developed at this time.

In January 1628 Oliver Cromwell was returned to Parliament as one of the two members for the town of Huntingdon; the other member was James Montagu, a younger son of the Earl of Manchester. He therefore witnessed the stirring events that took place there in 1628 and 1629. Montagu's brother Sidney had the previous year bought Hinchingbrooke from Sir Oliver Cromwell, who then moved to another large house at Ramsey some eight miles to the north.

At about this time a feud developed amongst the leading men of Huntingdon regarding the disposal of a sizeable bequest left to the town. One of the parties to the dispute persuaded the King to issue Huntingdon with a new charter, which amongst other things included a provision that their opponents, including Cromwell, should be banned from holding public office in the town. Cromwell was so incensed that he spoke violently against the ruling and was obliged to make a formal apology to the Privy Council in London. After that, he no longer felt that he could remain in Huntingdon. He sold most of his property and moved to the neighbouring town of St Ives, where he leased land, thus becoming little better than a tenant farmer. It is likely that his annual income as well as his status suffered a decline at this point.[1]

Also around this time, Cromwell became ill and, whether connected with his illness or not, he experienced what can best be described as a spiritual awakening. It is difficult to know whether the illness sparked off the spiritual crisis or whether the conversion came gradually over a number of years independently of the illness. All that can be said is that when he was in London in 1628 he went to see a well-known doctor, who told him that both his lungs and his digestion were affected and that he was suffering from melancholy. It is also known that in his early twenties he was no more than ordinarily interested in spiritual matters and that by his mid-thirties he had developed what can best be described as a religious obsession, which became the mainspring of his life.

Thereafter his speech and his writings are full of quotes from the Bible, mainly the Old Testament, and he regarded himself as having been 'saved'. He saw the hand of God in all sorts of everyday events and spent much time trying to work out from them what God wanted at any given moment. As he might have put it, he laboured to discover God's mind in the matter. He certainly felt that the Church of England had not gone nearly far enough in sweeping away the superstitions of the old religion; he would have felt more at home with the Calvinists than with the middle-of-the-road Anglicans. He had no time for Arminians: his only speech in the 1628–29 Parliament consisted of a somewhat confused attack on this group.

Early in 1636 Cromwell's fortunes changed for the better when his mother's brother died, leaving him a number of long leases of Church lands in and around Ely; he also took his uncle's well-paid job as the collector of Church tithes in the area. At this time he moved to a house in Ely and added to the long leases by taking additional ones from the church. Financially he was now comfortably placed, if not rich. This was fortunate for his family, which had been growing steadily since his marriage. By this time he had four sons and three daughters, with one more daughter still to come. Of his four sons, the eldest, named Robert, died in 1639 whilst still being educated. This left Oliver, born in 1622, Richard, born in 1625, and Henry, born in 1627. His four daughters, Bridget, Elizabeth, Mary and Frances, all married in due course, the younger two, who lived to a great age, to members of the aristocracy. Despite his religious enthusiasm Cromwell is depicted in the late 1630s as a happy family man who enjoyed dancing and singing and who made good use of the pleasure to be found from drinking ale and smoking his pipe.

In 1637 Cromwell became involved in a dispute regarding the drainage of the Fens around Ely which was being carried out by a syndicate headed by the Earl of Bedford. A number of landowners who lost their rights to common grazing were upset by this, together with many poor people, such as wild-fowlers, eel fishermen and reed cutters, whose livelihoods depended on the Fens. Cromwell offered support to these people. At this point the King took over the drainage works from the syndicate, guaranteeing that all should remain in possession of their customary rights. On this occasion Cromwell discovered that the King was a better protector of the common people than the well-off members of the Earl of Bedford's syndicate. Soon afterwards he supported some commoners near St Ives who found that land which they had been accustomed to graze had been enclosed by the Earl of Manchester. By 1640 the King had been obliged to call a new Parliament, in which Cromwell sat as one of the members for Cambridge, and the dispute was referred to the House of Lords, which found in favour of Manchester. After further agitation by Cromwell a committee of the Commons was set up to examine the matter, but Cromwell's language was so immoderate that he was rebuked by the chairman and the case was lost. On this occasion Cromwell's failure to control his fiery temper worked against his interests and those of his friends.

All this time he was conscious of the fact that he had been 'saved' by God and that he was therefore different from the many who had not had that experience: he would naturally have been drawn to those that had. By 1640 there were a number of such people, most of whom were Calvinists. Like the Presbyterians, most disapproved of bishops,[2] but on the other hand they did not all agree with the Presbyterians when it came to the rigidity with which that sect held to their own system of worship. It is interesting to note that one understanding of a Puritan is a Calvinist who does not accept the authority of bishops. Another and more generally accepted understanding of the term is of people who are so conscious of God's immediate presence that they eschew any behaviour that they think might offend Him and disapprove strongly of such behaviour in others. Even as early as 1640 Cromwell, without being a kill-joy, probably fitted into both of these categories.

IT IS NOW NECESSARY TO cast an eye at certain events that had taken place in the country as a whole since Parliament was dissolved in 1629 in order to understand the situation that existed when it was recalled in 1640. In the absence of Parliament the King could not afford to go to war; this led to a period of peaceful prosperity at a time when the rest of Europe was in turmoil as a result of the Thirty Years War. For the common people of England it was a golden age, but for those sections of the nobility and gentry who were excluded from the conduct of affairs, but who were being taxed in ways over which they had no control, discontent was seeding. Additional discontent arose from developments within the Church of England, where the followers of Arminius were gaining ground. In 1633 one of their number, William Laud, became Archbishop of Canterbury and straight away started to impose his ideas on the Church in an attempt to achieve uniformity throughout the country. Laud, an unattractive man of humble birth, was deeply unpopular. He had a rasping voice and was bad-tempered, fussy and humourless. Far from unifying the Church of England, he split it down the middle by offending all those with Calvinist leanings who had nonetheless stayed within the Church so long as it tolerated their point of view. Most of these people, together with some committed Anglicans, were also worried that his reforms might be a prelude to reconciliation with Rome, although in this they had no grounds for fear, since both Laud and the King remained totally committed to a Protestant and Episcopal Church of England. In the end they both died for it.

Laud was not only Archbishop of Canterbury; he was also a courageous and determined member of the inner ring of Privy Councillors who helped the King govern the country. Another such person was Thomas Wentworth, whom Cromwell would have known during the Parliament of 1628–29, as he was one of the group, led by Sir John Eliot, that was most critical of the King. But Wentworth evidently felt that he and his friends had gone too far, because after Parliament was dissolved in 1629 he became one of the King's servants, being employed both as Lord President of the North and later as Lord Deputy of Ireland. In both appointments he proved himself to be a first-class and fearless administrator, rooting out corruption and archaic practices. Naturally he made enemies among the established families who were displaced from their lucrative positions to make way for his reforms.

During the long period of the King's personal rule, the country was, on the whole, governed well. Nonetheless, members of the government had to resort to some questionable practices in order to raise the revenue necessary for running the country and also to control trouble-makers. Although almost always working within the law, the government made good use of facilities such as the Court of Star Chamber, instituted by Henry VII to control the country in the aftermath of the Wars of the Roses, which were considered unnecessarily draconian by the 1630s. There was much litigation and excitement whipped up by pamphleteers and others who were at loggerheads with the system, and a constant demand for the recall of Parliament, which King Charles wisely ignored.

When eventually the King was obliged to call a Parliament, his reason for doing so had little to do with the discontent in England. The trouble came from his other kingdom, Scotland. When James came to England on the death of Elizabeth, he had been ruling Scotland for many years and had little trouble in continuing to rule it through his Scottish council which consisted of a mixture of the most powerful Highland clan chiefs and Lowland land-owning nobility. Charles, who never went to Scotland at all until 1633, tried to rule it in the same way as his father, but unlike his father, he had little understanding of the problems there or of the feelings of the people. When the King did eventually visit Scotland, he was misled into supposing that the people were reconciled to the concept of episcopacy, which his father had cautiously and in a limited manner imposed on them. Charles, throwing caution to the winds, decided to have a new prayer book prepared for Scotland that would bring his two kingdoms together from a religious point of view. It took the Scottish bishops a few years to produce one, but by the summer of 1637 it was ready. Charles then told his Scottish Council to impose it, but when they did, it was rejected with rioting inside and outside church. The unrest culminated in March of the following year when a group of prominent men including the Earl of Montrose set about getting signatures to a National Covenant supporting the Presbyterian religion traditional in Scotland. Copies of the Covenant were circulated throughout the country, attracting thousands of signatures. 'The Covenant' was to play an important role in England as well as in Scotland over the next thirteen years.

The King's reaction was to order an army to assemble at York to subdue the Scots. In the event there was no fighting in 1639 as it was apparent that the English force was no match for the Scots. The Lord Lieutenants of the counties, whose job it was to raise the levies in England, got little co-operation from the gentry who, already angry at the King's reluctance to call a Parliament, were strongly opposed to paying additional taxes to finance the war. Furthermore, a considerable number of them had Calvinist leanings and sympathised with the Presbyterian Scots.

Although thwarted temporarily, the King did not give up. Realising that he needed a really efficient adviser, he sent to Ireland for Wentworth, who, before leaving, set about enlarging the very effective army that he had built up there in case it should be needed on the mainland. Next the King made plans for the production of muskets, cannon, powder, shot and swords, which were to be stored in a great arsenal in Hull. Finally, accepting that he would not be able to raise enough money without Parliament, he ordered one to assemble in April 1640. When it did, the King made it clear that its purpose was to provide him with money so that he could deal with the threat of invasion by the Scots. But Parliament had no intention of providing Charles with the where-withal to wage war only to have him dissolve Parliament for another eleven years as soon as the money was safely in the bag. Sir John Eliot was no longer leader of the King's critics, having died a prisoner in the Tower some years earlier, but his place had been taken by a more for-midable Parliamentarian, John Pym. On 17 April Pym made a speech demanding reforms to prevent government offences against the liberty and property of citizens and the privilege of Parliament. He also demanded that Archbishop Laud should be controlled in the way that he was using ecclesiastical courts to promote the King's wishes. The King replied that he would not consider reforms until he had the money for his campaign. Seeing that he was making no headway, the King dissolved Parliament on 5 May after it had sat for only three weeks.

In July the Scots army marched towards England. Wentworth, now Earl of Strafford, had done his best to prepare the north of England to withstand the assault, but without the necessary funds it was impossible to put well-found troops into the field. On 28 August the Royal army was defeated at Newburn, and Newcastle surrendered next day. In England the war remained unpopular. Some people in London openly celebrated the Scottish victory and twelve peers petitioned the King against continuing the war. The King summoned a great council of peers to attend him at York, but when they did, the general consensus was to end the war and to call another Parliament. A truce was arranged with the Scots, who remained in possession of Northumberland and Durham while their demands were being considered. Meanwhile the King had to pay to maintain them there.

The new Parliament, known as the Long Parliament, met on 3 November 1640; parts of it lasted until the eve of the Restoration almost twenty years later. When it assembled its mood was very different to that of the Short Parliament although over half of the members were the same. This time it was far more aggressive in its approach to the King and his ministers. The two most powerful members of the Privy Council, Strafford and Laud, were both sent to the Tower. Within a few weeks Strafford was beheaded. His accusers could not afford to spare a person who had governed so well on behalf of the King at a time when they were trying to transfer much of the King's executive power to a Parliament. Parliament could never hope to use it as effectively or as fairly as Strafford had done. Laud was imprisoned for a further four years before he too was beheaded.

As time went by it became apparent that Pym was attacking on two fronts. First, there was the purely political assault designed to rob the King of much of his power, such as his right to raise money in various ways without Parliament's consent. Pym also wanted a bill that would oblige the King to call a new Parliament every three years.

Second was an attack on the episcopacy designed to introduce the full Presbyterian system, or if this proved impracticable, at least to remove the bishops from the House of Lords and to restrict them to a limited number of unimportant religious and administrative activities. Both these alternatives were repugnant to the King. Although the mainspring of this attack was to prevent a slide towards Rome, it is also worth remembering that whoever controlled the pulpit also controlled the main means of communication at a time when there were few news publications and the vast majority of the population could not read. Under the Presbyterian system the minister was responsible to a group of church elders in each parish; they would by and large follow the lead of the local squire, who was more likely to be in sympathy with Members of Parliament than with the King. Under the Anglican system the priest was responsible to the bishop, who was appointed by the King and directed by the archbishops. Of Pym's two lines of attack it was the second that was most popular both with the King's opponents in Parliament and with the Scots, who were in close touch with Pym. Indeed, for a time Pym was subsidising them to stay in the northern counties as a threat to the King, who could not afford to be rid of Parliament while they were still there.

From the start of the Long Parliament Cromwell played an active part in furthering Pym's designs. Undoubtedly the promotion of religious reform was his chief interest but he also became involved in the other aspects of Pym's programme, judging by the large number of committees on which he sat and the duties he carried out. It must however be recorded that he had no part in the judicial murder of Strafford. It would seem likely that the amount of business given to Cromwell at this time was due to the family links that he had with some of Pym's principal supporters such as Hampden and St John.

One of the first eyewitness descriptions of Cromwell dates from the early days of the Long Parliament. Sir Philip Warwick, writing some time after the event, states:

> I came one morning into the house well clad, and perceived a
> gentleman speaking, (whom I knew not), very ordinarily apparelled,
> for it was a plain cloth-suit, which seemed to have been made by an ill
> country tailor; his linen was plain, and not very clean ... his hat was

without a hat-band, his stature was of a good size, his sword tight to his side, his countenance swollen and reddish, his voice sharp and untuneable, and his eloquence full of fervour, for the subject matter would not bear much of reason. [3]

As in Huntingdon and later in Ely, it was excessive fervour that was letting him down. He had not yet learnt how to use his righteous indignation and his direct line to the Almighty to promote his aims.

AS THE MONTHS PASSED, Pym and his supporters forced more and more unpalatable legislation on the King, much of which bore no relation to the traditional balance between Crown and Parliament. Although some thought it justified by the way in which the King had treated Parliament during the 1630s, many others were as unhappy with the radical measures introduced by Parliament as they were with the way in which the King had formerly stretched his own power. Meanwhile, although the King never abandoned his underlying position, he often disguised it and appeared to compromise in order to attract support, a game that Pym could also play on occasions. After a full year of the Long Parliament a number of important people who had formerly been opposed to the King's policies had rallied to his support and nearly succeeded in preventing Pym from passing a gratuitously offensive bill known as the Grand Remonstrance.

It is not unlikely that the tide would have turned in favour of the King at this point had it not been for an uprising that had taken place in Ireland a month earlier. In the absence of Strafford, the careful balance of the various factions and interests broke down and the army that he had built up to maintain order was disbanded to prevent the King bringing it to England to intimidate Parliament. As a result a vast horde of hungry and suppressed Roman Catholic peasants turned on the largely Protestant gentry in an orgy of rape and bloodshed. The Irish government responded with all the force that they could muster and a veritable bloodbath ensued. The King, who was in Scotland when this occurred, immediately sent a brigade of Scottish troops commanded by Monroe to

Ulster. Both King and Parliament realised that English troops would also have to be sent, but Pym was not prepared to leave control of such a force in the King's hands. He wanted Parliament to appoint the officers and direct their activities, which meant depriving the King of one of his most fundamental functions. Throughout December Pym pressed for the passage of a Militia Bill which would give Parliament control not only of the forces sent to Ireland but also of the part-time county levies and city trained bands throughout England. In order to force through this and some other legislation concerning the position of the bishops, Pym organised city mobs to intimidate the King's supporters and produce a crisis situation. It was even thought possible that he intended to impeach the Roman Catholic Queen, who was blamed for encouraging the Irish rebels and who was known to be looking for help from her brother the King of France and from the Dutch. At this point the King decided to act.

On 4 January the King with a detachment of his guards went down to the House of Commons intending to arrest Pym and four of his principal helpers, Hampden, Hazlerigg, Holles and Strode. He also tried to arrest one of Pym's allies in the House of Lords, Viscount Mandeville, son-in-law of the Earl of Warwick and soon to accede to his father's title as Earl of Manchester. But, as the King put it, the birds had flown. Uproar followed. Six days later the King left London, making his way via Hampton Court, Windsor and Dover to York. The Queen meanwhile slipped away from Dover and sailed to the United Provinces, where she started to collect men and weapons: it took some time before the first blow was struck, but war was now inevitable.

FOR THE FIRST SIX MONTHS of 1642 Cromwell remained at Westminster, giving his support to those in both Houses which were preparing for war. During this time various groupings of like-minded people emerged, so that Cromwell got a fair idea of those whose thinking most closely resembled his own. One such group was the members of the board of the Providence Company, which had been set up in the 1630s to establish a settlement on Santa Catalina in the Caribbean. Members of the board included the Earl of Warwick, who was a big landowner in Essex, Lord Brooke, who was influential in Warwickshire, Viscount Saye and Sele, another strong Puritan from north Oxfordshire, and John Hampden. Pym was the company secretary and St John its solicitor. During the 1630s, board meetings had provided opportunities for these people to discuss political matters of a subversive nature without attracting suspicion. Cromwell had access to Warwick through his cousin Thomas Barrington and to Viscount Saye and Sele through St John and John Hampden.[4] It was at this time that he came to the notice of these two important peers, who were as determined as Pym to subject the King to Parliament and who would have such an important part to play in Cromwell's rise to power.

In June Cromwell subscribed the considerable sum of £500 to Paliament to help raise its army, and in the following month sent arms worth £100 to his constituents in Cambridge. He also arranged for a vote to be taken in Parliament authorising his constituents to train and exercise volunteer companies in the use of the arms. Soon afterwards the King asked the University of Cambridge to send him their silver, together with a money contribution, to assist his war effort. At about this time Cromwell himself went to Cambridge. On 10 August, assisted by two of his brothers-in-law, Valentine Walton and John Desborough, he gathered together a number of men and intercepted the consignment outside the town. Five days later this unofficial gang seized the county magazine, containing much silver which he sent to Parliament. At the same time he forcibly prevented the men nominated by the King from exercising their commission of array and topped off his activities by arresting the heads of three of the University's colleges whom he suspected of favouring the King, and sent them as prisoners to Parliament. Cromwell did these things without authority, thus exposing himself to the danger of being hauled before a court. He had however shown himself to be efficient, energetic, and above all decisive. Parliament quickly passed an act of indemnity making his actions retrospectively legal. Shortly afterwards he received a commission to raise and command a troop of horse. His military career had begun.

2 · Gone for a Soldier

For a time after the King left London, deputations from Parliament waited on him at the various places where he stopped in order to ask for his assent to the bills that they had passed. One such bill was designed to remove the bishops from the House of Lords, to which the King assented. Another was the controversial Militia Bill. The King rejected this as being inconsistent with his ancient and unquestionable prerogative. Parliament then issued it as an ordinance, which did not require the King's assent. The Militia Ordinance governed the way in which Parliament raised its forces, using Lord Lieutenants and their deputies to appoint officers, raise the men and collect the necessary funds. Lord Lieutenants and Deputy Lieutenants who refused to do this were replaced. By contrast the King made use of the old system of issuing Commissions of Array to selected people throughout the kingdom, including those Lord Lieutenants and their deputies that Parliament had dismissed, together with Justices of the Peace and other leading members of the gentry. Three Commissioners acting together were entitled to issue commissions to an individual to raise and command a regiment of horse or foot or a troop of horse. Both sides tried to gain possession of the arms held locally for use by the trained bands.

At this time the only military units in existence were the trained bands in the larger towns. They suffered from two major disadvantages. First, they were neither obliged nor organised to operate outside their own locality and second, they were not trained. The only exception were the London trained bands, which since January had been commanded by Philip Skippon, a veteran of the European wars.

In order to go to war, both sides had to find enough professional officers and soldiers to train and direct the raw levies that they were collecting together. Although England and Scotland had been at peace for years, many Englishmen and Scots had seen action on the Continent. Some had fought under de Vere for the Elector Palatine, before being incorporated into the army of the United Provinces when the Elector's cause foundered. The United Provinces also employed four English and four Scottish regiments of foot and some troops of horse in its war with Spain. Many others, including a contingent of 9,000 Scots, fought in the Swedish army of King Gustavus Adolphus when in 1630 he swept through Germany to revitalise and assist the Protestant states. For two years Gustavus carried all before him, before being killed at Lützen. Meanwhile the Elector Palatine had died, but in 1638 his son tried to recapture the Palatinate with a small army which was soon routed by Imperial troops. A number of English volunteers took part in the Elector's expedition, which was commanded by a Scots officer called James King, formerly one of Gustavus Adolphus's generals. In addition to these people who were fighting for Protestant rulers, a considerable number of Englishmen, including many Roman Catholics, were serving in the armies of France, Spain and the Holy Roman Empire. It can be seen therefore that there was a reservoir of trained officers and men available, but it would take time before those still serving could be recalled from the Continent, and the war would not wait for them.

The earliest outbreaks of violence occurred in June as opposing groups clashed while trying to take possession of the arms belonging to the trained bands. At the end of June the King tried to gain control of the fleet by writing to each ship's captain individually instructing him to ignore orders from the Lord Admiral, the Earl of Northumberland. But Parliament moved quickly and appointed the Earl of Warwick, an experienced seaman and soldier, to command the fleet. Thus Parliament gained control of the navy whereas the King offended the powerful Northumberland, a moderate Calvinist, who became a firm supporter of Parliament.

By July all hope of resolving the dispute between King and Parliament by peaceful means had passed and both sides started to appoint their commanders. The Earl of Essex became Lord General of Parliament's forces at the age of 51. His military experience went back to 1620 when he commanded a company of foot in de Vere's force, after which he served as a colonel in the forces of the United Provinces. In 1625 he was vice-admiral of the expedition to Cadiz and in 1640 he was the King's lieutenant general in the war against Scotland. Son of the Earl of Essex, executed by Queen Elizabeth, he was a staunch Presbyterian and a first cousin of both the Earl of Warwick and the Earl of Northumberland. He subscribed to the official Parliamentary line that the aim of its army was to free the King from his evil advisers and restore him to his loyal Parliament. If this could be achieved by negotiation, well and good. If not, the war would have to go on until the Royalists could fight no more. The young Earl of Bedford, who had recently succeeded his father to the title, but who had no military experience, was appointed General of Horse. Skippon would be sergeant-major general of foot. ('Major general' was often used as an abbreviation for this military rank and will be used in his book, but technically they were sergeant-major generals.)

As a legislature Parliament was not organised to exercise executive authority in normal times; that was the job of the Privy Council, which was responsible to the King. Parliament therefore gave the task of dealing with its army in the field to the Committee of Safety, which had been set up in January to handle the unrest then sweeping the country. Members of the committee were chosen by vote and they gradually became Parliament's executive body so far as the war was concerned.

On the Royalist side the King was Captain General of all his forces and managed military matters through a council of war. His Privy Council handled other matters in the normal way. In July the King appointed the veteran Earl of Lindsey, aged 60, whose military experience dated back to the time of Queen Elizabeth, as his Lord General. Prince Rupert, a young, austere though charismatic Calvinist, son of the former Elector Palatine and a nephew of the King, became General of Horse. Sir Jacob Astley, who had once been Prince Rupert's tutor, commanded the foot. All three of these men had substantial operational experience, although in Lindsey's case it was very out of date. On 22 August the King set up his standard in Nottingham in a gesture which marked the official opening of hostilities, although by this time a number of sizeable and violent confrontations had taken place between Royalists and supporters of Parliament in different parts of the country.

ALTHOUGH IT IS NOT NECESSARY to go into great detail regarding the weapons, organisation and procedures adopted by Parliament's forces in order to assess Cromwell's ability as a commander, it is difficult to follow events without a broad understanding of these matters. Each army was divided into foot, horse, dragoons and an artillery train. The most senior officers such as Essex, or on the Royalist side the King, had a life guard, consisting of various-sized detachments of foot and horse whose job was to escort and guard the commander concerned in battle, on the move and in camp.

A regiment of foot or horse was raised by its colonel, who could be a senior officer in the army or a local magnate. Sometimes a group of people might club together to raise a regiment, in which case one of their number would be nominated as colonel. Alternatively an individual could be commissioned to raise a troop of horse, in which case, once raised and prepared, it would join up with a number of other troops to form a regiment. Sometimes troops were moved from one regiment to another. A few powerful men, such as Lord St John, might raise a regiment of foot and a troop of horse.

Regiments took their colonel's name, for example the Earl of

Warwick's Regiment of Foot or the Earl of Essex's Regiment of Horse, and troops of horse took the name of the captains who raised them. A regiment of foot was supposed to be 1,200-strong divided into ten companies, each consisting of one-third pikemen and two-thirds musketeers. One company would be commanded by the colonel of the regiment, one by the lieutenant colonel, one by the major and the rest by captains. If the colonel was not present with the regiment, for example because he was a general, or perhaps a prominent local magnate, or even fully occupied as a politician in London, his regiment would be commanded by the lieutenant colonel, and his company by the lieutenant of that company. The colonel would however draw his pay as colonel of his regiment and as a captain of his company and, if a senior officer, his pay in that capacity as well. The same system applied to a regiment of horse, which was supposed to consist of six troops totalling 500 men. One troop was commanded by the colonel, one by the major and the other four by captains: in theory there were no lieutenant colonels of horse in Parliament's army as there were in the Royalist army, although sometimes such an appointment was made.

Foot soldiers seldom wore armour, although pikemen were sometimes weighed down with back and breast plates. When deployed for battle the pikemen would be in the centre and the musketeers, who never wore armour, would be on either side of them. They were armed with the matchlock musket, which was clumsy, heavy and took up to a minute to reload. It was dangerous up to 100 yards; when the enemy closed, it could be used as a club.

A few regiments of horse were equipped with three-quarter-length armour, that is to say armour covering the front, back, arms and thighs with a helmet that gave protection to the head and neck. They were known as cuirassiers. Most regiments had no more than back and breast plates and a simple pot helmet and were known as harquebusiers. Troopers carried a sword and two pistols. Most officers managed to get hold of quality horses of about fifteen hands, but troopers usually had to make do with heavier animals. The value of a troop or regiment of horse depended greatly on how well it was mounted, first with regard to the size and quality of the horses, and second with regard to the evenness of performance of the horses throughout the troop or regiment. Even a small number of less good horses in a troop reduced the performance of the whole to the speed and stamina of the weaker ones.

Dragoons were musketeers mounted on cheap, small horses or ponies. They were expected to fight on foot and to use their nags only for getting from one place to another. Like regiments of foot they had ten companies, but there were no pikemen and they were armed with firelocks instead of matchlocks.

The main purpose of the artillery train was to demolish defences when a strongpoint was being stormed, but cannon were also used in set-piece battles to kill and frighten the enemy before the two sides became locked together in combat. There were ten different sizes of cannon, each with its own name, which could be included in the train, the largest of which had a bore of eight inches, weighed 8,000 pounds, fired a shot weighing 63 pounds and needed sixteen horses to pull it. By contrast the smallest had a bore of 1½ inches, weighed 120 pounds and fired a shot of twelve ounces. The mainstay of the field artillery was the saker. with a 3½ inch bore, which weighed 2,500 pounds. The main problem with the artillery train was the slowness of its movement and the need to provide escorts for it, especially if separated from the main body. Usually the larger cannon were used only for a major siege and did not accompany the army when it was involved in mobile operations.

When possible, soldiers in the field were issued with two pounds of bread or biscuit and one pound of meat or cheese a day. Men normally carried up to seven days' supply with them and they would be replenished as needed from the regimental wagons. Each army had a wagon train, which transported food from base areas to detachments in the field. When not on operations troops were often quartered on the civilian population, who housed and fed them in return for tokens which were theoretically redeemable for cash at a later date.

IN EARLY SEPTEMBER Cromwell was commissioned to raise a troop of horse, and on the 10th of that month he received orders to march to

Northampton to join Essex's army. His troop was to become part of Essex's own regiment of horse. By this time Cromwell had raised about 60 men. His brother-in-law Desborough accompanied him as quartermaster. Valentine Walton also raised a troop, enrolling his son as his cornet, and he too hastened to join Essex's army. Cromwell's own son, Oliver, became cornet in a troop raised by Lord St John, a second cousin of Oliver St John. When Cromwell joined the Parliamentary army he found that Essex's regiment was commanded by a Yorkshire MP, Sir Philip Stapleton, who was also a member of the Committee of Safety. Lord Brooke commanded one of the other troops, but as he was also colonel of a regiment of foot and a regiment of dragoons, he was not with it in person. Brooke's quartermaster was John Okey, who became well known in future years as a colonel of dragoons.

On 13 September the King left Nottingham for Shrewsbury, arriving there on 20 September. On 19 September Essex also moved west to Worcester, from where he would be well placed to prevent the King moving south to occupy Bristol. From Worcester he could also oppose any move that the King might make to recruit in Monmouth or Herefordshire, and he would also be able to intercept the King if he moved towards London. Naturally he would only be successful if he could get timely information as to the King's movements. It would be the responsibility of the Earl of Bedford as General of Horse to provide this.

The day before Essex reached Worcester he sent a detachment of horse ahead to approach the town from the south in order to secure a bridge which the army would need to cross next day. Here they came in contact with a force of eight troops of Royalist horse and some dragoons, commanded by Prince Rupert in person. Although the two sides were of approximately equal strength the resulting action saw the total rout of the Parliamentary detachment, the fugitives flying for many miles until they met the main body of Essex's army. The effect on the morale of both sides was considerable. Rupert added to his reputation as an inspiring commander and the Parliamentary army was correspondingly discouraged. The Parliamentary detachment seems to have been made up of troops from a number of regiments. Stapleton's troop was present at Powick Bridge, but not Cromwell's.

For the next month there were no further engagements between Essex and the King's army, but there was much that needed doing in order to prepare the hastily gathered men into a force capable of meeting their opponents in battle. So far as the horse was concerned, the Earl of Bedford, as Parliamentary General of Horse, had to train them in accordance with some sort of acceptable tactical doctrine, sort out and standardise the various bits of equipment that had been acquired by the different troops as they formed, replace unsuitable animals and teach the men how to handle their weapons whilst riding a horse. And while this was going on it was necessary to send out patrols to establish Royalist movements and to raid their outposts. Finally regiments had to scour the countryside for food and forage, not only for themselves but also for the army as a whole. It is not possible to know exactly what Cromwell's movements were at this time, but he must have been engaged in some or all of these activities.

Although the Earl of Bedford had no military experience, his lieutenant general, Sir William Balfour, did, having served for many years in the army of the United Provinces. Sir James Ramsey, the commissary general of horse, was also an experienced professional. In preparing a doctrine on which to train and fight, they would doubtless have based it on one or other of the standard works available at the time such as John Cruso's *Militarie Instructions for the Cavallrie*.[1] This particular work, published by the printers to the University of Cambridge in 1632, was a comprehensive document describing how mounted forces should be raised, officered and trained and how horses should be exercised and schooled. It discussed the use of guides and spies, how marches should be organised, quarters and camps established, how scouts, outposts and sentinels should be employed. It also covered the tactics of beating up the enemy in their quarters, of laying an ambush, of mounting a charge, of attacking enemy infantry and of defending against enemy attack. The manual had been written in accordance with conditions in the Dutch army which would have been familiar to Balfour but less so to the professional officers who had served in the Swedish army of Gustavus Adolphus. Some of it, particularly where it dealt with the co-ordination of action between cuirassiers, lancers and harquebusiers, was irrelevant and could be discarded, as the Parliamentary army had very few cuirassiers and no lancers. Other alterations would be needed to take account of the ideas of the Parliamentary commanders. But the instructions that Cromwell received and the exercises that he underwent, based on decisions made by Bedford, Balfour and Ramsey, provided the rock on which he would build his own ideas.

THE FIRST MAJOR BATTLE OF the Civil War, known to history as the battle of Edgehill, was fought on 23 October. By then the King's army, which had been pitifully weak when he left Nottingham, had received a large number of men and was heading for London. On the night of 22 October its regiments were billeted in a number of villages spread across an extensive area to the east of Kineton. On 19 October Essex moved east from Worcester to intercept him. By the evening of 22 October the head of his army reached Kineton and the troops started to disperse around the nearby villages. Neither side seems to have realised that their enemies were so close until a Parliamentary scouting party blundered after dark into the very place where Prince Rupert was planning to spend the night. From then on, the Royalists at least knew what was happening, although it is said that Essex himself only discovered when he went to church at Kineton early next morning and saw some of the Royalist horse drawn up about a mile away on the forward slope of Edgehill. They were covering the deployment of the whole of the Royalist army. It then became a race to see which side could deploy quickest.

At this time Essex's army was more spread out than the King's, partly because he had garrisons in Hereford, Worcester, Coventry, Northampton and Banbury and partly because he had been obliged to leave John Hampden with two regiments of foot and a regiment of horse to escort the artillery train. As a result he only managed to deploy around 14,900 men to face the King's 14,300. Essex had twenty regiments of foot, seven of horse and two of dragoons against the King, who had thirteen regiments of foot, ten of horse and three of dragoons. The Royalists deployed on the slopes while Essex deployed on the plain below. In the customary manner, both sides put their foot in the centre with their horse on either flank. The general idea was for the horse to try and dispose of the enemy horse opposite them and then turn inwards to attack the exposed flank of the enemy's foot. On each side regiments of foot were grouped into brigades, known then as tertias.

Essex placed two of his brigades forward with the third one behind his left forward brigade. Behind his right forward brigade Essex placed two regiments of horse, which he held in reserve: Balfour's and his own, although for one reason or another Cromwell's troop was not with it at the start of the battle. Most of the rest of Essex's horse was on his left wing, where the ground was open under the command of Sir James Ramsey. Only one regiment, under the command of Lord Feilding, was on the right, because the ground there was broken and difficult for a Royalist assault.

The Royalist horse deployed on either flank. Prince Rupert led the right wing with Sir John Byron's regiment in the second rank, whose job it was to attack the left flank of the Parliamentary foot if Rupert's men succeeded in dispersing Ramsey's horse. Lord Wilmot commanded the left wing, opposite Lord Feilding. Behind him were two weak regiments to attack the right flank of the Parliamentary foot.

Because of the way in which both sides were dispersed the previous evening, they were not fully deployed until 12.30 pm. The slight Royalist inferiority in numbers was made up for by the strength of their position on the ridge. Essex,who would gain in strength when the garrisons of Warwick and Coventry and the escort to the artillery train caught up, was in no hurry to attack. The Royalists had much to lose by delay because not only did they not want Essex to be reinforced, but they were also short of rations and could get no more until after the battle. They therefore abandoned their strong position and advanced to the plain opposite Essex in the hope of sparking off a Parliamentary attack. This was a tricky manoeuvre and was not complete until about 2.15 pm. Still

Essex did not attack although some of his cannon started firing at the King and his entourage as they rode along the line of battle. Soon after 3 pm, the whole Royalist line moved into the attack.

From the Parliamentary point of view the opening stages of the battle were alarming. Ramsey's men on the left saw Prince Rupert's regiments advance first at a walk, then at a trot, and finally for the last 200 yards at a canter. According to all the textbooks they should have halted in front of the Parliamentary horse to fire their pistols and then either retire to reload or else continue at a trot to engage in a sword battle. But Rupert's troops did not stop or fire their pistols. Instead they crashed into their enemy, causing their horses to turn tail and ride into the ranks behind them, so that soon the whole of Ramsey's horse were in flight pursued by Rupert's men, who were able to cause havoc with their swords and pistols. They also overran some musketeers that had been placed in gaps between Parliament's troops. So great was the panic in Parliament's ranks that the whole of their left forward brigade of foot also broke and ran. A similar situation arose on Parliament's right wing, Lord Feilding's regiment being easily disposed of by Wilmot's three regiments, but in this case only the right-hand regiment of foot took to its heels. The only Parliamentary forces now left in the field were the eight regiments of foot in the two remaining brigades and the two regiments of horse standing behind the right forward brigade.

Luckily for Essex, a serious mistake was made by the Royalist second line regiments of horse on both flanks. They should have supported the advance of their foot by turning inwards onto the flanks of Essex's foot, but instead of doing so they followed the leading regiments in the chase. No one has ever understood why this happened, because it is clear from reports written by participants that the regiments concerned knew what was required of them and had received specific orders to that effect.

Meanwhile Essex's two remaining brigades were being attacked by the Royalist foot and were just managing to hold their own. Although weaker in numbers, they had better weapons and equipment. Both sides were suffering heavy casualties at this time and gradually Essex's men were being worn down. But just as things were looking bad, Balfour decided to launch the two regiments of horse that he was holding in reserve. This enabled the Parliamentary foot to exploit the ensuing confusion so that for a time in that particular part of the field things seemed to be going so well that the King's standard was captured from his life guard. But at that moment the Royalist Sir Charles Lucas, who had managed to gather together 200 horse from Wilmot's second line, returned to the battle and charged into the rear of Essex's position, scattering two of his foot regiments, causing many casualties and recovering the royal standard. Shortly afterwards some of the Royalist horse from Prince Rupert's wing also reappeared and together with the remaining foot managed to stabilise the Royalist position. By this time the light was beginning to fade and both sides fell back a few yards so that they were no longer in close contact with their opponents, although they kept firing their muskets until it was fully dark. Later the Royalists fell back further still so that Regiments on both sides were able to start collecting up men who had become separated from them in the fighting.

Two questions arise so far as Cromwell is concerned. First, what did he see of the battle and second, what did he learn from it that influenced him as he rose up the ladder of command over the next two years? The first of these questions is not easy to answer. Although one contemporary account referred to by Firth implies that Cromwell was with Essex's regiment during the battle,[2] Cromwell himself, talking some time after the event, said that when he first went into the engagement he saw that Essex's men were beaten everywhere, which implies that he was not present at the start. It seems likely that his troop had been billeted for the night some distance from the battlefield and that he had arrived late.

All that we know for certain is that on 9 November 1642, Viscount Saye and Sele's son, Captain Nathaniel Fiennes, published in London what he described as a 'True and Exact Relation' of the events in order to clear his brother John's name of the suggestion that he had been the first to fly. In this account, amongst much else, he says that after Ramsey's wing broke, his brother gathered some of the fugitives near Kineton, where, after a time, they were joined by a troop commanded by Captain Keightly. Later still, Cromwell's troop arrived, after which he marched them all towards the town where many of the enemy's horse were and eventually joined up with Hampden's brigade and together they came to the army.[3]

Whether he saw the opening stages of the battle personally or whether he heard about it from others, Cromwell quickly realised that Rupert's system for charging the enemy without pausing to fire pistols was likely to succeed, if only because it was difficult for those being charged to prevent their horses from swinging round to go with their attackers. The sheer momentum of a large number of fast-moving horses bearing down on a line of stationary or slow-moving ones would have that effect. An added problem was the men's lack of experience of riding a horse whilst wielding their weapons, especially as the horses would be as inexperienced as were the men. Cromwell's own son could have told him what it felt like, as he had been caught up in the rout of Ramsey's wing and had seen his troop leader, Lord St John, killed in front of him.

Cromwell himself made another point in discussion with his cousin John Hampden some days later when he drew attention to the discrepancy between the quality of the men on both sides. According to Cromwell, recalling the conversation many years after the event, he said to Hampden:

> Your troopers are most of them old decayed serving-men, tapsters, and such kind of fellows, and their troopers are gentlemen's sons, younger sons, and persons of quality. Do you think that the spirit of such base and mean fellows will ever be able to encounter gentlemen that have honour, and courage, and resolution in them? You must get men of a spirit that is likely to go on as far as gentlemen will go, or else I am sure you will be beaten still.[4]

THE MORNING AFTER THE battle saw the two armies standing to arms watching each other. Despite the fact that Essex now had the troops that had joined him too late to fight in the battle, he could not make up for the loss of at least 1,000 men killed and the disintegration of one of his brigades and most of his horse, some of whom, including Ramsey himself, had by now reached London with tales of a terrible defeat. Not only was Essex unable to renew the fight, but he had also lost most of his baggage train, which Rupert's men had destroyed in and around Kineton after their original charge. This meant that he could not even move his army any distance until he had replaced it. On the following day, Essex started to withdraw his army to Warwick, harassed by Rupert, who managed to capture a further 25 of his baggage wagons. From the point of view of the Royalists, who had lost half as many men as their opponents, the road to London was open.

Luckily for Parliament, the King now made a decision that blighted his hopes for a quick victory. Prince Rupert, strongly backed by the Earl of Forth, now Lord General in place of Lindsey, who had been killed in the battle, urged a rapid descent on London, spearheaded by a flying column of 3,000 horse and foot with no heavy guns to delay them which would march on Westminster and secure Parliament. Such a force would be able to cover the 70-odd miles before the end of the month, while the capital was still stunned by the news of Essex's defeat. The rest of the army would arrive well before Essex could get there, which, in the event, he did not succeed in doing until 7 November. But a number of the King's civilian councillors felt that a better peace could be arranged by negotiation and the King, who had been shaken by the casualties in the battle, took their advice. On 29 October he occupied Oxford, which would be his capital for the rest of the war. Rupert captured and wrecked Broughton Castle, the home of Lord Saye and Sele.

While Essex and the remains of his army moved towards London the King's army moved into the Thames valley. On 4 November, when the Royalists occupied Reading, Essex reached Woburn. In London the Earl of Warwick, who had taken charge, was frantically throwing up fortifications to defend the city and Skippon was mobilising the trained bands. In a bid to gain time, Parliament offered to negotiate and the King agreed. Parliament also asked for a cessation of hostilities which the King neither accepted nor refused. On 7 November, when Essex finally reached London, Prince Rupert, who had occupied Maidenhead, attempted to take Windsor Castle but found it too strong for him. Two days later the King met Parliament's negotiators at Colnbrook, and on the same day Essex, together with the trained bands and some regiments that had been stationed near London, moved out to confront the Royalist army. The King responded to Essex's advance by pushing his outposts towards Brentford. Then, realising that he would be in a dangerous position if Essex established himself in the town, he ordered Rupert to capture it. Brentford was held by Brooke's regiment and Holles's regiment. Early in the morning of 12 November, under cover of fog, Rupert attacked, scattering the two regiments and sacking the town, an action which led to accusations that the King had broken the agreement about cessation of hostilities. By this time Essex had arrived at Turnham Green some three miles away, his total force amounting to nearly 24,000 men. This was too strong for the Royalists, who retreated down the Thames valley covered by Rupert. At this point both sides went into winter quarters.

Little is known of Cromwell's doings in the days following Edgehill. During this period he must have realised the damage that Rupert's horse had done, not only during the battle, but also by his constant activity thereafter which contrasted so strongly with Essex's leisurely progress back to London. It is even possible that he worked out the danger that London was in from a sudden descent by Royalist troops immediately following the battle and he would certainly have understood what an energetic and tireless commander such as Prince Rupert could achieve with well-mounted and well-motivated men.

AS MEN'S COMMITMENT to one side or the other took shape it could be seen that Parliament would have control of London, the home counties and most of the prime sources of wealth including all the main ports apart from Newcastle. Parliament was therefore in a better position than the King to pay and equip its forces. The King's strength lay in the traditional loyalty felt for his position by those of the nobility and gentry not specifically committed to Parliament as a result of their personal prospects, their family connections or their attachment to the Puritan interest. Geographically his hold was strongest in the north and west of the country. Naturally each side had some supporters in areas mainly controlled by their opponents. From a material point of view everything favoured Parliament except for the fact, made clear during the early months of the war, that the Royalist army was much better at fighting. If the King was to win he would have to do it before Parliament's armies overwhelmed him by sheer weight of numbers backed by superior equipment and supply, which would ultimately offset superior tactics and morale. There was also the danger that Parliament's armies would get better at fighting.

By the end of 1642 Essex's army had recovered from the setback it had suffered at Edgehill and was firmly between the King and his capital around which new and extended fortifications were being built. London could no longer be captured by direct assault of the main Royalist army. On the other hand Parliament could no longer hope to 'free the King from his evil advisers' while the balance of the two armies remained as it was.

In the panic following Edgehill, Parliament had contacted the Scots for help; although nothing had come of it so far, there was always the chance of substantial reinforcement from that quarter. In the same way, the King was desperately trying to patch up a truce in Ireland that would enable him, first, to extract the English regiments that had been sent there, and second, to get help from the Protestant-led Irish army that Strafford had built up. Parliament always suspected that the King might even try to get assistance from the Roman Catholic rebels themselves on the grounds that he would be less of a danger to them than a Puritan Parliament.

Meanwhile both sides started to build up forces throughout the country so that they could upset the existing stalemate, or alternatively gain control of enough of the country to force their opponents to accept terms. As a result, what started by looking like a war between two armies, spread and took on the appearance of a country-wide struggle in which Parliament tried to attract support from the King's adherents while the King tried to regain the allegiance of those of his subjects who had rebelled. Both sides vied for the allegiance of those hoping to remain neutral. The primary role of the forces being raised around the country was therefore to enable local leaders to gain physical possession of their area, thus helping them to attract prominent people to their side by rewarding support and penalising opposition. The role of each side's main field army was to destroy their opponent's field army if possible, to assist local forces when necessary, and to maintain communications between them. By the beginning of 1643 Parliament had set up regional associations in different parts of the country, each consisting of several counties and each association with its own little army.

Although Cromwell was certainly with Essex's army at Turnham Green, he would not remain with it for much longer. He was already earmarked for greater responsibility than command of a troop.

3 · Learning the Trade

Early in 1643 Cromwell was sent from Essex's army outside London to the Eastern Association, run by Lord Grey of Warke, a Northumberland peer, who commissioned him as a colonel to raise a regiment of horse. The Eastern Association covered the counties of Norfolk, Suffolk, Essex, Hertfordshire and Cambridgeshire. Huntingdonshire was also included in the Eastern Association from May 1643. Each county within an association had its own committee for raising men, money and supplies. Cromwell, by reason of his connections in the area, was a member of both the Huntingdon committee and the Cambridge committee.

Of interest to Cromwell was the neighbouring East Midlands Association, run by the young Lord Grey of Groby, son of the Earl of Stamford (unrelated to Grey of Warke). Lincolnshire, which was basically a Royalist county, was not initially included in any of the Parliamentary associations, although Parliamentary forces there were commanded by Lord Willoughby of Parham.

Equally interesting to Cromwell was the way in which the Royalists were organised to pursue the war. By the turn of the year the King had established two main regional commands. The first of these covered the whole of England north of the Trent, and the second covered Somerset and the counties along the south coast as far as Hampshire. The King from his position at Oxford covered the land in between. There was no Royalist command structure in London or in the counties to the south-east or north-east of it.

The Royalist commander in the north was the Earl of Newcastle, and in the south-west the Marquess of Hertford, who happened to be Essex's brother-in-law. Both were very large landowners with great influence in their areas. Both were in their fifties and neither of them had any military experience. As commanders-in-chief their task was to tie together all the strands of war-making, including the raising of money and the filling of civil and military appointments. Each gradually established a military chain of command, employing professional soldiers to plan and fight the campaigns.

1643 WAS CROMWELL'S formative year. In it he raised his famous regiment, subsequently known as the Ironsides, and developed his own tactical skills in a number of small-scale engagements with the enemy. He also had the opportunity of serving with two fine professional officers, Meldrum and Sir Thomas Fairfax, from whom he learnt much. Finally he showed that he had the quality which has always proved indispensable for true success in war: a determination to do more than is required by one's superiors in order to further the overall aim.

In raising his regiment Cromwell was faced with the task of finding better recruits than the serving-men and tapsters that he had decried to Hampden. His method of doing this was to chose such men as had, to use his own words, 'the fear of God before them, and made some conscience of what they did'. But he was not only looking for pious personnel, he also wanted men that could think and fight. Initially he looked out for men that he had known around Huntingdon and Ely, such as young yeomen farmers or freeholders from the towns. He thus started with people of a higher social class than most cavalry troopers. When it came to finding officers he started by getting hold of people he knew well, such as relations and other members of the gentry. If he could not get enough of them, he dipped down the social scale to find sound men that he could trust.

Amongst those that he collected were his cousin Edward Whalley, who had served as a cornet in John Fiennes's troop at Edgehill. Whalley was given a troop and was soon afterward promoted major and therefore Cromwell's second-in-command. Cromwell's brother-in-law Desborough was promoted from quartermaster to command another troop. Cromwell's nephew Valentine Walton and his son Oliver each got troops. Later in the summer Henry Ireton, who was to become Cromwell's son-in-law, transferred with his troop to Cromwell's regiment. Other troop leaders included James Berry, formerly a clerk in an ironworks, Robert Swallow and Ralph Margery, considered by some as being too far down the social scale to be entrusted with such a command. By March 1643 Cromwell had raised five of the six troops required, but he went on recruiting until by October he had ten troops. Ultimately he raised a total of fourteen troops.

Cromwell not only recruited this remarkable regiment, but also trained it hard and insisted on very strict discipline. In addition he used all his great knowledge of horses to ensure that his men were mounted on the best animals that money, cajolery or even theft of the 'finders-keepers' variety could provide. In building his regiment Cromwell showed great energy and practical sense. Although he did it all in the certainty that it was the Lord's work, he was also pragmatic. If a godly man turned out to be no use, he got rid of him. If a less godly man accidentally slipped through the recruiter's net, but turned out a good fighter, he kept him. Also, provided a man was in a general sense a man of conscience and a Protestant, Cromwell did not concern himself about whether he was a Presbyterian, Baptist or Congregationalist. He did not want heathens, rabble-rousers or Roman Catholics, but otherwise all were welcome.

In one way Cromwell was fortunate in that he was able to recruit and train his regiment in an area which was essentially sympathetic to the Puritan interest and Parliamentary cause. It was also rich in resources, although this did not mean that he could easily get money from the county committees. He was lucky that, for some months, there were no major operations in progress within the Eastern Association, although there were a series of skirmishes just beyond its borders which provided opportunities for the regiment to put their training into practice. There was also the threat of attacks by Newcastle's forces from the north, which frightened the county committees sufficiently to help Cromwell extract resources from them. His position was therefore more favourable than that of, say, the regimental commanders in Lord Fairfax's Northern Association, who were thrust into major operations from the start at the same time as they were trying to recruit and train their men.

At this time Cromwell appears to have been happy and fulfilled. In talking to his officers and men he was friendly and it seems that his liking for good company and jests, which was so much part of his nature before his religious conversion, had to some extent revived. He was certainly more relaxed than he had been in London and he seems to have enjoyed learning the business of war whilst dealing with the sort of problems concerning men and horses that he understood so well. Nonetheless he was totally single-minded so far as the war was concerned, and when considering the evils of the age he would burst into loud groans as he prayed, with tears running down his face. A modern psychiatrist would probably consider him to have been precariously balanced, and when in this condition his natural kindliness deserted him. And whether religious or relaxed, Cromwell was always prepared to be critical of his colleagues or superiors to an extent that owed little to traditional ideas of loyalty or military usage.

THE RAISING AND TRAINING of his regiment went on while Cromwell was engaged in assisting the Eastern Association in its work, including financing and equipping its regiments and countering threats to the security of its counties from within and without. Although the area was predominantly Puritan and therefore sympathetic to Parliament, there were Royalists spread around and in a few places they were even able to take control of a town to the extent that an operation had to be mounted to dislodge them. The enthusiasm with which Cromwell harried these people can be judged from old Sir Oliver Cromwell's description of a visit that his nephew and godson paid him at this time. Apparently Cromwell arrived with a good strong party of horse and asked for his blessing. He then stayed with him for a few hours, standing respectfully with his hat off throughout (hats were normally worn indoors at the time). But while this was going on, so Sir Oliver claimed, Cromwell's troopers not only took all the weapons, but also plundered the house, taking all his plate.[1]

In the early part of the year, when there was little external threat to the Eastern Association, the Earl of Essex ordered Lord Grey of Warke to join him with such force as he could muster. Early in April, therefore, Grey departed with about 5,000 men. They played their part in Essex's advance up the Thames valley and subsequent capture of Reading. Thereafter they stayed with him through the months of confrontation with the King's army based on Oxford, during which John Hampden was killed in a skirmish in June. Most returned home when Essex withdrew towards London in July.

Cromwell's regiment was not part of the force that went with Lord Grey because it was still in the early stages of being formed. Instead he was at first involved in some small-scale operations against local Royalists using those of his troops that were formed at the time. Thus in March he suppressed a Royalist uprising in Lowestoft on behalf of the Suffolk committee and then moved to King's Lynn, where he disarmed some Royalists who were preparing to seize the town. In April, on behalf of the Huntingdonshire county committee of which he was a member, he disarmed some Royalists in Huntingdon, despite the fact that it was not at the time part of the Eastern Association.

In the second half of April the Eastern Association became uneasy about the situation along its northern border with Lincolnshire. Cromwell with his regiment of horse, Sir Miles Hobart with his regiment of foot, and Sir Anthony Irby with a company of dragoons were therefore sent to occupy Peterborough, which they did on 22 April. A week later they captured the small Royalist garrison at Crowland, which was just inside Lincolnshire: it was commanded by Captain Cromwell, one of Cromwell's Royalist cousins.

Eastern Association and surrounding area

York
R. Ouse
Hull
R. Trent
NORTH
SEA
Saltfleet
Gainsborough
Lincoln
Winceby
NOTTINGHAM
Newark
Bolingbroke
LINCOLNSHIRE
R. Trent
Boston
Nottingham
Grantham
LEICESTERSHIRE
Stamford
Crowland
Kings Lynn
Norwich
Leicester
RUTLAND
NORFOLK
Peterborough
Ely
HUNTINGDON
NORTHANTS
Huntingdon
SUFFOLK
Cambridge
CAMBRIDGESHIRE
BEDFORDSHIRE
Ipswich

0   10   20 miles

53

IN MAY ESSEX ORDERED the Eastern Association to combine its remaining forces with those of the East Midlands Association with the aim of relieving the pressure on Lincolnshire and then move north to assist Lord Fairfax in Yorkshire. The operations that subsequently took place in pursuit of Essex's instructons were largely influenced by the way in which the war had developed so far, both in the midlands and in the north, which must now be outlined.

In the midlands at the end of 1642 Parliament had gained the ascendancy and captured both Nottingham and Derby. The King then established a number of garrisons south of the Trent, including one at Lichfield. Parliament retained control north of the Trent.

In Parliament's Northern Association the position was somewhat similar. At first Lord Fairfax, aided by his son Sir Thomas who was his lieutenant general, took control of Yorkshire, containing the local Royalists in York. But in December 1642, the Earl of Newcastle, having secured Northumberland and Durham for the King, moved south into Yorkshire, pushing Lord Fairfax back to the cloth-making towns of the West Riding. Early in January Newcastle put a Royalist garrison into Newark, a place of great strategic importance because of its position on the road between Oxford and the north. He also established garrisons to cut the West Riding towns, from Parliament's other strongpoint, Hull. This done, he started to push south into Lincolnshire and Nottinghamshire.

Essex wanted the Eastern Association to join their forces with those of the East Midlands and Lincolnshire in order to contain Newcastle. Although the commonly recorded notion that the Royalists were pursuing a strategy of a three-pronged attack on London by Newcastle, Hertford and the King was almost certainly not being implemented at this time,[2] there was still ample reason for Parliament wanting to control the East Midlands and Lincolnshire to prevent Newcastle from threatening the rich lands of the Eastern Association together with its wool, fish and farm produce that was of such value to Parliament.

MUCH OF THIS WOULD HAVE been understood by Cromwell; despite the fact that many of the regiments being raised in the Eastern Association were unwilling to leave their own areas and join up with forces from the midlands and Lincolnshire, he set off to do so on his own. He first went to Stamford, where he was supposed to rendezvous with Lord Grey of Groby, but he did not find him there and so went on to Sleaford, where he found Lord Willoughby with some of his men.

Willoughby's first aim was to capture Newark, about seventeen miles to the west. The Royalist commander at Newark, Henderson, together with the Royalist commander in Lincolnshire, Sir Charles Cavendish, had some weeks earlier established an outpost at Grantham. In order to head off Willoughby's attack on Newark, they took some more men to Grantham and then moved forward to confront Willoughby. On 13 May the Royalists overran three Parliamentary troops of horse a few miles north of the town and then drew up in front of Willoughby's force, which probably consisted of two regiments of foot, one regiment of horse and some dragoons plus Cromwell's regiment.

Late in the evening Cromwell's regiment and some extra troops of horse (possibly the balance of the regiment whose troops had been overrun) found themselves facing a larger number of Royalist horse, and some dragoons, commanded by Cavendish. Cromwell in his account of the affair estimated that Cavendish had 21 troops to his twelve, many of which, in his own words, 'were so poor and broken down, that you shall seldom see worse'. The Royalists evidently thought that it was too late to fight and contented themselves by exchanging shots with Willoughby's force at long range. But then, in the gathering dusk, Cromwell charged Cavendish at a round trot, which so surprised the enemy that they were thrown into disorder. It is recorded that Cromwell chased them for two or three miles, causing a considerable number of casualties. But Willoughby's men had also sustained casualties and he decided to withdraw to Lincoln.

This was Cromwell's first serious action and he was elated to find that his training and methods had worked so well. He wrote a glowing account of events giving all the glory to God, which was a procedure that he followed after most of his subsequent encounters with the enemy. Although undoubtedly sincere, it had the advantage of publicising the fact that he had taken part in a battle, and Cromwell certainly understood the value of publicity. Sometimes he added that, after the Almighty, the chief credit belonged to one or more specified people, thereby ensuring that his colleagues' or subordinates' actions were not overlooked.

At the end of the month Willoughby moved to Nottingham, taking Cromwell and his regiment with him. Here they met up with Lord Grey of Groby and some troops from the midlands and Derbyshire. The combined strength of this force was about 6,000. But although this constituted a sizeable Parliamentary concentration, the commanders of it could not agree whether they should move north to assist the Fairfaxes in Yorkshire, or whether they should threaten Oxford to assist Essex. On 19 June the professional Sir John Meldrum was sent by Essex to relieve Lord Grey of Groby and also to take command of the combined force. Willoughby himself had already returned to Lincolnshire.

On 20 July Willoughby with some Lincolnshire men captured Gainsborough, but they were soon besieged by a detachment of Newcastle's army which had been placed under Cavendish's command. Meldrum therefore went with some horse and dragoons from the forces around Nottingham to relieve it. Shortly before this, Royalists from Newark had taken Stamford and were moving on Peterborough. Cromwell with his regiment and some musketeers, together with one or two cannon, was therefore sent by Meldrum to deal with this raid. He soon turned the Royalists out of Stamford, following them to Burleigh House where they made a stand. Here Cromwell attacked them with such gusto that they quickly surrendered. Cromwell then set off to rejoin Meldrum, which he did on 27 July some thirteen miles south of Gainsborough.

Early next morning, Meldrum with four regiments of horse and four companies of dragoons advanced towards Gainsborough. Cavendish, abandoning the siege, deployed his men on a hill commanding Meldrum's approach. In order to relieve Gainsborough, Meldrum would have to attack. As Cavendish showed no intention of abandoning the favourable ground on which he was standing, Meldrum ordered an advance up the hill, which was led by some troops of the Lincolnshire horse. They brushed aside light opposition before reaching the summit after which the whole force tried to form into line. This proved to be difficult, especially as the ground where they were trying to deploy was pitted by rabbit holes.

At this moment Cavendish launched his troops against Meldrum's men. Cromwell, whose regiment had been last up the hill, was now on the right of the line. Not wanting to be charged by Cavendish while stationary, he countered by ordering a charge of his own. According to Cromwell, 'we came up to them horse to horse, where we disputed it with our swords and pistols a pretty time, all keeping close order, so that no one could break the other.' In other words, Cromwell avoided being carted by his horse turning to join the movement of the enemy, because he moved forward himself before his line was hit. But equally, because the enemy were also moving forward, they did not spin round when Cromwell hit them. As a result, both sides had to fall to with sword and pistol in the old-fashioned way. In this case the superiority of Cromwell's men, equipment and horses eventually told and the Royalist horse were put to flight.

Cromwell's regiment and most of the Lincolnshire horse set forth in pursuit, but, looking back, Cromwell noticed that Cavendish had kept a regiment of horse in reserve and that he was about to attack the few troops of the Lincolnshire horse that had been kept back from the chase to occupy the captured ground. Like Lucas at Edgehill, Cromwell would now have to stop enough of his men and return to the field of battle before Cavendish destroyed the remains of Meldrum's force. This was no easy task. Aided by Whalley, Cromwell eventually gathered three troops together with which he fell upon the rear of Cavendish's regiment. Being greatly surprised, the regiment was forced down the side of the hill. In the course of this encounter Cavendish's horse got stuck in mud and Cavendish, son of the Earl of Devonshire and cousin of the Earl of Newcastle, was killed by the commander of Cromwell's own troop,

Berry from the ironworks. According to Cromwell he 'slew him with a thrust under his short rib' in true Old Testament fashion.

Gainsborough was now relieved and re-supplied in case of a further siege. Meldrum, on hearing that another small body of Royalist horse and foot was in a position on the other side of the town, took the musketeers from the Gainsborough garrison together with his horse and set off to attack them. Cromwell encountered two enemy troops and drove them back into a village, but on advancing to the top of the next hill he saw a large body of foot and horse. It was apparent that the main body of Newcastle's army lay before him and that Meldrum's force was in grave danger. There was nothing for it but to get the musketeers back into Gainsborough as quickly as possible and then for the rest of Meldrum's force to withdraw in the first instance to Lincoln.

A fighting withdrawal is, and always has been, one of the most difficult operations of war. In this case Cromwell was put in charge of a covering force consisting of four troops from his own regiment, commanded by Whalley, and four troops from Lord Willoughby of Parham's regiment of horse, commanded by Captain Ayscough. Whalley and Ayscough withdrew by bounds, that is to say first one would hold a feature that the enemy would have to deploy in order to attack, while the other withdrew to another similar feature some way to the rear. As soon as the feature to the rear was occupied, the first detachment would withdraw through it to a third position further to the rear, and so on. In this way the enemy's follow-up could be delayed sufficiently to enable Meldrum's main body to reach its destination. It is recorded that in this case the whole business was managed with great skill by Cromwell and without loss, although shots were exchanged on a number of occasions.

On reaching Lincoln it was decided that Meldrum's force would have to split up. Meldrum returned to Nottingham and Cromwell withdrew to Peterborough and then back to the Isle of Ely, of which place he had been appointed governor on 28 July. Newcastle's army first recaptured Gainsborough. Soon afterwards Lincoln was occupied by Royalist forces while Newcastle pushed on as far as Nottingham intending to capture it.

Cromwell's energy and willingness to take part in these operations outside the association's area between May and July had not gone unnoticed in London. Alone of the Eastern Association regimental commanders he had done his best to fulfil Essex's desire that the association should help the Midlands Association deal with the Royalist threat from the north. He had taken part in a cavalry skirmish outside Grantham in May, had recovered Stamford from a Royalist raiding party and then captured them at Burleigh in July and finally at the end of that month taken part in Meldrum's attempted relief of Gainsborough. On 4 August he received the special thanks of the House of Commons for 'his faithful endeavours to God and the kingdom'. He was also voted £3,000 for the maintenance of his troops.

BY THE TIME THAT CROMWELL got back to Ely he found that much had changed in the Eastern Association. In July Lord Grey of Warke had returned from Essex's army with the survivors of his force, but soon afterwards he was deprived of his command. With most of Lincolnshire lost and with Newcastle's army outside Nottingham, the Eastern Association was now directly threatened.

On 10 August, the Earl of Manchester was appointed to command the Eastern Association with powers to build up its army to a strength of 10,000 foot and 5,000 horse and to raise the money to pay and maintain it. Manchester, like Cromwell, came from a great Huntingdonshire family. He married as his second wife the daughter of the Earl of Warwick, as a result of which, in the period leading up to the Civil War, he had been at the heart of the Presbyterian movement in Parliament. He was considered to be a kind, gentle and austere man with great ability as a political organiser. He was therefore well equipped to draw together prominent people within the association and get them to contribute their time and money to the cause, and he also had links with those in Parliament best able to help him. Although he had fought at Edgehill, he had no worthwhile military experience and would have to learn as he went along. From the start he took care of his men and was liked by them in return. Like Cromwell, he wanted to fill his regiments as far as possible with sober and godly men, and in the early days of their working together they co-operated well together. At this time Cromwell was still happy to take Presbyterians, and Manchester had not yet developed a distaste for the excesses of the Independents.

The relationship between Essex as Parliament's Lord General and the commanders of the regional associations was difficult. Essex issued them with their commissions as major generals of Parliament's army and generals of their own associations. He considered them to be under his command, to which end he gave them their tasks and where necessary summoned them to join him with some of their troops, as he had done with Lord Grey of Warke. Essex also had to approve the commissioning of colonels to raise regiments and the appointment of a lieutenant general of horse and a major general of foot in each of the regional armies when they grew big enough to warrant such appointments. It was fully accepted that he had the right to do these things. On the other hand the commanders of the regional associations were responsible to Parliament, not Essex, for raising the money to pay and maintain their units, and it was Parliament that laid down the amount of money that could be extracted from each county for this purpose. In this respect they were in competition with Essex for funds, as he too had to go to Parliament for the money he needed to maintain his army. Funding was therefore a source of irritation between Essex and the regional commanders. Occasionally Essex issued orders direct to individual colonels without asking their regional commanders, which was another cause of friction. There was thus plenty of room for misunderstanding between Essex and the regional commanders, and in the case of his relationship with Sir William Waller this grew into fierce dislike despite their long association which went back to Bohemia in 1619.

As both Manchester and Cromwell knew, it was not only the Eastern Association that was in peril. August marked the high point of Royalist success throughout the country. The whole of the north-east was under Newcastle's control, with the exception of Hull. In the south-west an army that had originated in Cornwall and which was commanded by Hopton had fought its way through Somerset and then defeated the

Parliamentary commander Sir William Waller near Devizes in Wiltshire. This army then invested Bristol on the south side while Prince Rupert with troops from Oxford took up a position to the north. Rupert, who was as expert in the conduct of sieges as in his use of cavalry, took Bristol by storm within three days at the end of July. Not only had he taken the second city in the kingdom and a major port, but he also captured eighteen merchant ships and four ships of Parliament's navy, all of which changed sides. Soon afterwards most of Dorset fell to the King, so that the south-west, except for the ports of Plymouth and Lyme Regis, was now in his hands. Apart from parts of the north-west and Gloucester, Parliamentary control was limited to London, the south-east and the Eastern Association, together with some isolated strong points such as Nottingham.

Naturally there was gloom in London. Early in August Pym only just managed to defeat a proposal in Parliament for peace to be made with the King. By the middle of the month the King was besieging Gloucester, and if this was not enough, Essex's General of Horse, the Earl of Bedford, together with Warwick's brother the Earl of Holland and the Earl of Clare, made their way to Oxford to make their submission to the King. Parliament could not afford to lose Gloucester without making an effort to relieve it.

On 24 August Essex set off from Hounslow, reinforcing his army with five regiments of foot and one of horse from the London trained bands, which seriously denuded London's defences. By 5 September he was within ten miles of Gloucester, and the King withdrew to the south-east. Three days later Essex relieved the city, but Parliament was now in grave danger. If the King could get between Essex and London and defeat him in battle, London, with its defences weakened, would be at his mercy. On 20 September the King brought Essex to battle outside Newbury on roughly equal terms, that is to say about 14,500 men on each side. At the end of the day both sides were exhausted and short of ammunition. Although Rupert urged the King to stand fast, the King withdrew during the night towards Oxford. Essex with a sigh of relief pushed on to London. Although the Royalists were able to re-occupy

Reading, it was in all other respects a victory for Parliament. The King had, for the second and last time, lost the opportunity of capturing London.

While these events were destroying the King's hopes of gaining his ends by occupying London, Parliament was engaged in further negotiations with the Scots. In an agreement ratified in London on 25 September, the Scots undertook to send an army of 18,000 foot, 3,000 horse and an artillery train into England, providing that Parliament reformed the religion of England in accordance with the 'word of God and the example of the best reformed churches'. The agreement also committed the English Parliament to pay the Scots £30,000 per month to keep their army in the field. To direct the war a Committee of Both Kingdoms would be set up, consisting of fourteen members of the Commons, seven members of the Lords and the Scots Commissioners in London led by Lord Maitland. This committee would supersede the Committee of Safety that had hitherto been directing the war.

The religious clause in the agreement gave scope for misunderstanding. By agreeing to reform the religion of the country in accordance with the word of God and the example of the best Reformed Churches, the Scots intended Parliament to enforce the Presbyterian religion on England, and that is what many English Presbyterians thought as well. But the English negotiators, headed by Sir Henry Vane the younger, took it to mean that all forms of the Reformed religion that excluded bishops would be permitted. Vane was an Independent, that is to say a Puritan in the sense of being a Calvinist who did not want bishops, but one who did not favour the exclusive arrangements of the Presbyterians. Independents wanted freedom for all Puritans to worship as they liked, but though in that sense they were more tolerant than the Presbyterians, they tended to be more earnest about their religion. In modern parlance, the Presbyterians were the establishment Puritans, whereas the Independents were of the charismatic or born-again variety.

Cromwell was an Independent and, largely as a result of his influence, first his own regiment, then the Eastern Association horse, and finally much of the Eastern Association army leant in that direction.

These people developed a degree of religious commitment bordering on fanaticism that was completely different from the outlook of the officers and men in the armies of Essex, Waller and Fairfax, to say nothing of the Scots. And although in terms of the enthusiasm engendered it made the Eastern Association army more formidable, it also led to great strains within it, especially as its commander, Manchester, was himself a Presbyterian. The tension later increased when he appointed another Presbyterian to be his major general of foot, but this is to jump the gun by several months.

WHILE THE DECISIVE EVENTS of August and September were in progress elsewhere, a period of operational inactivity descended on the Eastern Association following the withdrawal on 8 August of Newcastle's army from Nottingham to lay siege to Hull. All efforts were now bent on building up the new regiments and on raising the money to pay and maintain them.

During August when Manchester was busy in this way, Cromwell raised a regiment of foot to act as a defensive force for the Isle of Ely. He also continued to enlarge his regiment of horse, which, by September, consisted of ten troops. It is clear that by this time some people were becoming worried about the religious enthusiasm of his troopers and the social standing of his officers. His two letters to the Suffolk county committee, extracts from which are sometimes quoted together as though forming one letter, date from this period. In the first he begs the committee to be careful when choosing captains of horse saying that if godly men are chosen, honest men will follow them. He goes on famously to add 'I had rather have a plain russet-coated captain that knows what he fights for and loves what he knows than that which you call a gentleman and is nothing else. I honour a gentleman that is so indeed.' In a second letter to the Suffolk committee he explains himself in more detail by adding 'It had been well that men of honour and birth had entered into these employments, but why do they not appear? … But seeing it was necessary the work must go on, better plain men than none'. The truth of the matter was that the rate of expansion made it impossible to be as selective as the colonels of regiments would have liked. Nonetheless, Cromwell's method of going for godly and effective people rather than socially reliable but less effective people was raising concern that he might undermine the social fabric of the country, which was the last thing he would have wanted to do. He was certainly aware that some were criticising him for employing religious fanatics, as a letter he wrote to Oliver St John in early September included the lines 'I have a lovely company; you would respect them did you know them. They are no Anabaptists, they are honest, sober Christians.'[3] At that time the term 'Anabaptist' was used to denote fanatics and rabble-rousers.

Allegations were also being made that Cromwell was particularly involved in destroying church statues, crucifixes and other adornments. Undoubtedly Puritans as a whole disliked such objects and had done so since long before the Civil War. It is also true that many of Parliament's soldiers did damage of this sort when they could. But there is little evidence to suggest that Cromwell was any worse than other commanders in this respect, except possibly in his hatred of music in church, which did result in the destruction of organs and the dismissal of choirs. (In this respect he seems to have been out of tune with the Old Testament, which encourages the praising of God on the harp, to say nothing of trumpets, timbrels, stringed instruments and even organs: see Psalm 150.)

On 20 September Parliament decided that Lincolnshire should be joined to the Eastern Association. This gave Manchester control of the area through which enemy thrusts directed at his other counties were most likely to come, and it also increased the forces available to him, although Lord Willoughby of Parham was kept on as their commander for the next few months. Altogether the Eastern Association army would ultimately consist of 23 regiments of foot, ten regiments of horse, eight regiments of dragoons and an artillery train,[4] although many of these regiments were only usable as garrison troops and were neither trained nor backed to carry out mobile operations. Out of this total, Lincolnshire provided three regiments of foot, three of horse and one of dragoons.

THE ADVANCE OF NEWCASTLE's army into Lincolnshire in July had revitalised the hopes of Royalists in various parts of the Eastern Association territory, notably in King's Lynn, where they had succeeded in capturing the town. By the second week in September the Earl of Manchester was ready to recapture it. Not wishing to have his operation interfered with by Royalists from Lincolnshire, he sent Cromwell to establish a screen between his main body and any possible enemy advance. At this time Manchester had three regiments of horse capable of taking the field: his own, Cromwell's and Vermuyden's; Cromwell must have been reinforced by one or both of the other two regiments to carry out this task. In fact no Royalists appeared and Manchester captured King's Lynn on 16 September.

Before Newcastle's army tightened its grip on Hull in August, Lord Fairfax and his son Thomas managed to get some of their forces from the West Riding into the town. Once the town was besieged, it was naturally cut off from the outside world but, thanks to Warwick's ships, it could not be starved into submission. Although Lord Fairfax needed all the foot he could get to man the defences, Thomas together with his regiments of horse could be better used elsewhere.

It was therefore decided that with King's Lynn secured Cromwell should take his detachment of horse to secure a landing point on the Lincolnshire coast at Saltfleet. When he appeared there on 18 September, Fairfax started to ferry his 21 troops of horse across from Hull in a fleet of small boats that he had managed to assemble under the protection of Parliamentary warships. Four days later Cromwell himself crossed into Hull to obtain arms and ammunition from the arsenal there and for the first time met Thomas Fairfax, his future commander-in-chief. It was two days after the great battle at Newbury.

Meanwhile news of what was going on reached Newcastle, who sent a body of horse into Lincolnshire to try and intercept Fairfax and Cromwell before they could reach the safety of Boston, which was held by Lord Willoughby, but in this he failed. On 7 October Manchester too arrived at Boston, where he joined Fairfax and Cromwell with the regiments of foot with which he had captured King's Lynn.

On 9 October Newcastle's army launched a concentrated attack on Hull, which was repulsed. Next day Manchester, who now had a sizeable force at his disposal, moved north about fifteen miles to reduce the Parliamentary garrison at Bolingbroke Castle. A Royalist relief force commanded by Cavendish's successor in Lincolnshire, Sir William Widrington, together with reinforcements from Newark led by Henderson, was on its way to oppose them. Manchester sent Fairfax forward with his horse to form a covering force behind which his men could deploy. He then drew up his own men on a ridge outside the village of Winceby with his foot in the centre and his horse on either flank. Some dragoons were sent forward as the 'forlorn hope' to do what damage they could to the enemy as he advanced. Fairfax's horse would form up in the rear when they had completed their duties as covering force.

The Royalists took up a position on another ridge 600 yards from Manchester's line with dragoons in front and their horse on the flanks of the foot. The action started with an exchange of fire between the dragoons and then the horse on both sides closed with each other. Cromwell led the two regiments immediately under his command, but when still short of the enemy, his horse was hit by a bullet fired by one of the Royalist dragoons and it fell heavily, rolling on him as it did so. Cromwell extricated himself and jumped to his feet, only to be felled once more by a Royalist. But he was not seriously hurt and again got to his feet, to see his men fighting it out with their opponents some way ahead of him. Eventually he managed to find a trooper's horse, but it was too late for him to play any further part in the battle.

While this was going on, his two regiments had fought with such determination and effect that they had pushed the Royalist horse back onto their reserves, but owing to the sheer weight of numbers they were unable to break the Royalist horse. At this moment Fairfax brought his troops round the right flank of the battle and charged into the Royalist left. This caused the enemy line to break and Fairfax pursued the fleeing Royalists for some miles. 200 Royalists were killed and many more are known to have drowned trying to cross a river. A further 2,000 were taken prisoner. It would seem that the foot on both sides never became engaged, as the Royalist line disintegrated with the defeat of their horse.

Fairfax rightly got most of the credit for the victory in Manchester's report to Parliament, but it was the Eastern Association horse and Cromwell's regiment in particular that had held and weakened the enemy before Fairfax's decisive charge. This fact was not lost on Widrington, who later reported to Newcastle that the Eastern Association horse was very good, a fact that was by now becoming generally recognised.

The combined forces of Manchester and Sir Thomas Fairfax now set about clearing the rest of Lincolnshire, which took up most of the next two months. Gainsborough was the last place to be restored to Parliamentary control after being taken by Meldrum on 20 December. At the end of the year Fairfax departed from Lincolnshire, as he was required by Parliament to take a force into Cheshire.

Fairfax was usually a silent and mild man, but he became a whirl-wind of skilfully directed ferocity whenever the enemy appeared. He was tall, with black hair and very dark eyes, and was generally known as Black Tom. He was hugely admired and even loved by his men. He had started his military career at the age of seventeen in the United Provinces under Sir Horace Vere, whose daughter he later married. He had further experience commanding a troop of dragoons in the Bishops War of 1639, and he had been constantly on operations in Yorkshire since the end of 1642 with a string of successes and some gallant failures to his credit. He was still only 31 years old.

AS THE OPERATIONS DIED down, Cromwell returned to the Isle of Ely. Then at the end of the year, for the first time since the summer of 1642, he went to London to take his place in Parliament. He had cer-tainly had a successful year as a colonel of horse and he had built up a large and highly efficient regiment. Indeed by the end of the year it was exactly twice as big as it should have been and was known as a double regiment. He had also played a major part in building up the Eastern Association. It is probably true to say that he played the leading role in the absence of Lord Grey in the early part of the summer, and when Manchester arrived he continued by supporting him to the hilt. In terms of persuading, and if need be coercing, the local notables to play their part he was second to none. His single-minded determination to prosecute the war was impressive.

His performance in the various operations that took place was equally impressive. The training of his regiment soon paid off in terms of the control that he had of them in the early skirmishes, and whenever he did lead his regiment into contact with the enemy, he was successful. He was still short of experience of moving and fighting with a major force, but he must have learnt something of the business from his contacts with the competent professional Meldrum and with the resourceful and gallant Fairfax. He was not yet a major military figure, but he had made a start.

Where he had been outstanding was in his ability to choose captains for his troops of horse and then teach them how to get hold of the sort of men that would really fight and at the same time submit to a strict discipline. In this way he raised a body of men who promoted the aims of Parliament, not only when fighting but also by their behaviour amongst the population as a whole. In this he was unique and on it hung his future success. That he did it as a product of his religious leanings made it no less effective from a military point of view, although the political repercussions would ultimately cause a rift among the supporters of Parliament.

4 · Manchester's Lieutenant General

Pym died in December 1643. For the last five years of his life he had dominated Parliament and had dragged it into the war against the King. He was the champion of Parliamentary supremacy and considered that this could not be established until the King had been severely weakened. Although a rough and unscrupulous politician, he was in many ways a moderate and by no means a Puritan. It was Pym who held Parliament together throughout the disasters of 1643 and prevented a deal with the King that would have given up much of the political ground gained since 1640. His final great act was the negotiation of the treaty with the Scots which would, in 1644, reverse the run of Royalist success.

This was the scene that greeted Cromwell when he returned to the Commons in January 1644 after an absence of sixteen months. Despite Pym's success at bringing in the Scots, there was a strong peace party headed by Denzil Holles which opposed the most influential of Pym's successors, Oliver St John and Henry Vane. But it was the war party in the House of Lords led by Viscount Saye and Sele that was in the ascendant, and Cromwell, who was recognised for his military actions in the Eastern Association, was regarded by Saye as a valuable ally. From being a person of small account in Parliament his reputation as a soldier had turned him into a man of some influence.

It did not take long for Cromwell to become involved with an important issue being considered by Parliament concerning the financing of the Eastern Association army. As mentioned earlier, each county was obliged to find a certain sum each month for the maintenance of the military units raised in that county. In the case of the Eastern Association, the total amount was too little to finance the number of units authorised by Parliament. Furthermore, the system by which each county had to support its own units took no account of the fact that the number and type of soldiers maintained by each county varied, whereas the amount of money allotted was the same. Also, the fact that each county was supposed to support its own units meant that the system did not allow for the bulk buying of equipment required by the Eastern Association army as a whole. In January an ordinance was being discussed in Parliament to centralise the raising of money throughout the Eastern Association and to increase the overall amount authorised to be raised. This business was highly contentious as it cut across tradition. That the ordinance was passed on 20 January was largely due to the persistence and persuasive powers of Cromwell, and it was this above all that enabled Manchester to set up a uniquely successful system for funding and administering the Eastern Association in the coming months.[1]

On the day before this ordinance was passed the Scots army crossed the border into England. Three days later Cromwell was appointed Manchester's lieutenant general. One of the matters that he felt needed sorting out was the position of Lord Willoughby of Parham, who he considered to be totally inadequate for the command of the Lincolnshire regiments. He accordingly attacked him vigorously in Parliament and introduced a bill requiring him to give up his command. This struck a sideways blow at Essex's authority, as he had appointed Willoughby, and it fitted well with Saye's desire to weaken Essex's position since he regarded Essex as insufficiently committed to all-out war. Saye therefore put his weight behind Cromwell's bill, which was passed. When Willoughby finally gave up his command in March his regiments were placed directly under Manchester.[2] Saye, who was influential in the selection of the fourteen members of the Commons to be on the Committee of Both Kingdoms, rewarded Cromwell by including him on the list. Other members of the committee included Essex and Sir Philip Stapleton, Waller, now commander of the South East Association, and his lieutenant general Hazlerigg, Manchester, Warwick, Northumberland, St John and Vane. Shortly afterwards, this committee took over the running of the war from the Committee of Safety.

One of the conditions under which the Scots had invaded England was that all those people in both England and Scotland holding important appointments should take the Covenant. At the end of January Cromwell. having delayed to the last possible moment, took it. In doing so he pledged himself to the spirit of the treaty with the Scots, which was designed to extirpate Popery and prelacy and to preserve the rights of Parliament and the King's person, to punish malignants and to keep the two kingdoms together. On the other hand he and many others had reservations about the original purpose of the Covenant, which was to support Presbyterianism. Whatever his reservations, Cromwell could not be Manchester's lieutenant general or a member of the Committee of Both Kingdoms without taking it.

In early February the Scottish professional Lawrence Crawford was appointed to the Eastern Association as major general of foot. Twelve years younger than Cromwell, he had served in the Swedish and Dutch armies and had been a member of the Elector's life guard at the time of his attempt to recover the Palatinate in 1638. He thus knew the Elector's brother Prince Rupert, and also Newcastle's military commander, Lord Eythin, both of whom had taken part in that disastrous campaign. He subsequently served under the Earl of Ormonde in Ireland for three years before briefly returning to Scotland and then taking service with the English Parliament. Altogether, he had been in military employment for seventeen years.

AS LIEUTENANT GENERAL OF horse Cromwell had two jobs. First, he was responsible for the fighting efficiency of all the regiments of horse in the Eastern Association, which meant that he would have to try and raise them to the high standard achieved by his own large regiment. Second, as Manchester's second-in-command he would, in conjunction with the major general of foot, have to advise Manchester in all operational matters and be prepared to act as a task force commander should Manchester decide to detach part of his force to carry out a particular mission. And of course such a detachment might include regiments of foot and dragoons, possibly backed by part of the artillery train.

Once again Cromwell was fortunate in that he could get on with the first part of his task for some weeks without operational distractions. Newcastle, being fully taken up with repelling the Scots invasion and defending himself against Lord Fairfax, was in no position to interfere with the Eastern Association. At the same time Meldrum was assembling a large force to attempt the reduction of the Royalist stronghold of Newark, which meant that no threat was likely to develop from that quarter.

In the early months of 1644 there were ten regiments of horse in the Eastern Association. Of these, one was soon disbanded and the three Lincolnshire regiments were sent to reinforce Meldrum, two of them combining under Colonel Rossiter shortly afterwards. Two of the remaining regiments were garrison troops. This left four regiments, which would take part in the operations of Manchester's army up to August 1644. They were Lord Manchester's, consisting of eleven troops, Cromwell's of fourteen troops, Fleetwood's of six troops and Vermuyden's of five troops. Both Manchester's regiment and Cromwell's were in terms of troops the equivalent of two regiments.

It was important from Cromwell's point of view to have good men in command of these regiments. From the middle of 1643 Manchester's regiment was commanded by Colonel Algernon Sidney, a younger son of the Earl of Leicester, aged 22, who had formerly been commanding a troop of horse in Ireland. He was a brave and capable commander who subsequently held a number of important posts in the service of Parliament. Cromwell's regiment was commanded by Whalley. Charles Fleetwood, aged 25 and brother of a baronet, originally commanded a troop in Essex's army until he was wounded at the battle of Newbury.

When recovered, he was given a regiment in Manchester's army. He had a long association with Cromwell ahead of him. Vermuyden, the commissary general of horse, was a Dutch professional with experience on the Continent. He had been employed by Parliament as a colonel since the middle of 1643. Rossiter had been in command of his regiment since April 1643 and had therefore some operational experience. Altogether Cromwell's commanding officers were by the standards of the time an imposing bunch, some middle-aged, some young, and all well capable of transmitting his ideas both in terms of tactics and discipline to his regiments of horse.

While Cromwell was busy imposing his ideas on the Eastern Association horse as a whole, Manchester was rearranging the Eastern Association's financial and supply system in accordance with Parliament's new ordinance. This was a task that called on all his qualities of tactful determination backed up by his position as a great magnate. The result was an administrative system that was far superior to that of Parliament's other armies and which was extended to the New Model Army when it was formed in the following year.

In March Cromwell led a number of troops drawn from several of his regiments on a raid almost as far as Oxford, in the process of which he drove off a large number of cattle destined for the Royalist garrison. Also in March, his son Oliver died of smallpox in Newport Pagnell, which was, from time to time, held by troops from the Eastern Association army.

WHEN SIR THOMAS FAIRFAX departed from the Eastern Association army in December, he crossed to the west of the country to relieve Nantwich, which was being beseiged by Royalists. Nantwich was important to Parliament because forces based there could interfere with the deployment of Royalist reinforcements from Ireland landed at Chester. On 25 January Fairfax and Parliamentary forces from Lancashire defeated the Royalists outside Nantwich, a serious setback to the Royalist cause. The King now had to recover his position in the north-west, not only to make it safe for the arrival of fresh regiments from Ireland, but also to use it as a base and recruiting ground for operations designed to help Newcastle in his battles with the Scots. He therefore sent Prince Rupert to take command in the north-west. Rupert immediately started recruiting and collecting together the defeated Royalists and some incoming Irish. But before he could put together an army capable of restoring the Royalist position in Lancashire and Cheshire, an urgent call came from the Royalist commander in the midlands for help in fending off Meldrum's assault on Newark. Rupert soon appeared outside Newark with 3,000 foot and 3,500 horse, most of which he collected from Royalist garrisons on the way. Meldrum, who had 5,000 foot and 2,000 horse, had no idea that Rupert was within 50 miles of him and in the ensuing battle fought on 21 March he was shattered. Not only was Newark saved for the King, but Parliament had to abandon Lincoln, Gainsborough and Sleaford. The Eastern Association was now open to attack from Royalist forces in the midlands.

Rupert's relief of Newark has long been regarded as a classic. His ability to move a force rapidly was exceptional; within a few months Cromwell would have an opportunity of experiencing this at first hand. Movement was the main building block of strategy in that it enabled a commander to concentrate the maximum available force at a critical point in such a way as to surprise his opponent and take him at a disadvantage. Speed of movement depended partly on the state of the roads and of the bridges and fords across rivers, and partly on how the force could be supplied. An army on the move could be supplied either by taking the required food and ammunition along in carts, or by pre-positioning in magazines along the way, or by dispersing the force each evening into areas where small groups of men could get their own food by purchase or robbery, known as living off the land. Pre-positioning was the system that enabled the force to move the fastest, because it reduced the number of baggage wagons in a column. It also avoided wasting the time taken to disperse the force each evening over an area large enough to support it and then having to reassemble it next morning. But this system was not easy to manage when advancing into enemy country unless there were friendly fortified garrisons holding supplies surplus to their needs, or alternatively enemy magazines that could be captured and used. Another advantage of friendly garrisons was that some of the men in them could be temporarily removed to swell the force for an impending battle and then returned afterwards. Writers about the Civil War are often critical of the number of troops tied down in garrisons; there were certainly many serious disadvantages,[3] but these troops had, in addition to the routine task of dominating the surrounding area, the vital role of aiding the movement of friendly forces and of reinforcing them.

For a commander to become effective at moving a mixed force of horse, foot and artillery required study and experience. This would enable him to hold in his head data regarding the time needed to move the component parts of the army, under many different circumstances, over a given distance. Once gained, he would be able to apply this accumulated knowledge to planning and executing a particular operation. Competence in this field was one of the main things that distinguished the professional from the amateur. In due course Cromwell became effective in this business, with particular reference to his ability to make use of sea power, but for the time being the Eastern Association had to rely mainly on Crawford.

On 29 March Rupert was back in Wales building an infrastructure that would support a force large enough to go to the assistance of the hard-pressed Newcastle. On that same day Waller won a battle at Cheriton in Hampshire that turned the tables on the Royalists. As a result the whole of the area south of the Thames passed to Parliament, apart from a few fortified outposts. Waller and Essex, who both had armies of around 10,000, men were now free to concentrate against the King, whose Oxford army numbered no more than 9,000 because of the detachments it had been obliged to send to Rupert in the north-west.

Despite the ground lost by Rupert's relief of Newark, Parliament was also in a stronger position than it had been at the beginning of the year in the north. Early in February the Scots had reached the town of Newcastle; for the next two months they tied down the newly promoted Marquess of Newcastle in this area while Lord Fairfax was strengthening his position in the West Riding industrial towns.

Meanwhile Thomas Fairfax remained in Lancashire. Early in March Thomas heard from his cousin John Lambert, who was one of his colonels of horse, that his presence with his father would be enough to gain complete ascendancy over the West Riding towns. He started back with 2,000 horse but the Royalist governor of York moved out of the city to Selby with 1,500 horse and 5,000 foot to intercept him. A battle ensued in which Thomas was again wounded. But it was a victory for the Fairfaxes, who took 3,000 prisoners. As a result Newcastle had to abandon his position and withdraw to York which he reached in mid April. The Scots followed him up, meeting the Fairfaxes at Wetherby. The combined force, numbering 16,000 foot and 4,000 horse under the command of the Earl of Leven, proceeded to lay siege to York.

THE DEFEAT OF MELDRUM at Newark jerked the Eastern Association into a state of readiness for battle. Meldrum had withdrawn to Hull, and Manchester prepared to resist further incursions into his area, at the same time making preparations to reoccupy Lincolnshire. On 19 April Manchester received orders from the Committee of Both Kingdoms telling him to go north to join Lord Fairfax and the Scots outside York. This was not popular with some of his regiments, who feared that their homes in the Eastern Association might be attacked while they were in Yorkshire. Towards the end of April Manchester sent Cromwell ahead with his four regiments of horse and some dragoons, while he took the foot together with some horse from local garrisons to recapture Lincoln. Assuming that the four regiments of horse that Cromwell took with him were all up to strength, he must have had close on 3,000 horsemen, not to mention the five companies of John Lilburne's dragoons which would have added a further 500 men to his detachment.

When Cromwell arrived in Yorkshire he was initially sent to the Bradford area to guard against Royalist incursions from that direction. Meanwhile Fairfax and the Scots reduced a number of Royalist strongholds around York, coming gradually closer to the city. Meldrum also moved up from Hull and took a hand in reducing two strong points to the south of York, after which, early in May, he was sent to Lancashire to bolster the defences there against Prince Rupert. As Fairfax and the Scots moved in towards York, Cromwell closed up to give what assistance he could.

Manchester captured Lincoln on 6 May but because of the need to clear a number of Royalist positions in the county, his foot and artillery train did not reach York until 1 June. In the intervening period Cromwell had the opportunity to renew his contacts with Thomas Fairfax and his colonels, as well as meeting the Scots commanders, many of whom were very experienced soldiers. The Earl of Leven had served in the Dutch and Swedish armies for over 30 years. He was with the Swedish army at Lützen when Gustavus Adolphus was killed and remained with it until returning home in 1635. He commanded the Scottish army in the wars of 1639 and 1640. He had a great reputation as a general but by 1644 he was on the old side, being in his middle sixties. Leven's lieutenant general, William Baillie, commanded the foot instead of the horse and had served with the Swedes and then with the Dutch. Major General Sir James Lumsden was second in command of the foot; he had also fought with the Swedish army throughout Gustavus's campaign in Germany, remaining with it until 1639. The commander of the Scottish horse was Major General David Leslie, who served in the Swedish army as a colonel of horse. He was a competent commander, but not much liked by Cromwell.

Manchester brought with him six regiments of foot, one of which had been with Meldrum at Newark. His own regiment consisted of eighteen companies instead of the standard ten. The six regiments together numbered around 4,300. By this time Independents had been widely recruited into the foot regiments as well as into the regiments of horse and although Manchester's and Crawford's regiments were both mainly Presbyterian, the other four were composed largely of Independents. Furthermore the colonels of three of them, Pickering, Montagu and Russell, had close links with Cromwell, who encouraged them in opposing Crawford in matters of religion. Indeed, as early as March Cromwell had become involved in a dispute with Crawford when the latter had tried to get rid of one of his officers for his religious views.

On the arrival of Manchester's foot the whole of the allied army closed in on York and started to raise up batteries of guns in the approved manner. The Scots, who had with them about 13,000 foot, held the largest sector, stretching from the south to the north-west (roughly six o'clock to ten o'clock). Manchester held the sector from the north-west of the city to the north (ten o'clock to one o'clock). Fairfax, who mustered only around 3,000 foot, was given a regiment of Scots to reinforce him and held the whole of the eastern side of the city (one o'clock to six o'clock). To reduce the vulnerability of his supply lines from interference by Royalists, Manchester arranged for some of his supplies to come by sea, then up the Humber.

On 9 June Henry Vane arrived in the allied camp outside York as a representative of the Committee of Both Kingdoms, ostensibly to persuade the generals to send forces into Lancashire to assist in its defence against Rupert. But the real purpose of his visit was to discuss the future of the war with the senior officers. He suggested that as negotiations with the King were never likely to succeed, consideration should be given to overthrowing him altogether and replacing him with someone else such as the Prince of Wales or the deposed Elector Palatine.[4] Deposition of the King was strongly opposed by Leven, Fairfax and Manchester but found favour with some of the Independents in the Eastern Association army. Although these discussions had no significance at the time, they became one of the main causes of the rift that developed between Cromwell and Manchester later in the summer. Vane subsequently went on to Edinburgh to discuss the plan with leading members of the Scottish government.

On 16 June Crawford sprung a mine that had been dug under the city wall about 150 yards north-east of the river in the area then known as the Manor (now the Museum Gardens). He then put in an attack through the breach, but as the attack had not been co-ordinated with Leven or Fairfax, there were no diversionary attacks and Crawford was repulsed with the loss of 40 killed and 250 captured. This incident had the effect of discouraging further assaults, so that all attempts were now concentrated on starving the garrison out.

ON 16 MAY PRINCE RUPERT with 2,000 horse and 6,000 foot left Shrewsbury for Lancashire, where he overran many Parliamentary strongpoints. On 1 June he was joined by Lord Goring, who had brought with him 5,000 Royalist horse not wanted in York during the siege. He was also joined by Royalist detachments from Lancashire, Derbyshire and Cumbria.

While Rupert was subduing Lancashire, Essex and Waller closed with the King, reaching Oxford on 3 June, but during the previous night the King escaped with 2,500 musketeers, joining up with 5,000 Royalist horse outside the town. He then retired to Worcester. Essex now told Waller to follow the King, while he took his army into Devon and Cornwall. With no foot soldiers other than musketeers, the King felt unable to hold Worcester; so he moved north, intending to give Waller the idea that he was going to join Rupert. Waller swung north to prevent this and the King made a dash for Oxford to collect the rest of the foot. At this time, when his position was precarious, he wrote a confused letter to Rupert telling him to relieve York, beat the allied armies besieging it and get back to him as soon as possible. Rupert received the letter on 16 June, the same day that Crawford exploded his mine. Leaving Meldrum at Manchester, he headed off for York on 22 June with 7,000 horse, 6,000 foot and an artillery train.

Rupert's army moved to Preston, then up the Ribble valley via Clitheroe and Gisborn to Skipton, where it arrived on 26 June. Two days later Leven, Fairfax and Manchester heard that he was advancing towards them with 18,000 men, a considerable overestimate. The allied generals had already sent messages to Meldrum and Lord Denbigh, the Parliamentary commander in the west midlands, to join them. Together these two might have added as many as 12,000 to the allied strength, which would have enabled them to confront Rupert and at the same time maintain the siege of York. But by 28 June they realised that neither Meldrum nor Denbigh could arrive in time; so next day they abandoned the siege and moved to a position astride the road from Knaresborough to York, intending to fight Rupert before he could combine his army with Newcastle's troops in York.

The allies deployed facing west on Marston Moor behind the river Nidd, about seven miles west-north-west of York. The allied position covered not only the approach from Knaresborough but also the road from Wetherby, thus preventing Rupert from outflanking them to the south. The three generals had their headquarters in the village of Long Marston. When the allies took up their position, Manchester's army, having come from the northern sector, was on the right of the line with Cromwell's horse on the right flank. To reach his position Manchester moved his army across the river Ouse on a bridge of boats which he had built earlier at a place usually described as Poppleton but sometimes as being in Clifton Ings,[5] a few miles upstream of York. In case he should need to withdraw to the east of the river in an emergency, he left a regiment of dragoons to guard the bridge against a sally by the York garrison.

Cromwell arrived at the Long Marston headquarters ahead of the generals, just before midnight of 29 June. Soon afterwards he told Manchester's scoutmaster to send a message to the generals suggesting that orders should be sent to outlying troops of Lord Fairfax's army instructing them to join the main body so that 'by their absence they should not be made useless'.[6] Either as a result of this suggestion, or because the generals had already ordered such a concentration, there were no troops watching the approaches to York from the north-west.

Early on Monday 1 July the allied army saw a large body of Royalist horse appear in front of their position as though to screen the arrival of the rest of their army. During the morning the last of the allied regiments arrived from their entrenchments around York and took up their battle positions. As the day wore on, expectancy arose regarding the arrival of the Royalist foot but they never appeared. What had happened was that Rupert, realising that he could not attack an allied force that he reckoned to be 27,000 strong with his own army of 14,000, had decided to march round the northern flank of the allied position. Undetected, he crossed the river Ure at Borough Bridge and then the river Swale at Thornton Bridge before sweeping down the east bank of the Ouse to seize Manchester's bridge of boats. York was relieved and the garrison swarmed out to loot the allied trenches.

Although it was now dark, Rupert pushed his horse out towards Marston Moor to reconnoitre the rear of the allied position, at the same time sending Goring into York with a message to Newcastle instructing him to be at Marston Moor with his army by 4 am next morning. By marching his army 22 miles in one day, which was about twice what armies could normally manage, he had totally surprised the allies and increased the size of his army by the 5,000 men of the York garrison. If he could fight a battle while the allies were off balance, he had a good chance of making up for his numerical inferiority and winning a decisive victory.

When the allied generals discovered what had happened there was a difference of opinion as to what they should do. Fairfax and Manchester wanted to fight but Leven, who did not like the position on the moor, wanted to withdraw the whole army south to Tadcaster. At Tadcaster they would be well placed to join Meldrum and Denbigh and to intercept Rupert were he to strike south into Lincolnshire in order to draw them away from York. Rupert had deliberately fostered this idea by sending a detachment of horse south from York soon after reaching the city. Leven's view prevailed and early in the morning of 2 July the move to the south began with the Scots foot leading, followed by the English foot, followed by the artillery train. A little over half of the horse under Sir Thomas Fairfax, accompanied by Cromwell and Leslie, was deployed along a ridge of high ground south of the road between Tockwith and Long Marston to cover the withdrawal.

At around 8 am Fairfax saw a body of Royalist horse appear to his north on Marston Moor, but soon afterwards they withdrew. About half an hour later he heard that the leading Scots troops had reached Tadcaster; so he gave orders for a gradual thinning out of his force on the ridge. Shortly afterwards at about 9 am he noticed that a much larger number of Royalist horse, which he estimated as being around 5,000 strong, had arrived on the moor, followed soon afterwards by regiments of foot. Fearing a full-scale attack on the allied army, strung out as it was along the road to Tadcaster, he recalled the regiments that he had recently sent back and sent a message to the generals pointing out the danger and suggesting that they should turn the army around yet again and take up a proper defensive position.

Fairfax had every reason for concern, since Rupert's original idea was to attack the allies at the earliest possible moment to take advantage of the disarray that he had caused by getting behind them. But Rupert too was troubled, because Newcastle was unable to get his troops to the rendezvous by 4 am. Both Newcastle and Lord Eythin, his major general, were reluctant to fight a battle at such short notice and Newcastle, who had for so long been the King's commander in the north, was offended that Rupert had neither visited nor consulted him on his arrival outside York . But for all that, the main problem was that the garrison, having gone into the allied trenches to loot, got drunk and could not be collected together in time. Until they arrived Rupert felt that it would be too dangerous to commit his horse to a running battle with the retreating enemy since his own foot, unsupported by Newcastle's men, would be vulnerable to any counter-attack that might develop. Instead, he spent the coming hours deploying his army for battle.

For the allies, who knew nothing of Rupert's problem, the priority was to build up a strong enough position to repel an attack as soon as possible. They laid out their regiments along the ridge where the horse had been standing in the customary fashion, with a large block of foot in the centre and with bodies of horse on each wing, but as speed was so important the foot regiments were put into the positions that most needed filling as soon as they arrived. This naturally prevented a layout that reflected the command arrangements of the three armies.[7]

The allied centre consisted of 28 regiments; ten in the front line, eight in each of the second and third lines, and four in the fourth. The front line consisted of four of Manchester's regiments on the left, then two of Fairfax's and then four Scottish regiments on the right. The second line consisted of eight Scottish regiments. The third consisted of four of Fairfax's regiments, two Scottish and two of Manchester's. The fourth line consisted of two Scottish regiments. It is difficult to know how command was supposed to be exercised in this mass of foot, because

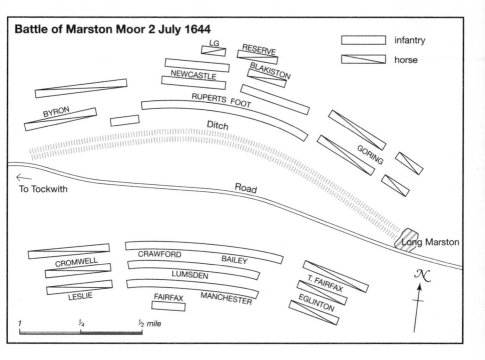

Battle of Marston Moor 2 July 1644

infantry

horse

LG
RESERVE
BLAKISTON
NEWCASTLE
RUPERTS FOOT
BYRON
Ditch
GORING
To Tockwith
Road
Long Marston
CROMWELL
CRAWFORD
BAILEY
LUMSDEN
T. FAIRFAX
LESLIE
FAIRFAX
MANCHESTER
EGLINTON
1   ¼   ½ mile

regiments from one army in the second and third lines were not necessarily behind their own regiments in the front line. But it is clear that Crawford was in charge of the left half of the front line and that Leven's lieutenant general Baillie was in charge on the right. It is also clear that Sir James Lumsden commanded the second line and that both Lord Fairfax and the Earl of Manchester stationed themselves in the third line. The total number of foot soldiers was about 18,500, of whom 1,000 musketeers were split between the two wings.

The left wing of the army was commanded by Cromwell and consisted of the Eastern Association horse, amounting to around 3,000 men, and three regiments of the Scottish Horse. In the front line, which was commanded by Cromwell in person, were the two large regiments, Manchester's and Cromwell's. In the second line, commanded by Vermuyden, was Vermuyden's regiment and Fleetwood's. The third line, consisting of the three regiments of the Scottish horse amounting to a further 1,000 men, was commanded by David Leslie. On the left wing there was also a regiment of Scottish dragoons and 500 musketeers, probably drawn from the fourth line regiments. Altogether, the left wing amounted to around 5,000 men.

The right wing of the army was commanded by Sir Thomas Fairfax. Because of the many intense engagements undertaken by the northern army, his ten regiments had been greatly weakened so that they amounted to no more than 3,000. These he divided into two lines, the front one, which he led himself, and the second, led by Colonel Lambert. Behind was a third line consisting of three regiments of Scottish horse amounting to a further 1,000 men. There were also around 500 dragoons and some musketeers, so that the total for the right wing was also about 5,000 men.

The area into which both sides were pouring their troops was the land either side of a two-mile stretch of road joining the villages of Tockwith to the west and Long Marston to the east. Although the allies to the south of the road had the advantage of slightly higher ground over which to deploy, their foot was drawn up in a large field of standing and sodden rye which, until trodden down, was both awkward and uncomfortable. Furthermore, the Royalist position to the north contained a number of terrain features that they could use to their advantage, in particular a deep ditch behind a stiff hedge which ran to the north of, and parallel to, the road.

By midday, at which time only about half of the allied army had returned, Prince Rupert had got his own army in position, although Newcastle's contingent had not yet appeared. Most of Rupert's foot regiments, which together numbered around 7,000 men, were drawn up in two lines in the centre of his position. When Newcastle's regiments, amounting to a further 3,500 men, arrived, they would be placed behind the second line on the right, while behind the second line on the left would be two weak regiments of horse, in the same way as Essex placed Balfour with two regiments at Edgehill. Opposite Cromwell was Rupert's right wing, commanded by Lord Byron. This consisted of 2,600 horse in two lines with 500 musketeers to fire in the gaps between troops. Another strong regiment of horse was placed between Byron's second line and the foot in such a way as to be able to go to Byron's assistance if required, or to be used to guard the flank of the foot regiments. In front of this regiment were two strong regiments of foot covering the ditch. Between Byron and the ditch were many rabbit holes, which would further break up the cohesion of an enemy attack. Rupert's left wing, which was opposite Sir Thomas Fairfax, was commanded by Goring, who had 2,100 horse against Fairfax's 4,000. Rupert kept a reserve of two weak regiments of horse under Sir Edward Widdrington together with his life guard behind the centre of his position.

Clearly Rupert understood that the greatest danger was to his right flank, the whole of his layout being heavily weighted to repelling an assault from this direction. It is well attested that he instructed Byron, if attacked, not to advance beyond the rabbit holes, so that his attackers would have to negotiate the ditch lined with musketeers, the boggy ground and the rabbit warrens before reaching him. Whilst negotiating these obstacles they would be subjected to the fire of the musketeers drawn up between the bodies of his horse. Rupert's concern for his right was based partly on the fact that his left wing was more difficult to attack because of the juxtaposition of lanes, gorse and hedges there, and partly because he knew that the more heavily armed and better-trained Eastern Association horse was opposite Byron.

Newcastle's foot, less three regiments left to defend York, arrived between 2.30 and 4.30 pm, adding 3,500 men to Rupert's army, which must now have numbered about 17,500 men. But by the time they were in position so also were the remaining regiments of the allied army, numbering about 27,500 men. Thus although by his flanking movement Rupert had gained a valuable addition to the number of foot soldiers at his disposal, he had been unable to take advantage of the chaos into which he had temporarily thrown the allies earlier in the day. None the less, it would be necessary to attack the allies in accordance with the King's letter of 16 June, because without defeating them he could not abandon York to rescue the King. By this time he knew that the King had succeeded in getting back to Oxford, but he had not yet heard that the King had defeated Waller on 29 June at Cropredy Bridge and was now in no particular danger.

At 5.30 pm Rupert decided that, his men being tired after their exertions and the ground sodden by numerous heavy showers, he would postpone the attack to the next day. When shortly afterwards the Earl of Leven reconnoitered the Royalist position he saw that the Royalists were settling down for the night rather than preparing to attack and he also realised how heavily he outnumbered them. With a lifetime of experience he could see that he had a chance to achieve tactical surprise by attacking in the last hours of daylight. He ordered some of his own regiments to put down their arms and start cooking in order to lull Royalist suspicions. He then held a short meeting with Manchester, Lord Fairfax and Baillie to co-ordinate arrangements for an attack at 7 pm, by which time there would be just under two hours of daylight remaining.

As the allied foot rose to their feet and started to advance across the 800 yards that separated them from their enemy, a thunderstorm broke, which dampened the powder of the Royalist musketeers manning the ditch, thereby reducing casualties among the advancing allies. In several places allied regiments managed to get across the ditch and engage the Royalist foot. For a time they made good headway, but then Newcastle's regiments in the Royalist second line started to push the allies back. When the regiments of horse in the Royalist centre added their weight, most of the allied foot was obliged to withdraw across the ditch and the road until they merged with their own third line which was moving forward to support them.

When the allied foot advanced, so also did the allied horse on both wings. On the right Sir Thomas Fairfax's men ran into a lot of trouble amongst the hedges, ditches and gorse, where they suffered severely from the fire of the musketeers shooting in the gaps between Goring's troops of horse. Although Fairfax himself with about 400 horsemen on the right of his front line succeeded in breaking through, most of his wing were thrown into disorder when Goring charged. Carrying all before him, Goring chased his opponents off the field while his second line under Lucas turned inwards against Baillie's foot, causing some companies to break and flee. At this moment, with the allied foot in grave trouble in the centre and their right wing in retreat, things looked pretty black. Leven, watching from the ridge and receiving reports from various parts of the battlefield, evidently thought that the battle was lost. Having no reserve with which to influence events, he decided that discretion was the better part of valour and fled the field, stopping only when he reached Leeds. Lord Fairfax, taking a similar view, made for Hull. By contrast, Manchester took his place with pike in hand at the head of his own regiment of foot which, having started on the right of the third line, now constituted one of the isolated pockets of resistance situated somewhere between the ridge and the road. At this point the Royalists thought that they had won and sent word to York with the good news. Bells rang out and a messenger was sent to the King at Oxford with tidings of victory.

But Royalist rejoicing was premature. When the allies moved forward at the start of the battle, Crawford led the four regiments that were on the left of the allied front line across the ditch and engaged the two Royalist regiments of foot stationed close behind it, which fell back on the Royalist centre. As a result, the horse of the allied left wing led by Cromwell got across the ditch without breaking ranks. Had Byron stood firm as he was supposed to do, and allowed his musketeers to fire at Cromwell's men as they struggled through the mire and the rabbit warrens, they might have weakened Cromwell's horse sufficiently to make up for their lack of numbers. But Byron could not contain himself and charged into the mire, masking the fire of his musketeers. He was now no match for Cromwell's four strong regiments. Soon the Eastern Association horse defeated the Royalist front line and on their left they also put to flight the Royalist second line regiment. But by this time Sidney, commanding Manchester's regiment, was seriously wounded and Cromwell, grazed in the neck by a pistol shot, was bleeding profusely. Cromwell left the field to have his wound dressed and there was a brief pause in the action while both sides tried to sort themselves out. The Eastern Association horse then renewed their attack.

But now matters became critical as Rupert, apprised of the position, led his life guard and his two reserve regiments to Byron's assistance. Rallying what he could of Byron's regiments, he led them in a charge against Cromwell's men who, though shaken, stood their ground despite being charged in front and from the flank by the best of the Royalist horse. According to a contemporary account the enemy's horse, being many of them gentlemen, stood very firm a long while coming to a close fight with the sword and standing like an iron wall, so that they were not easily broken. But there were no more Royalist reserves, whereas Leslie's horse, which had followed Cromwell into the battle, had not yet been committed. At this point Leslie charged into the flank of the Royalist line, which broke under the impact and fled back across the moor pursued by Leslie's troopers. Cromwell's training and discipline had once again borne fruit. Having given their horses time to recover their wind, his four regiments re-formed and in good order waited for further orders.

The thunderstorm that had initially helped the allies had now ceased though the sky was overcast. As it started to get dark the battle still hung in the balance. Although some of the allied foot on the right had been swept away, Lumsden had managed to plug most of the holes in the first and second lines with regiments from the third and fourth line. Also Crawford on the left with his four foot regiments was still across the ditch facing Newcastle's foot regiments, which had angled themselves back facing west so as to protect the Royalist right flank, now that their right wing regiments of horse had been put to flight. Cromwell, who had returned from having his wound dressed, was standing with his four regiments on Crawford's left.

By now too Goring had managed to recall some of his regiments of horse from chasing the remnants of the allied right wing. He was standing with them on the ridge to the right of the allied foot in roughly the same place as Sir Thomas Fairfax had been standing when the battle started. Thus whereas at the start of the battle the allies had been facing north and the Royalists south, the allied foot was now facing north-east and the Royalist foot was facing south-west. Cromwell and Leslie had a strong detachment of horse at the western end of the battlefield, while Goring had a less strong body of horse in the south-east. The allies, having come near to disaster in the early stages, had recovered to some extent, but as darkness fell it was difficult to foresee how matters would fall out.

As Cromwell was deciding how best to use his regiments, he was surprised to be accosted in the gloom by Sir Thomas Fairfax, bleeding from a sabre cut to his face. It will be remembered that at the start of the battle Sir Thomas had pushed past the end of Goring's line and had headed off towards York, doing what damage he could in the Royalist's rear area. At some point he returned with two or three troops to the area occupied by Goring's horse at the start of the battle. Here he came upon his second-in-command, Lambert who had also managed to collect together two or three troops after Goring's charge and was trying to rejoin Fairfax. The area in which they found themselves was alive with Royalists; so they removed from their hats the white handkerchiefs which the allies were wearing that day as a distinguishing mark and rode round the rear of the Royalist position until they met up with Cromwell.[8]

Fairfax told Cromwell what was happening on the opposite wing and urged him to bring his regiments round the back of the Royalist line to attack Goring, thereby disposing of the last of the Royalist horse remaining in the field. Cromwell, who knew the ground well from having been stationed on it when the allies were expecting an attack from Knaresborough two days earlier, managed to take his whole body of horse round the back of the battlefield as Fairfax suggested. When shortly afterwards he lined up opposite Goring he must have greatly outnumbered him, but Goring, not waiting to receive Cromwell's attack, charged straightaway. Cromwell's regiments then overwhelmed Goring's troopers and drove them from the field, after which Cromwell turned back to help in the final destruction of the Royalist foot.

By now it was fully dark but the clouds had passed and a bright harvest moon lit up the scene. Under pressure from Crawford on the left, the whole line had been pushed back even further, so that both sides were now lined up from north to south. Cromwell, moving in from the east, therefore took the Royalist line from the rear. Gradually gaps appeared in the Royalist line and some of their regiments were surrounded, others being withdrawn by their commanders, who marched the survivors off the field. After this the remainder either surrendered or broke up and disappeared. The very last to continue resistance were the men of Newcastle's own regiment of foot, the famous Whitecoats, who continued to fight until almost the last man was killed or wounded. By this time it was nearly midnight.

MARSTON MOOR WAS BY far the largest battle of the Civil War and was a total victory for Parliament and its Scottish allies. It is impossible to know how many men perished but it could easily have amounted to 6,000, mainly Royalists. Eight Royalist colonels were killed and 1,500 prisoners taken, including Rupert's major general of foot, to say nothing of Goring's two principal subordinates. Rupert had failed to regain the north, which had effectively been lost to the King from the time that the Scots invaded, and it remained under Parliamentary control for the rest of the war. York itself surrendered within two weeks, after which the Scots moved north to reduce the town of Newcastle and make safe their tenuous lines of communication. Lord Fairfax set about regaining control over Yorkshire. The Marquess of Newcastle and Lord Eythin retired to the Continent.

This was Cromwell's first major battle and his contribution was first-class. He used the splendid weapon that he had forged to great effect, defeating the best of the Royalist horse in a slogging match, holding his regiments together afterwards and giving them enough rest to enable them to re-enter the fray within a relatively short time. He grasped the opportunity pointed out to him by Fairfax, led his troops round the north of the battlefield in the dark, and then destroyed the last of the Royalist horse having withstood their charge. Finally he again rallied his regiments sufficiently to lead them into the rear of the remaining Royalist foot to help with their ultimate destruction. He had played a major part in turning what looked like a very dangerous situation into a victory. Rupert had laid out a strong defensive position which, with luck, might have made up for his lack of numbers, but the Eastern Association horse burst through his heavily defended western flank, which finally enabled the allies to break up his centre.

But Cromwell had only commanded a small part of the allied army and other allied leaders had also made valuable contributions. It was Leven who saw the opportunity and daringly struck at exactly the right moment. It was Crawford whose four regiments of foot opened the way for Cromwell's horse to get across the ditch and who fought and held the Royalists on the left when the rest of the allied line was giving way. He was also involved in the final destruction of the Royalist line. Credit is due to Lumsden, who stabilised the centre when it was in grave difficulties. And it was Leslie who led the charge that finally broke Rupert's counter-attack on Cromwell's men and it was he who chased the enemy off the field at this time, thereby giving Cromwell the opportunity to re-form and rest his regiments before their next contest. Last but not least, it was Thomas Fairfax who recognised the need to beat Goring's horse at the end of the battle and who managed to get himself from one side of the battlefield to the other to tell Cromwell of the opportunity that existed for doing so.

The generals' despatch after the battle was understandably brief and made no attempt to commend individuals, but many other letters winged their way to London and elsewhere, to be followed by second-hand accounts written by people who were not even present. Cromwell justly received much praise but many of the writers failed to mention other deserving people, which naturally led to bad feeling. Cromwell was by no means pleased at being singled out in this way. To his mind, all the glory was due to God alone. But inevitably pro- and anti-Cromwell stories started to appear, which usually reflected the political position of the writer. A Presbyterian minister attached to the Scottish army, and Denzil Holles, the Presbyterian leader of the peace party in Parliament, both wrote protesting at the amount of praise lavished on Cromwell. Holles in his memoirs went further, belittling Cromwell's performance, suggesting that he was a prey to indecision at critical moments and on one occasion left Crawford to give orders to his men as he did not know what to do,[9] a most unlikely tale. Cromwell himself wrote no official account but he did write to his brother-in-law Valentine Walton after the battle to break the news that his son was dead; his letter is worth quoting, as it shows Cromwell at his best and most compassionate.

> England and the Church of God hath had a great favour from the Lord in this great victory given unto us, such as the like never was since this war began. It had all the evidences of an absolute victory, obtained by the Lord's blessing upon the godly party principally. We never charged but we routed the enemy. The left wing, which I commanded, being our own horse, saving a few Scots in our rear, beat all the Prince's horse. God made them as stubble to our swords. We charged their regiments of foot with our horse, and routed all we charged. The particulars I can not relate now; but I believe of 20000, the Prince hath not 4000 left. Give glory, all glory, to God. Sir, God hath taken your eldest son away by a cannon shot. It brake his leg. We were necessitated to have it cut off, whereof he died. The gallant young man, exceeding gracious, exceedingly beloved in the army of all that knew him, who had died full of comfort, lamenting nothing save that he could no longer serve God against his enemies, and rejoicing in his last moments to see the rogues run.

WHEN THE THREE ARMIES broke up and went their separate ways, Manchester set off for Lincoln. On the way he was ordered by Parliament to capture Welbeck and Sheffield Castle, both of which tasks were completed by 7 August. Thereafter he remained at Lincoln for the rest of the month.

After Marston Moor, Rupert and Goring withdrew via Lancashire to Shrewsbury along a route which Rupert had already prepared in case of need. They arrived on 5 August together with around 6,000 survivors of the battle and with many from the garrison of York who had joined him. Rupert also collected various regiments that he had left to guard the north-west when he marched to relieve York. His force was therefore sufficiently numerous to defend the Royalist position in Cheshire, Shropshire and Wales. Before the march to York the King had asked Rupert to send Goring to him, but Rupert had not then been able to spare him. Now he sent Goring to the King, putting the remains of Newcastle's horse under the command of Sir Marmaduke Langdale; they were henceforth known as the Northern Horse.

Meanwhile Waller, after his defeat at Cropredy Bridge, wrote to Parliament saying 'until you have an army merely your own that you may command, it is impossible to do anything of importance'. This was the first of a number of demands made by different people to the effect that Parliament should reduce its regional forces and concentrate on getting a sizeable army, properly paid and supplied. It was these demands that eventually materialised in the New Model Army almost a year later.

The King now decided that it would be safe for him to follow Essex into the south-west with a view to crushing him between his own army and that of Prince Maurice besieging Lyme Regis. He reckoned that if Waller tried to put together a large enough force to rescue Essex he would arrive too late, and that if he appeared with the small number still with him he would do no good. In the event Essex relieved Lyme, and Prince Maurice retired into north Devon. Essex then went on to relieve Plymouth and the King moved to Exeter, where he was joined by Maurice, so that together they had 16,000 men. Essex then moved into Cornwall with his 10,000 men. On 4 August the King reached Boconnoc, a short distance to the east of Essex's position at Lostwithiel. Essex was effectively trapped between Lostwithiel and the sea. Unless rescued by Waller he had no hope, and Waller could not get his army to march any farther west than Abingdon. By now Goring had reached the King and taken over command of the Royalist horse.

By the end of the month Essex realised that Waller was not going to rescue him and gave orders for his horse to break out under Balfour. This they succeeded in doing. On 1 September Essex also escaped in a fishing boat, leaving Skippon, his major general of foot, to negotiate the surrender of the rest of the army to the King. All their weapons, including 42 cannon and 5,000 muskets, were taken, but the men were let go on the understanding that they took no further part in the war until they reached Southampton. On 3 September the King started the long march back to Oxford.

WHILE THESE STIRRING EVENTS were in progress Manchester remained at Lincoln, declining to use his victorious army either to help the Parliamentary forces in Cheshire or even to attack Newark as suggested to him in late July. The reasons he gave were that he had lost many men from sickness and desertion as well as from the casualties sustained in the battle and that the pay of the rest was gravely in arrears.

It was during this period that Cromwell and Manchester fell out. The cause of the trouble was the hostility between Cromwell and Crawford. Crawford in his determination to promote Presbyterianism got rid of one of his officers for being an Independent. Cromwell, supported by several of his colonels, threatened to resign unless Crawford was removed. Cromwell went further and started to weed out some of his Presbyterians, thus destroying the accord which he had previously had with Manchester, based on a common policy of employing any godly person regardless of whether he was Presbyterian or Independent. Manchester patched up a compromise between Cromwell and Crawford, but he no longer trusted Cromwell and the whole wretched business undermined his determination to pursue the war.[10] He was thoroughly alarmed at the political ambitions of the Independents, and the threat that they posed to the social structure of the country. Vane's suggestion that the King should be deposed was a further worry and he felt that it was high time to reach an agreement with the King.

It is against this background that Manchester's reaction to the destruction of Essex's army has to be seen. At the end of August Manchester was told to march to Essex's assistance, but it was already too late. It was however necessary for Waller to be reinforced before the Royalist army returned from the west. Without reinforcement the King might destroy Waller's small army, but if a junction could be achieved between Waller and Manchester before the King reached Oxford, the Royalists would themselves be in danger of defeat. All this was clear to Cromwell, but Manchester dragged his feet, saying that his army was raised by the Eastern Association to guard Eastern Association territory and that it should only go elsewhere if the Eastern Association agreed. This was in line with what he had written to the Committee of Both Kingdoms in July when he pointed out that if he left the Eastern Association, which raised and paid his men, it would not only have cause to cease paying and recruiting his army, but it might also be obliged to raise some other force to defend its territory.[11] Cromwell, who had little time for such considerations, became more and more direct in his dealings with Manchester, to the extent that those that heard him thought him downright rude if not insubordinate. On 8 September Manchester was at Huntingdon.

September saw the Royalist army moving slowly through Dorset, dislodging Parliamentary garrisons as it went. Waller, strengthening key positions along the Dorset coast, fell back as the King advanced. On 2 October the King arrived at Sherborne, by which time Manchester, reinforced by 1,800 men from London and with some extra money provided by Parliament to pay his army, had reached Reading. Essex was in London, blaming everyone but himself for the disaster in Cornwall. He then went to Reading. Essex's disarmed foot under Skippon, having been transported from Plymouth by the navy, were at Portsmouth, where they were being re-equipped. Here too they were reunited with Balfour's horse. Essex tried to co-ordinate a concentration of all these groups, but neither Waller nor Manchester was prepared to take his orders and he himself was ill. Parliament therefore decided that the army should be commanded by a committee consisting of Waller, Manchester and Balfour.

By 15 October the King was at Salisbury, Waller was at Andover and Manchester, having asked to be reinforced by the London trained bands, was at Basingstoke, where he hoped to be joined by Balfour and Skippon. Three days later the King attacked Waller at Andover, driving him back to Basingstoke. The King then swung north to relieve Donnington Castle to the north of Newbury. On 20 October Balfour and Skippon arrived bringing the combined Parliamentary strength to 17,000 (Waller 3,000, Manchester with reinforcements from London 8,000, Balfour and Skippon 6,000). At this time Cromwell still had the same regiments with him as he had had at Marston Moor, except for having Sir John Norwich's regiment instead of Fleetwood's regiment, which had been left in Lincolnshire to guard against sorties from the Royalist garrison at Newark.

Although the King's army had by now shrunk to no more than 9,000, he did not seem greatly concerned by the considerable concentration of Parliament's forces. He took up a strong defensive position north of Newbury, mainly between the Kennet and its tributary the Lambourn. The centre of the position, which was just to the north of the Lambourn, lay astride a heavily fortified house and its outbuildings, now known as Shaw House. Donnington Castle, relieved and replenished, covered the left rear of the position. South of it, between the Lambourn and the Kennet, was the village of Speen.

The combined Parliamentary army advanced from Basingstoke and drew up on Clay Hill to the north-east of Shaw House on 26 October, from where they could overlook the Royalists. What they saw led them to believe that the King's position was too strong to be taken by a frontal attack. The three commanders therefore decided on an ambitious plan. Waller would take Skippon with the remains of Essex's foot and two regiments of the London trained bands, together with all of Waller's and Balfour's horse and part of the Eastern Association horse under Cromwell, on a long night march round the north of the King's position with a view to attacking it from the rear. This force amounted to about 12,000 men. Manchester with the Eastern Association foot, the remnants of Waller's foot, three regiments of the London trained bands and the balance of the Eastern Association horse, a total of around 7,000 men, would put in a feint attack on Shaw House from Clay Hill the following morning to divert the attention of the Royalists. When Waller launched his attack Manchester would put in his main attack to prevent Royalist forces from the east being switched to the west. Waller was to fire a gun to let Manchester know when he was about to attack.

On the evening of 26 October the King, suspecting that Waller, well known for his flank attacks, might try something of the sort, sent a detachment of 500 foot and five cannon to Bloxford to guard the crossing of the Lambourn. He also sent Prince Maurice and his small west country army to hold a position on rising ground just to the west of

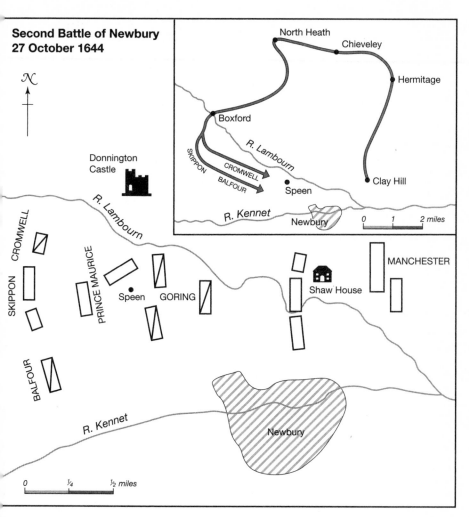

**Second Battle of Newbury
27 October 1644**

𝒩

Donnington Castle

R. Lambourn

CROMWELL

SKIPPON

PRINCE MAURICE

Speen

GORING

Shaw House

MANCHESTER

BALFOUR

R. Kennet

Newbury

0   ¼   ½ miles

North Heath

Chieveley

Hermitage

Boxford

R. Lambourn

SKIPPON

CROMWELL

BALFOUR

Speen

Clay Hill

R. Kennet

Newbury

0   1   2 miles

Speen in an area which consisted of a number of little fields and hedges. The front of Maurice's position was covered by the cannon in Donnington Castle and by some of his own guns sited behind his foot. The King stationed the rest of his foot and his two brigades of horse in a large open field between Prince Maurice's position in the west and the regiments around Shaw House, commanded by Lord Astley, in the east. The brigades of horse probably amounted to no more than 600–700 men each, being made up from a number of regiments that would have been considerably undermanned after the hectic summer campaign.

Late on 26 October Manchester sent 1,000 men to seize a bridge over the Lambourn near Shaw House. This attack was beaten off, but while it was going on Waller slipped away with his force from Clay Hill to Hermitage, thence west by north to Chieveley and North Heath, where they rested for the remains of the night. At dawn on 27 October he surprised the Royalist detachment at Bloxford and secured the crossing of the River Lambourn. Once across the river he swung left-handed and moved towards the rear of the Royalist position west of Speen. By now he was in sight of Donnington Castle, so that the King knew that an attack on Speen was likely to develop.

Manchester's feint attack was now directed on Shaw House. This turned the King's attention in that direction and may have caused him to underestimate the threat posed by Waller, but Manchester had committed too many men to his attack and it became difficult to disengage them when Astley launched a counter-attack.

Waller's force advanced from Boxford along two parallel routes; Cromwell with his horse and some musketeers on the northern or left route, and Balfour's horse and the foot regiments along the southern or right route. On approaching Prince Maurice's position they deployed with the foot in the centre and the horse on each flank. At around 3 pm the foot advanced and after a prolonged struggle eventually forced Prince Maurice back through Speen, capturing the Royalist guns behind his position. At this moment Waller launched his horse on both flanks.

On the right Balfour, about 500 strong, broke out of the small enclosures into the open ground beyond. Here they were attacked by a small body of Royalist horse, which they quickly dispersed. Soon afterwards the Royalist brigade of horse, commanded by Bennet, accompanied by the King's life guard of horse, attacked them and forced them back beyond Speen.

On the left, Cromwell too was unsuccessful. When, having manned the hedges with musketeers, he finally broke out of the enclosures into the large area of open grass, he was confronted by Goring in person with the other Royalist brigade commanded by the Earl of Cleveland.

Cromwell's men were soon forced back over a hedge into a small field, heavily pressed by Goring. Cromwell's second line mounted a counter-attack but this too was seen off by Goring, who then put the whole of Cromwell's force to flight. The only consolation was that during the mêlée the Earl of Cleveland[12] was captured and Goring lost a considerable number of men from the fire of Cromwell's musketeers.

Even then all might have been well had Manchester's main attack gone in at the same time as Waller's. This did not happen for two reasons. First, Manchester's feint attack in the morning had gone on too long and involved too many of his foot regiments, so that it proved impossible to get the men ready for another assault in time. Second, Manchester had difficulty in distinguishing Waller's gun signal from the guns fired from Donnington Castle. Only when the roar of battle was heard did Manchester know that it was time for his assault, but by then it was too late. In the event his attack did not go in until well after 4 pm,[13] by which time there was only another half an hour of daylight. At first he had some success but he was driven back by a violent Royalist counter-attack, and the battle ended in stalemate about an hour after dark.

Various reasons have been put forward for the failure of Cromwell's attack, such as the harassing effect of the fire from Donnington Castle. But bearing in mind the number and rate of fire of the cannon, the range, which was around 1,000 yards, and the speed at which Cromwell's horse was moving, this cannot have been the main reason. A more likely explanation is that the regiments that had recently won such acclaim for their performance at Marston Moor had lost some of their edge, or to put it another way, their morale was not as high as it might have been. Furthermore, Cromwell himself does not appear to have been as forceful as usual, which might well have resulted from the dissension that had recently been rife in Manchester's army. Being susceptible to emotional swings he may well have been depressed and therefore less capable of inspiring his men than he had been at Marston Moor. Admittedly this is no more than speculation, but the results were plain for all to see. At Marston Moor, despite commanding only a very small proportion of the allied army, he made a great impact on the course of the battle. At Newbury, where he commanded a similar proportion of the Parliamentary army, he made no impact, despite having as good an opportunity to destabilise the Royalist position as he had in the earlier battle. This battle, the second to be fought near Newbury, could have been decisive, but Parliament, with a superiority of two to one over the King, failed to defeat him.

The King, realising that he would inevitably be worn down if he renewed the battle next day, decided to withdraw. Waiting until the moon went down and exploiting an unguarded gap between Donnington Castle and Shaw House, he slipped away in the darkness, leaving his artillery and supply wagons in Donnington Castle. During the night Colonel Birch saw what was happening and tried in vain to get Manchester to react. Astley and Prince Maurice withdrew the Royalist army to Wallingford, where they crossed the Thames. The King, with an escort of 500 horse, rode to Bath to meet Prince Rupert, who was on his way to join him with the Northern Horse and 2,000 men recruited in Wales.

Early next morning Waller and Cromwell set out in pursuit with their regiments of horse, but could not follow through the close country beside the Thames without the support of foot soldiers. Leaving their men at Blewbury, Waller and Cromwell rode back to try and get Manchester to bring the army up, but it was too late. At a council of war Waller and his lieutenant general Hazlerigg proposed intercepting the King on his way back to the Royalist army, which was by now at Oxford. Manchester disagreed, telling Hazlerigg that he was a bloody fellow and calling on God to send them peace since none of their victories were ever clear-cut victories. Manchester did however agree to attack Donnington Castle in order to get hold of the Royalist guns, but this failed with heavy loss of life. Afterwards the whole army moved forward as far as Blewbury. By this time the King and Rupert were safely at Oxford, the Northern Horse being stationed at Burford.

On 6 November the King held a review of his forces at Burford. With Rupert's reinforcements and detachments from outlying garrisons, his army had risen to 15,000 men. He then announced the retirement as

Lord General of Lord Forth, who was over 70 years old, and appointed Prince Rupert in his place. Not wishing to cause jealousy, Rupert asked that the title of General should be held by the fourteen-year-old Prince of Wales, with him doing the job as 'the King's lieutenant general'.

When Manchester heard that the Royalist army was assembled at Burford, he held a council of war which decided that the army should return to Newbury. The Royalist army followed them back towards Newbury in order to collect their cannon and wagons from Donnington Castle. Having done this with no more than token opposition from the Parliamentary army, they drew up in battle formation, inviting an attack. Manchester held another council of war, at which Cromwell was in favour of attacking the Royalists, but the majority were of the contrary opinion. It was on this occasion that Manchester famously said 'If we beat the King ninety-nine times yet he is King still and so will his posterity be after him; but if the King beats us once we shall all be hanged and our posterity made slaves.' To this Cromwell replied 'If this be so, why did we take up arms at first? This is against fighting forever hereafter. If so let us make peace, be it ever so base.' In the event there was an exchange of cannon and musket fire in which the horse that the King was riding was hit in the foot, but there was no battle. The King withdrew to Oxford and after a short time Parliament's armies went into winter quarters. Manchester and Cromwell repaired to London to resume their quarrel in Parliament. Their association was at an end.

CROMWELL HAD BEEN Manchester's lieutenant general for nine months, during which he had learnt much from him regarding the raising and administering of an army. He must also have learnt a lot about handling a force of all arms from the professionals with whom he had contact, particularly Crawford, Vermuyden and Thomas Fairfax. On his own account he had done wonders with the Eastern Association regiments of horse, on the strength of which he had won a well-earned reputation as a general officer. He had fought in the two largest battles of the Civil War, Marston Moor and second Newbury. In the first he had been largely responsible for turning defeat into victory. In the second he was partly responsible for turning what should have been a victory into a draw.

After Marston Moor he evidently found working for Manchester frustrating from a military point of view, because Manchester was dragging his feet at the very moment that Cromwell, full of new-found confidence, was raring to go. But in one sense he was himself partly to blame, because it was his religious and political activities in quarrelling with Presbyterians and promoting Independents that were the cause of Manchester dragging his feet. Presbyterians such as Crawford who quarrelled with Cromwell were also to blame.

When he returned to Parliament at the end of November his military reputation as a military commander gave him increased political influence. Much more important was the influence he exerted as a result of the growing strength of the Independents in the army, of whom he was by far the most important. The rise of the Independents in 1644 started a change in the very nature of the revolution which Pym had brought to fruition. Within four years the war between the King and Parliament would be at an end, to be replaced by a political struggle between Independents and Presbyterians. It was as Manchester's lieutenant general that Cromwell fired the first shots in this new conflict.

5 · New Model Army

The return of Manchester and Cromwell to Westminster led to a period of bitter recrimination followed by some highly creative legislation. Cromwell led off with a number of speeches and a detailed paper attacking Manchester's handling of the Eastern Association army in the aftermath of Marston Moor. His criticism was not confined to the purely military aspects of the business but included the accusation that Manchester was deliberately pulling his punches in order to avoid 'bringing the King too low', as he put it. According to Cromwell, Manchester sought a negotiated peace that would avoid excessive social upheaval and which could only be achieved if the King retained much of his power. Cromwell's main line of attack was therefore essentially political and was seen as such. Furthermore, as with his attack on Willoughby a year earlier, it was partly intended to undermine Essex, who shared Manchester's views, a fact that was also clearly understood, particularly in the Lords.

Manchester's counter-attack, which was put together by Crawford in conjunction with Essex's friends in the Lords, defended his conduct of operations point by point from a military point of view and then turned to the political implications of events. Here Manchester not only defended his own record but vigorously attacked Cromwell for his excessive support for Independents and for promoting hostility towards the Scots and the Presbyterian interest in England. Manchester even went so far as to suggest that Cromwell's indifferent performance in the battle of Newbury and his failure to act against the Royalists in their advance to rescue the guns and wagons at Donnington Castle was deliberate. He implied that Cromwell did not want to beat the King too soundly at this time as he felt that the resultant peace negotiations would strengthen the hands of the Presbyterians at the expense of the Independents. This was the mirror image of Cromwell's criticism of Manchester and, although little short of ridiculous, was received sympathetically by many members in both Houses worried by the suspected social aims of the Independents. So strong was this feeling in the Lords that some would have liked to see Cromwell charged as an incendiary, although in the Commons Cromwell was better supported because of his fine military record.

Cromwell's main ally in the Lords, Viscount Saye and Sele, was as determined as Cromwell to defeat the King, despite the fact that he was a firm Presbyterian. Faced with stalemate, Cromwell changed tack. As mentioned earlier, there had for some months been a strong feeling that the whole command structure of Parliament's forces needed remodelling. On 9 December 1644, after a statesman-like speech in the Commons by Cromwell, Saye in the Lords and Zouch Tate in the Commons proposed that all members of both Houses should voluntarily give up all offices, both civil and military, conferred on them by Parliament. Although this was instantly thrown out by the Lords, it formed the basis for the Self-Denying Ordinance that eventually became law in the following April. In another speech on 9 December Cromwell, recognising not only that he was not going to undermine Manchester but that the new approach would result in Manchester's disappearance anyway, magnanimously withdrew all his charges against him. During the first weeks of 1645 Cromwell together with Saye and Vane used their influence to get agreement to a total reorganisation of Parliament's armies: they went on to get Essex replaced with Sir Thomas Fairfax, who was neither an MP nor a member of the Lords.[1] Once this was agreed,

Cromwell was made a member of a sub-committee of the Committee of Both Kingdoms charged with making decisions regarding the reorganisation of the new army and with formulating the regulations under which it should be managed.

WHILE RECRIMINATION AND reorganisation were monopolising the attention of Parliament, the Royalists were working out their future plans. Their difficulty was that they had lost their hold over so great an area in the north, and to a lesser extent along the Welsh border, that they did not have enough territory left to support their armies. They therefore had to do two things; secure what was left and recover what was lost. To this end in early 1645 the King made the fourteen-year-old Prince of Wales commander-in-chief in the south-west with his own council and with Hopton as his military commander. His task was to make this vital area impregnable. He also sent Prince Rupert to the Welsh border to join Prince Maurice in Cheshire and recapture Shrewsbury, which had recently been taken by local Parliamentary forces. When these operations were complete, the King intended to take his main army to join Rupert and Maurice. Their combined force would then move north to attack the Scots, who were already worried about the situation in their own country as a result of victories won by the King's general in Scotland, the Earl of Montrose. Once in possession of the north, the King hoped that with further reinforcement from Ireland he would be strong enough to defeat Parliament, once and for all.

Meanwhile in early December 1644 the King sent Goring with a force of 3,000 horse and 2,000 foot to harry Parliamentary forces south of the Thames. At the same time he initiated a further round of negotiations with Parliament. From the King's point of view, talks were necessary to satisfy his supporters that he was trying to achieve a negotiated settlement. They also gave time for his other plans to develop. The Presbyterians in Parliament and the Scots embraced them as affording an opportunity to reduce the growing influence of the Independents. Saye, Cromwell and their friends felt that they gave time for the reorganisation of Parliament's armies. Waller was left to deal with Goring.

At the end of November 1644 Waller sent some of his regiments to relieve Taunton, which was done in mid December. Waller himself with the rest of his force was pushed back into Surrey by Goring, but by early March 1645 he had launched a counter-attack, reaching Winchester with 3,000 horse and dragoons. By this time work was starting on the formation of the new Parliamentary army which would be formed from the remains of Essex's army, the Eastern Association army and Waller's army. Cromwell, who had been so influential in the early stages of planning, but who would have to give up his military rank if the Self-Denying Ordinance became law, was now called upon to take the field once more. On 4 March he was sent with 2,000 horse and dragoons to work under Waller's command. In this capacity over the next six weeks he took part in a number of small actions against Royalist troops.

The first of these took place on 8 March, when Waller and Cromwell dispersed a small Royalist force near Andover, during which they captured Lord Henry Percy and some of his followers. Percy was the brother of the Earl of Northumberland, and Waller, who was unwell, asked Cromwell to entertain their unwilling guests on his behalf. Cromwell later told Waller that amongst Percy's retinue 'was a youth of so fair a countenance that he doubted of his condition; and to confirm himself, willed him to sing; which he did with such daintiness that he scrupled not to say to lord Percy that being a warrior he did wisely to be accompanied by Amazons; on which that Lord did in some confusion acknowledge that she was a damsel'. This evidently led to the prisoners being mocked for their loose living and for bringing the King into disrepute.[2]

Waller and Cromwell subsequently became involved in minor actions at Westbury, Devizes, and then at Pitminster just to the south of Taunton. Later Cromwell, who had been sent to Dorchester, was attacked by Goring and scattered. Cromwell rejoined Waller at Cerne Abbas, where they received orders from the Committee of Both Kingdoms to return with their men to the New Model Army, as Fairfax's force was now known. By this time the Self-Denying Ordinance had become law; so

Waller and Cromwell, both of whom were Members of Parliament, would have to retire.

Waller was a highly experienced and successful professional soldier, so his opinion of Cromwell as a subordinate is of some interest. He said that at this time Cromwell showed no exceptional ability nor did he seem to think of himself as exceptional. He was blunt but neither proud nor disdainful of others. As an officer he was obedient and never disputed his orders.[3]

IT IS NOW TIME TO EXAMINE the New Model Army that was being put together by Fairfax assisted by Skippon. Although set up hurriedly in a state of confusion, it would, under Fairfax, become the instrument that finally defeated the King. Subsequently, under Cromwell, it would crush resistance in Ireland and Scotland before turning out the Parliament that had brought it into being. In the end it would find itself the agent by which Cromwell governed the country. Its birth pangs are therefore of interest.

The New Model Army contained fewer regiments than there were in the combined forces of Essex, Waller and Manchester. This meant that it would be necessary to dispense with the services of a number of officers. Fairfax was allowed to select the ones he wanted to keep, but his selection had to be confirmed by Parliament. All the other ranks would be needed because so many of the old regiments were under strength: indeed, Parliament was obliged to conscript 8,600 more in an attempt to fill up the foot regiments and reach the overall manpower target for the new army of 22,000 men. The advantage of maintaining such a relatively small army was that it would be within the powers of Parliament to ensure that it was paid, equipped and supplied in such a way that it would not need to plunder the countryside in order to exist. Nor, it was hoped, would its men mutiny or its regiments melt away from lack of pay and supplies. At the same time the New Model Army would be large enough to detach one or more small task forces and still outnumber anything the Royalists could put into the field.

The New Model Army consisted of eleven regiments of horse, each of 600 men divided into six troops. One of these regiments was formed from one half of Cromwell's old regiment, and a second from the other half. Fairfax himself became the colonel of one and Whalley of the other. Vermuyden's regiment was transferred complete into the New Model Army as were Fleetwood's, Rossiter's and much of Manchester's former regiment, the colonel of which was now Nathaniel Rich. Thus six of the eleven regiments of horse were the ones that Cromwell had trained and led in the old Eastern Association. Of the rest, Sheffield's and Graves's were both from Essex's army, Butler's regiment, formerly famous as 'Hazlerigg's Lobsters', was from Waller's army, and Ireton's was from the garrison of Gloucester. The last of the eleven was made up partly from Essex's army and partly from Lord Fairfax's northern army and was commanded by Sir Robert Pye.

There was to be one regiment of dragoons consisting of ten companies and totalling 1,000 men. It came mainly from Essex's army but with two companies from the Eastern Association. It was commanded by Okey and had the reputation of being composed of fanatical Independents.

There were twelve regiments of foot, each of ten companies and 1,000 men. Fairfax's regiment consisted of six companies from Essex's army and four from the Eastern Association. Montagu's, Pickering's, Hammond's and Rainborough's were all from the Eastern Association. Skippon's regiment was partly from London and partly from the Eastern Association. Harley's came mainly from Essex's army, as did Lloyd's, Ingoldsby's and Fortescue's regiments. Weldon's regiment was formed partly from Essex's army but mainly from Waller's, and Sir Hardress Waller's regiment came entirely from Waller's army.

In building up the New Model Army the opportunity was taken to get rid of most of the Scots professionals. Probably for good military reasons, Independents outnumbered Presbyterians in the higher ranks. No one knew for certain whether Fairfax was a Presbyterian like his wife or an Independent like many of his friends, but everyone knew that he was committed to fighting the war to a finish and that he would not tolerate dissension in his army. As a result, both groups worked comfortably together. Skippon was his major general of foot and Vermuyden became commissary general and temporarily commander of the horse. The artillery train was commanded by Lieutenant General Hammond, uncle of the Robert Hammond who commanded one of the foot regiments. The comptroller of the artillery train was Captain Richard Deane.

From the outset, the New Model Army contained many officers who would become famous during the next fifteen years. In addition to Fleetwood, Ireton and Whalley, all of whom ultimately became generals, there was another future general in Fleetwood's second-in-command, the fanatical Thomas Harrisson, and in the major of Fairfax's regiment of horse, Desborough. Harley's lieutenant colonel, Pride, later became well known for his 'Purge' as did Robert Hammond because, as governor of the Isle of Wight, he was for many months the King's gaoler. Deane and Montagu both became generals-at-sea. Redundant officers joined one of the few remaining regional commanders such as Brereton in the north-west, Sydenham Poyntz in the north, or Massey at Gloucester.

ON 19 APRIL CROMWELL met Fairfax at Windsor to take his leave of him. When he did so, he found fresh orders from the Committee of Both Kingdoms instructing him to take the forces that he had recently commanded under Waller, together with Colonel John Fiennes's regiment from the garrison of Abingdon, into the area north of Oxford. Cromwell's task was to make it difficult for the King to join Prince Rupert in the Severn valley. In particular, he was to remove as many of the draught horses from the Oxford area as he could find, in order to prevent the King using them to drag his artillery train. Cromwell could hold on to his military commission for the time being because, under the final form of the Self-Denying Ordinance, he did not need to surrender it for 40 days.

Cromwell moved rapidly via Watlington to Islip, where he ferried his men across the River Cherwell. Next day he was attacked by the Earl of Northampton with four regiments of horse. Cromwell quickly rallied his force and put in a counter-attack, which routed the Royalists, killing 40 and capturing 200. Cromwell next turned his attention to

Bletchingdon House, one of the ring of outposts of the main Oxford garrison. Although not well fortified, it contained 150 men and should have been capable of holding off an attack for a few days, as Cromwell had no foot other than a small number of dragoons. But Cromwell by a show of boldness caused the governor to surrender at once; he was later court-martialled and shot. Cromwell moved further west to Bampton-in-the-Bush, where he cornered a force of 350 Royalist foot who barricaded themselves into the town. This time he had to make two assaults on successive days, losing some of his men before they surrendered. While this was going on, Colonel Fiennes took a number of prisoners in a second engagement nearby.

Emboldened by these successes, Cromwell, who had recently been reinforced by 600 foot from the garrison at Abingdon, decided to attack Farringdon Castle on 29 April, but this proved too tough a nut to crack. Indeed he was now in a dangerous position, because Prince Rupert and his brother Prince Maurice were approaching Oxford from the north-west to escort the King with his retinue at the start of the 1645 campaign. Goring also was closing on Oxford from the south-west, and any combination of these groups could have destroyed Cromwell's small force should they succeed in bringing it to battle. Cromwell, however, moved rapidly south to Newbury, having denuded the area of draught horses. Throughout this operation he had been back on the top of his form.

At the end of April the New Model Army was due to take the field and the Committee of Both Kingdoms had to decide what to do with it. Some favoured an advance on Oxford, some a move into the south-west to relieve Taunton, once more besieged by Royalist forces, and some dividing the army and doing both at once. In the end, the whole army, less four regiments of foot still under-recruited, set off for Taunton via Reading, Newbury and Andover. On 5 May it reached Salisbury and by 7 May it was at Blandford. On this day the King with the two Princes and Goring left Oxford, moving by easy stages to Evesham. Here he mustered his forces, which amounted to 6,300 horse and 5,300 foot. In view of the threat posed by the New Model Army, Goring with 3,000 of the King's best horse was sent back to the south-west.

But the Committee of Two Kingdoms was now uneasy, having just heard of the arrival of the Princes at Oxford. In a letter written to the Eastern Association the Committee admitted that they did not know what the King had in mind. New orders were sent to Fairfax that he should detach a suitable force to relieve Taunton and then act on the basis of such intelligence as Cromwell could provide. Fairfax therefore gave Colonel Weldon four regiments of foot (Weldon's, Fortescue's, Ingoldsby's and Lloyd's) together with detachments of foot from the garrisons of Chichester and Lyme. He also gave him Graves's regiment of horse together with three other horse regiments from local garrisons. This force proved strong enough to relieve Taunton on 14 May, the Royalists being under the impression that the whole of the New Model Army was approaching. Fairfax then retraced his steps.

On 10 May Cromwell was ordered to take his force to Warwick and be prepared to cover the Eastern Association, should the King swing in that direction, or to join Sydenham Poyntz and the Scots, should the King move north. Three days later Vermuyden was told to take four regiments of horse to join the Scots, the regiments to be his own, Rich's and Pye's from the New Model Army and John Fiennes's regiment, which had formerly been with Cromwell. He also took 500 dragoons. By 15 May Fairfax was back at Newbury. There he received orders to move towards Abingdon and in conjunction with that garrison to besiege Oxford in the hope of diverting the King from his northern venture. Cromwell too was to move south from Warwick to take part in besieging Oxford. Fairfax's main army set down outside Oxford on 22 May.

Fairfax's siege of Oxford had the desired effect, and the Royalists instead of moving north towards the Scots turned east. The King, still worried about Oxford, felt that were he to attack Leicester, Fairfax would abandon the siege and head north. By this time the Scots who had been in Derbyshire had decided to withdraw northwards because of a further victory won by Montrose in Scotland. This made Vermuyden's mission pointless; so he met up with Rossiter's regiment, which was also in Derbyshire, and together they moved to reinforce Leicester. But they were too late. Only Pye's regiment, which was moving to join Vermuyden, managed to reinforce the garrison in time.

By 29 May the King's army reached Leicester and Prince Rupert made preparations to take it by storm. Next day at 3 pm, having unsuccessfully called for the town to surrender, he assaulted it. After a furious resistance the town fell, the casualties on both sides being high. Pye himself was captured but soon exchanged for a Royalist taken at Marston Moor. Fearing that the King might now move into the Eastern Association area, Cromwell was ordered back to Cambridgeshire and told to take all the local forces of the Eastern Association under his command.

The loss of Leicester thoroughly alarmed Parliament. Hitherto Fairfax, Cromwell and Vermuyden had been driven hither and thither by the Committee of Both Kingdoms in accordance with the information that they were receiving, which was usually out of date. The orders sent out by the committee were even more out of date by the time they reached the recipient, and the New Model Army itself had been dangerously weakened by the loss of these detachments. Fairfax now had with him only seven regiments of horse and eight regiments of foot, including the four that he had left behind when he set off for Taunton and which had now joined him. On 3 June, realising that day-to-day interference from London could only bring disaster, Parliament gave Fairfax a free hand to take whatever steps were needed to destroy the King's army.

The first thing Fairfax did was to raise the siege of Oxford and head north. At the same time he ordered Vermuyden to rejoin him at once. When on 8 June Vermuyden met Fairfax at Stony Stratford he asked Fairfax to accept his resignation, saying that 'there were special occasions requiring him to withdraw beyond the sea'. Fairfax felt obliged to let him go, but this left him without anyone capable of commanding the horse. He appointed Ireton as commissary general and that very evening wrote to Parliament requesting that Cromwell should be sent to him as his lieutenant general. This was authorised by Parliament on 9 June, and on 10 June the Committee of Both Kingdoms passed the

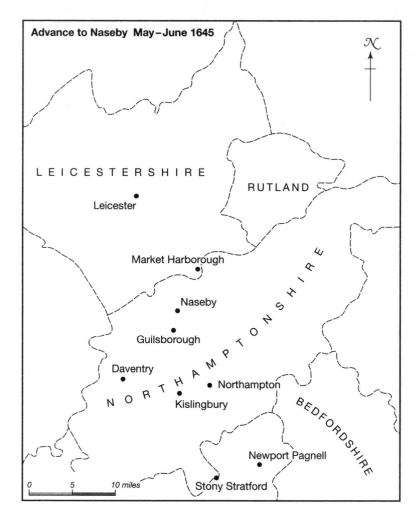

Advance to Naseby May–June 1645

LEICESTERSHIRE

Leicester

RUTLAND

Market Harborough

Naseby

Guilsborough

Daventry

NORTHAMPTONSHIRE

Northampton

Kislingbury

BEDFORDSHIRE

Newport Pagnell

Stony Stratford

0   5   10 miles

order to Cromwell to move instantly with whatever he had raised in the Eastern Association counties to join Fairfax. Cromwell received the order late on 11 June; early on the 13 June he arrived with 600 horse and dragoons at the New Model Army's camp at Kislingbury just to the west of Northampton. It is recorded that he was received with shouts of joy, especially by the regiments that he had formerly commanded in the Eastern Association army.

In many ways the appointment of Cromwell as lieutenant general of horse in the New Model Army was a major turning point in his life, since it gave him the military power base that he needed for his future political activities. It is often said that Fairfax always wanted him as his lieutenant general, which may well be true, but it was the particular circumstances following the loss of Leicester and Vermuyden's unexpected resignation that provided the opportunity. Only an emergency of this nature could have persuaded those in Parliament who recently wanted to indict Cromwell as an incendiary, and in particular Essex, Manchester and the hostile representatives of the Scots, to approve of such an appointment. Cromwell arrived in the nick of time.

IT IS NOW NECESSARY TO view the situation that existed in the Royalist camp following the storming of Leicester. Some, led by Rupert, wanted to stick to the original plan of defeating the Scots and recovering the north, as this was the only chance of winning the war. Others, aware of the disparity of strength between the King's army and their opponents, wanted to move west to meet up with 3,000 foot marching to join the King from Wales and with Goring, who been ordered to return to the King without delay. A third group, unduly concerned for the suffering of their wives and children in Oxford, felt that they should return and confront the New Model Army there.

A disastrous compromise resulted. The Royalist army, depleted by the losses incurred in storming Leicester and also by the need to garrison the place, turned south towards Oxford just at the time that Fairfax decided to lift the siege and seek out the King's army. On the same day that Vermuyden joined Fairfax, the King's army arrived at Daventry, where it stayed for three days rounding up cattle and sending them under escort into Oxford. By the time this unnecessary operation was complete, Fairfax was only ten miles away at Stony Stratford. The King now decided to pull back to Market Harborough in the hope of joining up with his Welsh reinforcements and Goring. He had not received a letter written by Goring saying that he could not leave the south-west until Taunton was captured: it had been intercepted by Fairfax's troops. Fairfax followed the King closely when he started his withdrawal from Daventry.

On 12 June Fairfax was at Kislingbury, and on 13 June he marched to Guilsborough. That same day the King reached Market Harborough. In the evening an advanced guard of the Parliamentary army overran a detachment of the Royalist rearguard at the village of Naseby some five and a half miles south of Market Harborough, which brought home to the King how closely he was being pursued. In a council of war that night Rupert, realising that the New Model Army was much stronger than the King's army, recommended a further withdrawal towards Leicester in order to gain reinforcements from the garrison there and possibly from Goring or the men from Wales. But overconfident civilians around the King, such as his secretary-of-state Lord Digby, persuaded him that it would be bad for the soldiers' morale to make a further withdrawal. Surprisingly, foolishly and disastrously, the King backed them rather than his general and Rupert was told to seek out and attack the New Model Army. In the early hours of 14 June 1645, the Royalist army deployed along a ridge about two miles south of Market Harborough.

FAIRFAX TOO HAD GOT his army on the move early that morning and was advancing on Naseby about four miles ahead. Then together with Cromwell and his other principal commanders he went forward to make a reconnaissance of the ground. At this time Cromwell had been a member of the New Model Army for less than 24 hours, but he would have been briefed on the general situation and on the state of the regiments of horse. He would also have met the officers commanding the regiments of horse and some of the troop commanders.

On the reconnaissance Fairfax at first favoured the idea of deploying over an area of low ground between Naseby Ridge and Dust Hill, that is to say, about a mile and a half north of the village of Naseby. But on close examination this area was found to be too wet for the operation of the horse regiments and Cromwell suggested a withdrawal of a few hundred yards onto the slopes of Naseby Ridge. By chance Rupert, who had moved forward to reconnoitre, saw Fairfax and his party withdrawing up the slope to this better ground. Thinking that this denoted an intention of the New Model Army to move further south, he sent word to the King to bring up the army and occupy a new position ahead of the one into which they had moved earlier. Meanwhile Cromwell and Skippon started to work out in detail where they would place their regiments of horse and foot respectively.

It is reported that as Cromwell moved around on the position he was in a state of euphoria, smiling and praising God for the victory that he now saw as inevitable. An eyewitness said that he was laughing out loud. Some weeks later recalling his mood, he wrote in a letter:

> when I saw the enemy draw up and march in gallant order towards us and we a company of poor ignorant men to seek how to order our battle... I could not (riding alone about my business) but smile out to God in praises in assurance of victory, because God would, by things that are not, bring to naught things that are.

Quite why he regarded the New Model Army as a body of poor ignorant men is difficult to know, since it contained his own Eastern Association regiments of horse, described by the veteran Leslie as the best cavalry in Europe, to say nothing of the pick of the foot regiments. Also, ignorant or not, it outnumbered the King's army by 14,000 to 9,000.

But even in this oddly elated state Cromwell was still capable of deploying his resources with skill. First he allocated to Ireton the regiments that were to fight on the left wing of the army: a total of 3,400 men together with the New Model Army's regiment of dragoons. Ireton put his own regiment, Vermuyden's and Butler's in his front line, and Fleetwood's, Rich's and one of the two Eastern Association regiments that were temporarily with the New Model Army, in his second line. Four of these six regiments were well experienced, three being veterans of Marston Moor and the fourth, Butler's, having formerly belonged to Hazlerigg. Each regiment was divided into two halves, or squadrons, standing next to each other, with a gap between so that musketeers could fire at the advancing enemy before contact was made. Ireton himself commanded the front rank and Fleetwood the second. At the last moment Cromwell placed Okey's dragoons

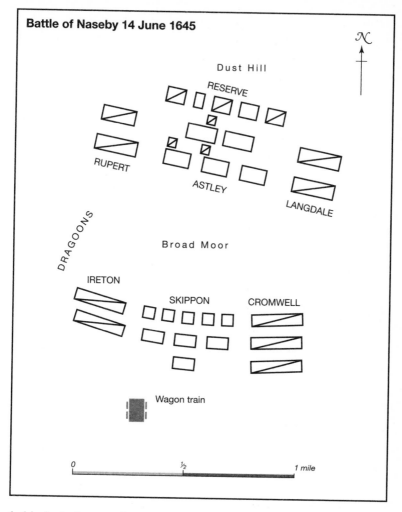

Battle of Naseby 14 June 1645

Dust Hill

RESERVE

RUPERT

ASTLEY

LANGDALE

DRAGOONS

Broad Moor

IRETON

SKIPPON   CROMWELL

Wagon train

0   ½   1 mile

behind a hedge running north and south covering Ireton's left flank.

Having done this, Cromwell set out the regiments that he would command on the right wing, amounting to a total of 3,900 men. Cromwell had seven regiments plus Fairfax's life guard of 150 men, standing in squadron blocks of half a regiment each. In his front rank he placed Fairfax's regiment and life guard, half of Pye's regiment and Whalley's regiment. In his second rank he placed half of Fiennes's regiment, the other half of Pye's regiment and the whole of Sheffield's regiment. In the third rank as a reserve he had the other half of Fiennes's regiment, and the second of the Associated Horse regiments. Soon after he had completed his layout Rossiter's regiment, which had been away on outpost duty, returned, and he placed half on the extreme right and slightly behind his front and the other half in the third line as an additional reserve. Whalley was placed in command of the front line. Cromwell took charge of the second line.

In the centre were the eight regiments of foot, commanded by Skippon, who placed five in his front line and three in his second. Between the gaps in the front line regiments were eight cannon planted in pairs. In front of the whole army was the 'forlorn hope' of 300 musketeers drawn from all the regiments; their job was to shoot at the advancing enemy to disorganise their attack.

While the new Model Army was deploying for battle, so too were the Royalists. First to arrive were the Northern Horse under Langdale, who secured the ground opposite Cromwell's right wing. Langdale had only 1,700 men to confront Cromwell's 3,900. They were the survivors of 25 old regiments each reduced to a remnant. He formed them into two lines; he commanded the front line and Blakiston probably commanded the second. Langdale also had 200 musketeers in support of his wing.

The veteran Lord Astley commanded the Royalist centre. This contained the remains of 26 old regiments of foot, mustered on this occasion in three tertias or brigades commanded by Lisle on the left, Bard in the centre and Astley's son Sir Bernard on the right. There is little doubt that these men constituted the best foot soldiers in the country, but there were only 3,200 of them to oppose Skippon's 6,400. Astley was also given a body of horse under Colonel Howard amounting to nearly 900 men. It consisted of the remains of seven old regiments and Astley deployed them in three divisions, two of which stood in front of his second line and one in rear of his second line.

Prince Rupert took command of the Royalist right wing, consisting of around 1,700 horse and 200 musketeers. They would have to dispose of Ireton's 3,400 horse and 1,000 dragoons. In Rupert's front line was his life guard and Prince Maurice's life guard, his regiment, Prince Maurice's regiment and the Queen's regiment. In his second rank were the three regiments of the Earl of Northampton's brigade, commanded by Sir William Vaughan.

In reserve on Dust Hill were, from left to right, half a regiment of horse from Newark, Prince Rupert's regiment of foot, the King's life guard of horse, the King's life guard of foot, and the other half of the Newark regiment of horse. The King himself commanded this sizeable reserve, which was designed either to be committed as a concentrated force to repel a major incursion or to be used in bits where a minor reinforcement appeared necessary.[4]

At some time between 10 am and 11 am Cromwell would have seen the whole Royalist line move forward to attack the Parliamentary position, the horse initially moving in time with the foot. Whenever the horse got ahead of the foot, they stopped to let the foot catch up. Then, if he had been looking in that direction, he would have seen far away on his left the horse led by Prince Rupert charge Ireton's wing. But it is likely that his attention would have been held by events nearer at hand, since as Langdale advanced, Whalley moved his front line towards them. But the front line regiments did not all advance at the same speed because of difficult going on his right. As a result, Whalley's own regiment on the left struck the right-hand regiment of the Northern Horse hard, dispersing three or four of its troops, who fell back and re-formed behind Prince Rupert's regiment of foot on Dust Hill. By contrast, in the centre his men were able only to push Langdale's main body back without breaking it. But as more and more troops got clear of the bad going, the Northern Horse was submitted to increasing pressure. In an attempt to restore the position, that part of the Newark Horse on the left of the King's reserve was sent to back up Langdale, whereupon Cromwell despatched reinforcements to Whalley, probably the reserve squadron of Pye's regiment. The remains of the Northern Horse, now heavily outnumbered and attacked from the flank by the forward squadron of Rossiter's regiment, fell back about a mile. Cromwell then sent orders to Whalley to make no further attack on the Northern Horse for the time being. Instead he was to stay watching them with two regiments while the remainder were to return.

Events elsewhere on the battlefield had gone less well. Despite the best efforts of Okey's dragoons, the horse led by Rupert smashed into Ireton's wing and managed to break through after some hard fighting. They then pursued their opponents as far as the Parliamentary baggage train, which was just to the west of Naseby village, about three-quarters of a mile behind the Parliamentary position. But the regiments on the left of Rupert's line had been unable to break through Ireton's regiment, which was on the right of his line, so that this regiment and a few troops of Vermuyden's regiment remained in their positions when the rest of Ireton's wing was put to flight. Whether in the confusion Ireton realised that most of his regiments, including both of his second line regiments, had been put to flight is unclear. Certainly he took no steps to rally them. Instead he turned the half of his own regiment to the right and led an attack on the Royalist centre. In the ensuing fight his horse was killed and he was wounded by a pike thrust before being knocked insensible and captured. His performance was gallant enough but reflected the fact that he had only commanded a regiment for a little over two months and had been second in command of the horse for a mere week. Towards the end of the battle his captors released him in return for their lives, since by then they were being attacked on all sides.

Nearer at hand, Cromwell was able to observe the fortunes of the Parliamentary foot. Here, despite their numerical superiority, things had not gone well to start with. Once again the Royalists were not strong enough to attack the whole of the Parliamentary front line in sufficient strength; so although the four regiments in the centre and left of the New Model Army were all hard pressed, Fairfax's regiment of foot on the right was virtually unassailed. After stiff fighting and many casualties, Skippon's front line was pushed back until the three regiments in the second line were sent forward by Fairfax to reinforce them. By this time Skippon had been seriously wounded, although he stayed at his post until the end of the battle.

At this point Cromwell, who had returned from a quick visit to assess the situation on Ireton's wing, launched a series of attacks against the left flank of the Royalist foot, and Fairfax directed his own regiment of foot to go to the rescue of Montagu's regiment on its left. From Fairfax's point of view, this was the critical moment. He had to destroy the Royalist foot before either the King launched his reserve or Rupert returned to the battle with his horse.

The King too was aware of the importance of the moment, and he even tried to lead his reserve into the mêlée, but as he did so an obscure Scottish earl, fearing for the King's life, seized his bridle and swung him away to the right. Instead of slaughtering the earl on the spot as Rupert would have done, the King allowed himself to be deflected. As a call of 'right turn' indicated a retreat, the whole of the reserve started to move back and there was a period of confusion before it could be halted and made ready for further action.

Meanwhile Fairfax had put himself at the head of his own regiment of horse, which had been sent back by Whalley after his initial attack on the Northern Horse. Fairfax led it round the Royalist position and attacked it from the rear. The Royalists were now being engaged from their front, left, and rear and to cap it all Okey re-mounted his dragoons onto their ponies and charged into the Royalist right flank. At this point the King's life guard of foot was despatched to repulse Okey's dragoons and Rupert's regiment of foot reinforced the Royalist centre, but it was too late for such piecemeal remedies to be of much use. Gradually the magnificent Royalist foot regiments started to crumble and after a time small groups whose position had become hopeless surrendered. Soon none remained. The few that had neither died nor surrendered dispersed; some drifted back to the King over the coming weeks.

By now Rupert with most of his regiments of horse had returned to the King, but it would take time before their tired and blown animals could be got ready for another charge. Some of Ireton's horse were also returning to the battlefield and were forming up under Fleetwood's command opposite the Northern Horse in roughly the same place as Cromwell had been in at the start of the battle. As the fighting died down, Fairfax redeployed his army so that it again presented a solid front with the foot in the middle and with horse on either flank. Naturally the horse was ready before the foot, but Fairfax refused to sanction any advance until the whole army was properly re-formed. He had no intention of allowing Royalists the satisfaction of overrunning any detachment that he could not fully support.

For a time a desultory fire was maintained at long range and the Royalists even considered mounting one last charge, but wiser counsels prevailed and after a time they turned about and rode off at considerable speed towards Leicester. Under these circumstances Fairfax was prepared to release Cromwell to follow up the Royalist horse, which he did. Cromwell followed the retreating Royalists to within two or three miles of Leicester, overtaking and cutting down a number of the fleeing horsemen.

Altogether the fighting had lasted for little more than two hours, but in this time the King's army had been totally defeated. Although most of the horse had got away, they had sustained heavy casualties, and the splendid foot regiments had been destroyed except for the few isolated groups that managed to disperse. The King also lost all his guns and his baggage train, including his coach with his personal papers containing damaging disclosures of his plans to bring over Irish troops to subdue his English subjects. It is estimated that Royalist losses amounted to around 1,000 killed and a further 4,500 captured, including many of the professionals needed to turn recruits into fighting soldiers. Contrary to the usual practice of disarming and releasing rank and file captured in battle, Fairfax sent all his prisoners to London.

A considerable number of female camp followers were also killed, on the grounds that they were Irish whores. In fact they were the usual collection of women who moved with the Royalist army to help with the cooking, washing and care of the wounded, many being the wives of the men in the ranks. Comparatively few were Irish, but there might have been a number of Welsh-speakers, judging by the composition of the army.

FEW ACCOUNTS OF THE battle of Naseby give any clear account of how it developed and the impression has got round that it was a rehash of Edgehill, with Rupert smashing the enemy on his wing and then taking all the best Royalist horse away from the battle in an uncontrollable pursuit, in marked contrast to Cromwell, who managed to break the opposing horse on his wing and then, keeping his men together, turn them on to the flank of the Royalist foot.

Certainly Cromwell handled his part of the battle with great skill, but his task was easy compared to Rupert's. With an even greater superiority than Ireton, Cromwell was able to despatch a suitable force under Whalley to beat off the Northern Horse, reinforcing it when he saw that he had not committed enough troops in the first place. This left him with four regiments to launch against the Royalist centre and when he saw that the Northern Horse was unlikely to take any further part in the battle, he was able to recall a fifth regiment for this purpose. In all of this, his coolness and efficiency was matched only by the strength and restraint of his front line regiments, two of which he had raised, trained and commanded for the two years prior to the formation of the New Model Army. At the end of the battle he quickly re-ordered the horse, and organised and conducted the pursuit. For all of this he deserves great credit, but the picture of Cromwell leading a charge and then, after a period of heavy fighting, wheeling his men away from the enemy to attack the foot is fictitious.

The comparison with Edgehill is also flawed so far as Rupert is concerned. At Edgehill the Royalist horse only had to appear for most of Parliament's horse to turn tail and fly, taking some of the foot with them. On this occasion it was Byron who failed to turn on the Parliamentary foot with the second line regiments as ordered. At Naseby, Rupert's right wing was faced with an enemy almost double its own strength and including three of Cromwell's old Eastern Association regiments. That Rupert was able to break through these veterans and chase most of them off the field was a tribute to his great skill in the heat of battle. Furthermore he achieved it only after heavy and prolonged fighting in which the officers commanding both his own and his brother's regiments became casualties, together with a number of other officers. Then, despite the ferocity of the struggle and the difficulties of control caused by the loss of the two commanders, Rupert was able to halt the pursuit. Although he got to the Parliamentary baggage park, he did not attack it, let alone loot it. Instead he reorganised his regiments and lead them back to the King. The big question hanging over Rupert's conduct of the battle was why he was on the right wing at all. As the King's overall commander he might have been more effective had he stayed with the King.[5]

Fairfax sent a letter soon after the battle to the Speaker of the House of Commons which, in a few lines, gave an account of the results in terms of prisoners taken and guns captured. He also said that the army would move on Leicester. At the end he said 'All that I desire is that the honour of this great and never to be forgotten mercie may be given to God in an extraordinary day of thanksgiving and that it may be improved to the good of his churche and his kingdome.'

Cromwell also wrote to the Speaker giving details of the prisoners and guns captured in a similarly concise manner, but the rest of the letter is worth comparing with the words of Fairfax given above. Cromwell wrote:

Sir, this is none other than the hand of God; and to him alone belongs the glory wherein none are to share with Him. The General served you with all faithfulness and honour; and the best commendations I can give him is that I dare say he attributes all to God and would rather perish than assume to himself. Which is an honest and a thriving way, and yet as much for bravery may be given to him in his action as to a man. Honest men served you faithfully in this action. Sir, they are trusty; I beseech you in the name of God, do not discourage them. I wish this action may beget thankfulness and humility in all that are concerned in it. He that ventures his life for the liberty of his country, I wish he trust God for the liberty of his conscience, and you for the liberty he fights for.

It is interesting to notice that the House of Commons deleted the last four sentences, which constituted a call for toleration of the Independents, from their record, whereas the House of Lords retained it in theirs.

It must have been a comfort to Fairfax, if he ever saw this letter, to know that his second in command had given him a good report, bearing in mind some of the things that Cromwell had said about his former commander! Certainly Fairfax deserved any glory that God could spare. In the short time since the Committee of Both Kingdoms had given him a free hand he had retrieved the various bits of his army from around the country, reorganised the command structure, raised the siege of Oxford and followed the King's army so tenaciously that his opponent was unable to shake him off or concentrate enough forces to oppose him. Having brought the King to battle, he conducted it effectively, personally committing his reserves at the right moment and at the culmination of the fighting putting himself at the head of his regiment of horse to administer the *coup de grâce*. For the first time since the start of the war, Parliament's main army knew that it was in the hands of a master tactician.

All battles are won by the men who fight them, and Naseby was no exception. No matter how favourable the circumstances engineered by Fairfax, errors, accidents or chance could have turned victory into defeat. It is a tribute to Cromwell, Skippon and their junior commanders that whenever things started to go wrong they were able to seize the initiative and turn each situation to their advantage, and in this respect Cromwell's horse was pre-eminent. But in the final analysis this was Fairfax's battle and on 14 June 1645 he won the war for Parliament, even though there were many more months of fighting before it could be finally concluded.

AFTER THE BATTLE FAIRFAX moved the army to Market Harborough, where he set up his headquarters. Estimates of his losses indicate no more than 200 to 300 killed and wounded. Next day he laid siege to Leicester, which surrendered on 18 June. By this time the King and his companions were approaching Hereford.

Fairfax immediately realised that his next target must be to destroy the Royalist position in the south-west. The Scots were returning south after their temporary concern about Montrose and were making their way towards Chester: it would not be long before they were threatening Hereford. The only place where there was still a worthwhile concentration of Royalist troops was in the south-west and it was likely that the King would take refuge in this area with his surviving regiments of horse and any other recruits that they could pick up on the way. It was important that Fairfax should forestall him before this could happen.

Parliament agreed with this appreciation of the situation and instructed Massey at Gloucester to send 2,200 horse and dragoons to join Fairfax in the south-west. Fairfax was also told to keep in close touch with the Scots, who in conjunction with Poyntz in the north-east and Brereton in the north-west would attempt to contain the King and reduce the remaining Royalist garrisons to the north of Fairfax's operational area. It was within this overall plan that the operations leading to the fall of Oxford in June 1646 took place.

For the purposes of this book it is necessary to follow only the fortunes of Fairfax and Cromwell, but the writhings of the King as he gradually accepted the impracticalities of his expectations and the ruin of his cause make interesting reading. His peregrinations between Hereford, south Wales, across England into Yorkshire, back to Newark, then to Oxford and Hereford, again then to Newark and finally to Oxford, all accompanied by a few thousand men, almost defy belief. On one occasion he even strayed into the Eastern Association, spending the night at Manchester's Hinchingbrooke.

But back to the New Model Army. At the end of June Cromwell was given the vacant colonelcy of Vermuyden's regiment of horse. Impelled by Fairfax and Cromwell, the army's march to relieve Taunton and confront Goring would have done credit to Prince Rupert himself. On 28 July it reached Marlborough, then, moving south to avoid confrontation with Royalist garrisons at Devizes and Bath, it went via Amesbury and Blandford to Beaminster in Dorset, where it arrived on 4 July. This involved marches averaging seventeen miles a day in hot weather and in the aftermath of a great battle, which had seriously reduced the number of horses available. A normal day's march in those times would have been between ten and twelve miles per day.

Meanwhile Goring had abandoned the siege of Taunton and moved out with around 7,000 men to confront Fairfax. His immediate aim was to hold Fairfax off for long enough to withdraw his guns and baggage train into Bridgwater and ensure that the town could withstand an attack. Prince Rupert also recognised the danger posed by Fairfax's advance and moved hastily to Bristol to put that place in a condition to withstand a siege. While these two places remained in Royalist hands it would be difficult for Fairfax to penetrate into the heartland of Devon and Cornwall.

Goring took up a position behind the river Yeo between Langport and Yeovil. Fairfax swung north from Beaminster to Crewkerne, from where he sent some horse forward to make contact. Riding out with Cromwell to reconnoitre, they found all the bridges across the river destroyed. An attack by the foot on 8 July secured a crossing at Yeovil, which surrendered, and the horse moved north of the river. Ilchester also surrendered without a fight.

On 8 July Fairfax received a report that Goring had left Langport and was heading back towards Taunton with a large body of horse and foot, presumably to take it for Parliament before Fairfax could intervene. In fact Goring had merely sent a body of horse under his lieutenant general, Porter, to distract Fairfax and cause him to split his army. Fairfax fell for the ruse and despatched some horse and dragoons after them, but thanks to Porter's inefficiency his men were taken by surprise and routed with many casualties.

Fairfax now turned west towards Langport, which lies at the junction of the Yeo and the Parrett. Goring decided to hold him at the point where a stream called the Rhyne Wagg, flowing north to south, crosses the road running east to west from Long Sutton to Langport at a ford just outside the village of Huish Episcopi. On 10 July the stream was in flood, so that the ford was up to the horses' bellies. To the west of the ford the country was enclosed by hedges, which Goring lined with musketeers. Behind them on a slight rise Goring placed his horse and two cannon covering the ford.[6]

Fairfax's first task was to silence Goring's cannon, for which purpose

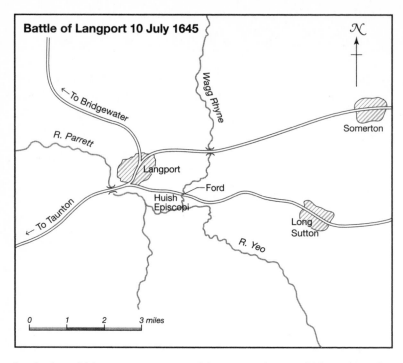

Battle of Langport 10 July 1645

To Bridgewater

R. Parrett

Wagg Rhyne

Somerton

Langport

Ford

Huish Episcopi

To Taunton

Long Sutton

R. Yeo

0   1   2   3 miles

he deployed his own cannon on rising ground some 700 yards to the east and soon disposed of them in a one-sided artillery duel. Next a number of musketeers were passed across the river to deal with the enemy musketeers in the hedges covering the ford. Fairfax then told Cromwell to push horse through the ford to tackle the Royalist horse at the top of the slope. This was an extremely hazardous proceeding, since there was only room for four horses to pass abreast over the ford and along the road. Goring's horse were drawn up at the point where it was possible to debouch off the road.

Cromwell ordered three troops of Whalley's regiment commanded by Major Bethell to carry out this task. Bethell led the first troop down the road at a good pace, through the ford and up the slope without deploying, so that it hit part of Goring's line on a narrow front and broke it. The next two troops crossed the ford and were then able to deploy at the point where the first troop had forced the Royalists back, before charging into the regiment that the first troop had run into head-on. For

Miniature portrait of Oliver Cromwell (*unfinished*), by Samuel Cooper
(*private collection / Bridgeman Art Library*)

Portrait of Oliver Cromwell, by Sir
Peter Lely (*Bridgeman Art Library*)

Henry Ireton, attributed to
Robert Walker, after Samuel
Cooper and Sir Anthony Van
Dyck (*National Portrait Gallery*)

Prince Rupert, attributed
to Gerrit van Honthorst
(*National Portrait Gallery*)

Charles Fleetwood
(*Corporation of London/HIP*)

The Earl of Manchester, by
Sir Peter Lely
(*Governors of Kimbolton School*)

Sir Thomas Fairfax (*Hulton Archive*)

John Lambert, after
Robert Walker
(*National Portrait Gallery*)

David Leslie
(*Clan Leslie Charitable Trust*)

Samuel Cooper's miniature of George Monk, Duke of Albemarle, c.1658
(*The Royal Collection © 2003 Her Majesty Queen Elizabeth II*)

King Charles II, after Adriaen Hanneman (*National Portrait Gallery*)

some moments chaos reined, but then weight of numbers began to tell and Bethell's men started to fall back. But Cromwell had already despatched another three troops of Fairfax's regiment under Desborough and they too deployed on the far side of the stream. In this case, on reaching the top of the slope they moved north for a short distance before turning left and ploughing into the flank of the Royalist horse. At the same time the musketeers who had crossed at the start of the battle moved forward and started shooting into the Royalist horse. After more troops had been fed into the battle and much hand-to-hand fighting had taken place, the Royalist troops fled through Aller up the road to Bridgwater. Contemporary reports tell of a great cloud of dust hanging over the Bridgwater road, which is strange, considering that there must have been heavy rain to produce the flooding of the Rhyne Wagg at the ford.

The battle of Langport was really no more than a rearguard action, but the terrain was such that it posed a difficult tactical problem. There can be no doubt that Fairfax's plan for dealing with it was exceedingly bold and depended on the horse being able to cope with exceptional circumstances. That victory was achieved was due as much to the splendid performance of Cromwell's old regiment as to Fairfax's bold concept and immaculate timing. Fairfax later considered Langport to be his greatest victory, placing it even above Naseby. This is an assessment that few historians would endorse, but Fairfax should know. It was certainly a remarkable feat of arms and one that cost Goring 2,000 prisoners, some of whom took the Covenant and joined the Parliamentary army. Goring, having left his guns and baggage at Bridgwater, moved rapidly west into Devon.

The fall of Bridgwater would mean a continuous line of Parliamentary garrisons running from the Bristol Channel through Taunton to Lyme on the English Channel, a desirable state of affairs for Fairfax. The New Model Army quickly closed up to the town but were then given a few days' rest by Fairfax, who was waiting for fresh supplies of powder and match. On 22 July he stormed Bridgwater. Next day the town surrendered with the loss of a further 1,600 prisoners.

Clearly Bristol was the next important target but Fairfax considered that before attempting it he should clean out the Royalist garrisons in Bath and Sherborne, which were impeding his lines of communication. There was also a problem caused by the appearance in the country of gangs of so-called clubmen, who were officially neutral as between the two sides but wanted to keep their homes clear of looting soldiers. Fairfax and Cromwell were obliged to spend time negotiating with these people before proceeding with their operations, but they were soon pacified. Fairfax then sent a brigade to invest Sherborne Castle, and Colonel Rich with his regiment of horse and Okey with his dragoons to try and seize Bath. Bath quickly surrendered although Rupert with a relief force was only a few miles away. Sherborne put up strong resistance, which obliged Fairfax to storm the town after battering its walls with his cannon. Its capture was complete by 14 August.

Throughout these operations it is difficult to know what Cromwell was doing. In addition to handling the horse he was probably exercising some influence on the running of the army as a whole. It is probable that Fairfax would have relied on him for advice on such matters as the detailing of officers for tasks, because Cromwell knew many of them well during his time with the Eastern Association. Probably for this reason the twenty-year-old Montagu was given the job of commanding the foot in the absence of Skippon. On the other hand Lambert, who had for long been Fairfax's chief support in Yorkshire, had joined the army at the end of June; so he too would have had Fairfax's ear. It is said that it was during this long series of operations that Cromwell got to know and appreciate Lambert's great ability as a commander.

On 22 August 1645 the New Model Army concentrated outside Bristol. As the first troops arrived to the south of the town Rupert sent out a body of horse led by the commander of his life guard, Sir Richard Crane, to harass them. In the ensuing fight Crane was killed.

The city of Bristol was built on land between the river Avon and its tributary the Frome. Between them, these rivers surrounded the whole city except for a short distance to the east, which was covered by the castle. Behind the rivers was the old city wall. But the Frome was easily crossed and the wall was crumbling in places, and in any case the city was closely overlooked to the west and north-west by a ridge of high ground, in places no more than 450 yards distant. The city was therefore hopelessly exposed to enemy cannon fire unless the ridge itself was held. For this reason there was an outer earthwork and ditch interspersed with forts around most of the perimeter which had to be defended, although this required a large number of men. If however the outer line, where most of the defenders were stationed, was breached, there would be insufficient men left to man the city walls. Rupert, who had only 800 horse and 700 foot with which to defend Bristol, well understood the problem. But having captured Bristol in 1643, he also knew that breaching the outer ring would cost the attackers dear. In recent weeks he had provisioned the city well and made arrangements to manufacture bullets and match for the muskets. He was confident of withstanding a siege for many weeks.

Fairfax had 12,000 men, excluding the contingent from Gloucester, which he placed to the south of Bristol to ward off any relief force that Goring might bring from Devon. He posted four regiments of horse on Durdham Down outside the outer defences to the north-west to prevent a breakout by the Royalist horse; they would also be well placed to intercept any relief force that the King might send, although there was little chance of this happening. Fairfax then raised a battery of guns outside the Temple Gate to the south of the city, through which Crane had led his harassing attack. Realising that it would cost him dear to storm the city, he first tried to arrange a surrender. To soften Rupert up, he and Cromwell wrote letters to many of the more important citizens urging them to take any action that they could to sabotage the defence and to persuade Rupert to surrender. Next on 4 September Fairfax wrote a long letter to Rupert, which started as a summons to surrender, but which continued as an eloquent personal appeal. Reminding him of all the support that Parliament had given to his family over the years and acknowledging his great military qualities, Fairfax said that if Rupert found himself able to spare the city from the inevitable result of an assault, it would endear him to the English people. Fairfax reiterated the usual declaration that he fought only to restore the King to his Parliament, the true guarantor of his crown and honour.

Rupert does not appear to have been unduly impressed, but he too was playing for time and first answered by saying that he might surrender if he could get the King's permission to do so, which would involve sending him a letter and waiting for the reply. Fairfax naturally refused. Rupert then wrote to say that if no relief force had arrived by a certain time he might surrender under conditions, which Fairfax could not possibly accept without asking Parliament. After exchanging a few more letters along these lines, Fairfax launched an all-out attack at 2 am on 10 September.

Fairfax's plan was that Weldon's brigade of four regiments would launch an attack from the south at the Temple Gate. At the same time three regiments of Rainsborough's brigade would attack the outer defences to the north-east of the city either side of Prior's Fort, while the fourth regiment would attack the fort itself. Behind Rainsborough's brigade would be three regiments of horse standing by to pour through any gap made. Fairfax retained a reserve of four regiments of horse and four regiments of foot on Durdham Down.

Weldon's attack to the south was unsuccessful, although it prevented Rupert from moving men from this area to boost the defence elsewhere. Rainsborough's men broke through the outer defences in several places after an hour's heavy fighting. Once through they opened up a way for their supporting regiments of horse, which by sheer weight of numbers beat off a counter-attack launched by some Royalist horse. One of Rainsborough's regiments, after getting through the earthworks, turned inwards to attack Prior's Fort from the rear. Pressed from both sides, the Fort surrendered after about three hours, all the defenders being put to the sword.

When it got light Fairfax could see that most of the defenders had withdrawn behind the city walls, with the exception of those in the forts, who fought on. Each time one of the forts was captured, the defenders were slaughtered. After a time, in one place after another Fairfax's men got over or through the city walls and the defenders were forced back on the castle. By now the battle had raged for a good six hours and Fairfax had lost many more men than he had lost at Naseby. As the day wore on, it was clear that Rupert could do no more than hold the castle with such men as he could cram into it, in which case all left outside would inevitably be killed. As there was no army capable of coming to his relief, this would serve no purpose. He accordingly offered to surrender on terms.

Fairfax sent Montagu, Rainsborough and Pickering to meet Rupert's representatives, and very generous terms were soon agreed under which Rupert and his entire force were permitted to march to Oxford with their swords, pikes, colours and drums, Rupert's lifeguard being permitted to carry loaded carbines. Next morning these three men escorted Rupert out of the city at the head of his men.

Outside the city walls Rupert was met by Fairfax and Cromwell who, showing all possible courtesy and respect, rode with him for the first two miles. Cromwell sent Butler's regiment of horse to escort them as far as Oxford to see that they were not attacked by clubmen. On the way to Oxford Rupert told one of the officers of the escorting regiment that he had 'never before received such satisfaction in unhappiness'.

It would be interesting to know how Cromwell felt when he saw Rupert at close quarters. Although defeated, he still looked impressive: six foot four inches tall in scarlet and silver on a magnificent black Arabian. Without doubt Cromwell had studied Rupert's methods in order to counter them and improve on them, and he had taken full advantage of his studies with regard both to handling cavalry on the battlefield and also to moving bodies of men at great speed over long distances. Rupert had been at war, or a prisoner of war, for most of the past twelve years and, although still only 25, was almost at the end of his career as a soldier. Cromwell had thought much about Rupert over the past three years. What was he thinking now and how much was he influenced by the barrage of black propaganda poured out by Parliament's supporters since 1642? Unfortunately we cannot know the answer directly, but Butler, who was well known for his hatred of Rupert, having escorted him to Oxford, changed his mind completely. He wrote to his former commander Waller saying that he was honoured to have been with him and that he was sure they were all mistaken about him. He asked Waller to use his influence to ensure that no Parliamentary pamphlet was published to Rupert's discredit for the surrender of Bristol, as he could not have held it without more men. By contrast, the King was so annoyed that he stripped Rupert of all his appointments.

After the storming of Bristol Fairfax asked Cromwell to write a letter to the Speaker announcing the results. As with his letter after Naseby Cromwell sent a full account of the action complete with details of the number of cannon and muskets captured, but as with his earlier despatch he could not resist a bit of embroidery. He wrote:

> Presbyterians, Independents, all had here the same spirit of faith and prayer; the same pretence and answer; they agree here, know no names of difference: pity it is it should be otherwise anywhere. All that believe have the real unity, which is most glorious, because inward and spiritual, in the body and to the head. For being united in forms, commonly called uniformity, every Christian will, for peace sake, study and do as far as conscience will permit.

As before, this passage was deleted from the House of Commons record and the whole despatch made to look as if it had come from Fairfax, but Cromwell's supporters had the deleted parts printed and circulated.

FAIRFAX NOW SENT Rainsborough with three regiments of foot north into Gloucestershire to capture Berkeley Castle. At the same time he sent Cromwell with four regiments of foot and three of horse to reduce remaining Royalist garrisons in Wiltshire and Hampshire. On 23 September Cromwell formed up in front of Devizes, which surrendered as soon as his cannon opened fire against the walls. On the same day Pickering with three regiments of foot captured a Royalist garrison at Laycock.

Cromwell's next target was Winchester, which declined to surrender when he summoned the city in the first place. Next day was spent preparing for an attack. Once a breach had been opened up in the walls

Cromwell again summoned the city, which on 6 October surrendered, thus saving much bloodshed. Up to this point Cromwell had gone out of his way to avoid shedding a drop more blood than necessary.

But now it was the turn of Basing House, a Royalist stronghold that had resisted many Parliamentary attempts to take it. Basing House belonged to the Roman Catholic Marquess of Winchester and some at least of the garrison were of the same persuasion. It was already under siege by 900 local Parliamentarians, who had enlisted the help of a Dutch engineer called Dalbeir. When Cromwell arrived he offered an opportunity to the garrison to surrender, which they refused. He then deployed his siege train to the south while Dalbeir watched the north, after which he subjected the walls to a heavy pounding with his cannon for five days until two gaps appeared. Cromwell spent the night of 13 October in prayer, searching through the Psalms for a text prophesying the destruction of idolaters. On the morning of 14 October he launched an attack with three regiments of foot. Convinced that they were attacking Papists, the men fought like tigers and were resisted with similar determination. This time there were no further offers of quarter and Cromwell allowed his men to put the enemy to the sword and pillage the house, which was burnt to the ground. Many perished, including some women.

Meanwhile Fairfax had taken the rest of the New Model Army into Devon, where on 19 October he captured Tiverton, another centre of Roman Catholicism. Fortunately he had ordered that anyone taken alive should be spared, so that there was little loss of life. From Tiverton he moved south towards Exeter, as the weather got wetter and colder and the army increasingly less able to slither around in the freezing mud. Cromwell rejoined the army by the end of the month and together they fortified a number of posts to the east of the Exe where the men could live until movement was again possible. Food was short and men were huddled twenty or so in a room, so that some became ill and died, including Pickering, who had commanded his regiment of foot so well since the early days of the Eastern Association. For the moment the war had literally got bogged down.

On 20 November Goring, decided that he had had enough, boarded a ship at Dartmouth and made off to the Continent. He was a brilliant commander of horse, witty, totally unreliable and a confirmed drunkard. Although officially the King's general of horse, he had been acting in support of the Prince of Wales's command for some months, following the Prince's instructions when they suited him and co-operating with the Prince's two little armies commanded by Grenville and Berkeley as and when he or they felt like it. Now the remains of Goring's force were put fully under the Prince of Wales.

In the last week of November Fairfax was obliged to send three regiments of horse (his own, Whalley's and Ireton's) to Buckinghamshire and Rainsborough's regiment of foot to Abingdon. The purpose of this deployment was to tighten the ring round Oxford in order to make it difficult for the King to make use of his forces there.

During December Fairfax pushed detachments to the west of Exeter to prevent supplies getting into the city and to hinder any relief attempt from Okehampton. It was at this time that Fulford House was captured and used as a base for troops moving against other Royalist garrisons in the area. In early January he took the bulk of the army south to push back a Royalist force, led by the Prince of Wales in person, from Ashburton and Totnes. It was as part of this movement that Cromwell led a body of horse and foot against Bovey Tracey, where three regiments of Royalist horse were stationed. In a daring night operation he surprised the enemy, taking 400 prisoners and dispersing the rest. Cromwell kept up the pressure by sending parties of horse into the west to prevent little bands of Royalists from joining together. Meanwhile Fairfax invested Dartmouth, which fell to another night attack on 19 January 1646. A few days later he raised a new regiment of foot to remain at Totnes and keep guard in the surrounding area to avoid detaching any of his own regiments.

The army returned to Exeter and on 27 January Fairfax sent an appeal to Berkeley to surrender the town to save bloodshed, but this was refused on the grounds that there was still some prospect of relief. Early in February Fairfax discovered that Hopton was assembling a force for this purpose around Barnstaple. Abandoning the siege, Fairfax headed off to confront him. The two sides met outside Great Torrington on 16 February, where the last battle of the war, worthy of the name, took place. Both sides occupied hedges along lanes leading out of the town, with the bulk of the Royalists in the buildings along the town's edge. After many hours of hand-to-hand fighting the Royalists were pushed out of the town during the night and retreated piecemeal over the Torridge into the countryside. Although some of the horse regiments remained intact, the foot was destroyed. Fairfax reinforced the troops blockading Exeter and Barnstaple and followed Hopton into Cornwall, which he occupied over the next few weeks. The Prince of Wales had already escaped by sea.

Fairfax then took the army back to Exeter via Plymouth, which he and Cromwell ceremoniously entered on 25 March to celebrate the end of its long siege. By the end of the month the New Model Army was once more outside Exeter and on this occasion, with no hope of relief from any direction, Berkeley surrendered to Cromwell, Fairfax having already left to accept the surrender of Barnstaple. On 18 April the New Model Army headed off for Oxford.

From the battle at Langport until the final destruction of the main Royalist bastion in the south-west had taken Fairfax and Cromwell nine hectic months, during which they had been continually on the move and frequently in action. They, together with their troops, must have been close to exhaustion. But the New Model Army had retained its cohesion. It was undoubtedly the most highly disciplined and formidable fighting force ever seen in England.

On 1 May the army assembled outside Oxford. But the King was no longer there, having slipped out in disguise on 27 April. A week later he handed himself over to the Scots army at Southwell outside Newark. Work continued for the reduction of Oxford, and it might even have become necessary to take it by storm. Luckily, before this could happen, the King ordered all his remaining fortresses and garrisons to surrender. Oxford did so on 16 June and the war was over.

6 · The Second Civil War

Cromwell's stature increased considerably in the period between the end of the first Civil War in June 1646 and the start of the second in April 1648. Although the events that took place at this time are only marginally relevant to an examination of his credentials as a military commander, it is nonetheless necessary to take a brief look at them in order to understand how his influence was growing.

For nearly a year after Cromwell moved to London following the fall of Oxford, he stayed there, attending Parliament most of the time. He also had a number of personal matters requiring his attention. Two of his daughters got married in 1646, the first, Elizabeth, to John Claypole and the second, Bridget, to Ireton. His own circumstances improved when Parliament rewarded him with estates worth £2,500 a year, a very large sum at that time. Then from the end of January 1647 until the middle of March he was seriously ill with what he described as an 'importune' of the head.

During the latter half of 1646 the army experienced the usual anticlimax felt by soldiers at the end of a long war. The religious fervour of the godly got out of control as some of the junior officers and men gave way to an orgy of preaching, on occasions turning priests and ministers out of their pulpits and treating their congregations to lengthy dissertations on religious matters. Not all of the army favoured these enthusiasts. Indeed, six months earlier some of the 'godly' had been taunted as 'Cromwell's bastards', one or two even being killed in brawls.[1] Now Fairfax calmed things down by forbidding unauthorised preaching. Eventually the ferment settled, but the religious fervour that had formerly been a positive factor in building up morale turned in some people into a desire for political action leading to social equality. Those affected in this way became known as Levellers.

The autumn of 1646 saw three other interesting developments. Essex died, thus weakening the hand of the Presbyterians in the Lords. Fairfax, taking advantage of contradictory instructions from Parliament, disbanded Massey's largely Presbyterian force based on Gloucester. Bishops and other senior ranks in the clergy were abolished, which freed up money which was used early in 1647 to pay off the Scots and get them to return to Scotland. As part of this deal, the Scots handed the King over to Parliament. By the spring of 1647 the Presbyterian influence was still uppermost in Parliament, strongly backed by the city of London. In the New Model Army the Independents were in the ascendant and the counterbalance to their power provided by Massey and the Scots had gone.

During the rest of 1647 three groups of people played out their conflicting interests. They were first, the Presbyterian majority in Parliament; second, the army; and third, Cromwell and his friends such as Viscount Saye and Sele in the Lords, and Vane and St John in the Commons. The Presbyterians wanted to limit the New Model Army to 5,400 horse and 1,000 dragoons and conscript the foot regiments into a new force under reliable (Presbyterian) officers to campaign in Ireland. This would lessen the possibility of coercion of Parliament by the army. In order to underpin their position they also wanted to restore the King on terms not greatly dissimilar to those envisaged by Pym at the start of the war. These terms were more favourable to him than anyone else was offering him, although he would need to make concessions regarding the Presbyterian religion.

The army did not want to disband until given their arrears of pay, an assurance that no one would be conscripted to serve outside England,

and a Parliamentary Act of Indemnity for all that had happened in the Civil War which, for safety's sake, would require the King's assent. The Independent majority in the army also wanted tolerance for all brands of the Calvinist religion, but not of course for Roman Catholics or Anglicans: the Prayer Book was already banned.

Cromwell and his friends wanted to avoid a conflict between the army and Parliament by making an agreement with the King, which would involve restoring him to his throne on more restrictive terms than those offered by Parliament. Naturally they would include a Toleration Act to prevent either the King or the Presbyterians from forcing their religious views on their countrymen. Such an agreement would also strictly limit the royal prerogative in other ways to prevent the King from reverting to his former methods of running the country.

In May 1647 Parliament, fearing that the army might openly defy its orders to disband, sent a deputation of its members including Cromwell to discuss matters with Fairfax and regimental representatives who together formed an Army Council. At the same time Parliament sounded out the possibility of the Presbyterian Scots returning to enforce the disbandment. Parliament also planned to strengthen its position by moving the King to London and by securing the army's artillery train, which was still in the area of Oxford.

At this time Parliament was holding the King prisoner in Northamptonshire. During the night of 2 June Cornet Joyce of Fairfax's regiment replaced the King's guards with his own men and two days later took the King to Newmarket, where the bulk of the New Model army was stationed. The army also secured its artillery train. Cromwell, now back in London, may have known that the army intended to take over guarding the King, but not that it intended to remove him from Parliament's control.

Up to this time Cromwell had been acting as a Member of Parliament rather than as an officer of the army, but he now decided to base himself with the army in order to pursue his plan. On 3 June he left London and joined Fairfax at Newmarket. For the rest of 1647 he acted mainly as Fairfax's second-in-command, although after the army moved nearer to London, he sat in Parliament when it suited him. Ireton too, now an MP, returned to the army.

Parliament's attempt to bounce the army into disbanding had stalled. It was now the army's turn and as a first step it moved towards London. Parliament set about organising the defence of the capital. On 14 June the army reached St Albans, from where it sent a strongly worded demand for its grievances to be rectified. It also insisted that Parliament should expel eleven of its members most hostile to its demands, including Denzil Holles. Although Parliament did not agree to the army's demands, the eleven members withdrew voluntarily and some money was sent to reduce the arrears of pay, whereupon the army retreated towards Bedford and dispersed its regiments around the countryside.

By this time Parliament's northern army, commanded by the Presbyterian Sydenham Poyntz, had mutinied, which further weakened Parliament's position. Some of its regiments moved south to join Fairfax, bringing Poyntz with them as a prisoner. Fairfax released Poyntz, and Parliament, recognising the reality of the situation, put the northern army, together with all other forces in the country, under Fairfax's overall control. Lambert became his major general in the north.

The next challenge to Parliament came unexpectedly from the city of London, which announced its own plans for a national settlement and sent mobs to bully Parliament into accepting them. Fairfax now found himself obliged to rescue Parliament, for which purpose he concentrated the army once more at St Albans and prepared to blockade the port of London. On 30 July the Speakers of both Lords and Commons, together with a number of members of both Houses, took refuge with the army. On 6 August Fairfax entered London unopposed with 16,000 men, occupying the city and the Tower. He then set up his headquarters outside London at Chelsea. Parliament, heavily in his debt, formally expelled the eleven members and took a more conciliatory attitude with regard to the army's future.

Meanwhile Cromwell was pursuing his attempt to achieve an agreement between the army, Parliament and the King, now held in honourable confinement at Hampton Court. To this end Ireton, in consultation with Fairfax and Cromwell, was busy producing 'Heads of Proposals' to underpin this hoped-for settlement. The proposals included an obligation on the King to call frequent Parliaments, and they envisaged reorganising the Commons franchise to make it more representative. They also gave Parliament the right to control the militia for ten years. During this period Cromwell, Ireton and other senior army officers had meetings with the King to try and get his agreement. Cromwell, who appeared to be getting on well with the King, even defended him vigorously in a speech in Parliament in October.

But as the summer wore on, a new difficulty made itself felt as the Levellers in the army, together with other extremists such as the Fifth Monarchy men, opposed what the generals were suggesting. Basically. these people wanted a far more radical solution involving a form of democratic government unthinkable at that time and one which neither Cromwell nor Fairfax nor Parliament, let alone the King, would contemplate. They also wanted the army to purge all the Presbyterians in Parliament opposed to their views, not just the eleven that Parliament had expelled. But although the Levellers were not strong enough to gain acceptance for their views, their very existence undermined the negotiating position of the generals by making it look as if they would be unable to get the army to back the agreement that they themselves were proposing. In order to instil some realism into the Levellers, Fairfax instituted debates at which their representatives could discuss matters with him and his senior officers. The first of these took place at Reading in July before the army entered London. A further series of debates took place at Putney in October and November at which time Cromwell deputised for Fairfax, who was ill.

As the year wore on, Cromwell lost some support in Parliament, where members felt that he was working more on behalf of the army than for them, and he lost support among the Levellers, who became suspicious of his dealings with the King. Furthermore, the agitation of the disaffected soldiers caused the King to worry about his personal safety, as a result of which he escaped from Hampton Court and handed himself over to Colonel Hammond at Carisbrooke Castle in the Isle of Wight, where he was once more held in honourable confinement. It has been suggested that Cromwell engineered the King's escape from Hampton Court to compromise him, at a time when the negotiations were making no headway. In fact this seems unlikely, although it is possible that he had wind of the King's plan and did nothing to stop him. It was undoubtedly a convenient way of bringing the negotiations, which were stalling under pressure from the Levellers in the army and lack of enthusiasm in Parliament, to a halt.

Soon afterwards Fairfax ordered a general rendezvous of the army at Ware in order to restore his authority, which had suffered from the behaviour of the extremists. There was a very minor mutiny in one or two of the regiments at the rendezvous, but it was speedily suppressed by Fairfax and other senior officers, including Cromwell. Throughout the summer and autumn Cromwell had been trying to achieve by negotiation what he thought to be consistent with good government, emphasising that anything achieved by force against the will of Parliament would not last.

As 1647 wore on, it became apparent that unrest was gathering throughout the country for a number of reasons including the Puritan insistence on interfering with traditional religious observance such as the celebration of Christmas. The main cause of discontent was, however, the weight of taxation needed to pay the army, and this was closely associated with resentment at the continued use of free quarter by the army in lieu of pay. Clearly major tax cuts could be achieved only by making a reduction in the size of the army.

Conscious of the army's power, Parliament at last agreed to finance a reduction in the army's strength. Fairfax suggested a reorganisation of the main field army which involved increasing the number of horse regiments to fourteen and foot regiments to seventeen, but reducing the numbers in each troop and company from 100 to 80. There would also be 30 independent companies of foot in garrisons around the country.[2] Everything else would go, except for five selected regiments of the northern army. The first to go would be ex-Royalists and anyone who had joined since the army entered London in early August. Next were units considered politically unreliable from the army's point of view, mainly Presbyterian-dominated regiments in Wales and the west of England. Then all the surplus men from the garrisons and castles throughout the land would go. Reductions would be complete by the middle of 1648, by which time the army would be cut by a half.[3] The important point was that the army would choose who should be selected for demobilisation, which meant that troublesome extremists would leave, together with a number of Presbyterians.

Early in 1648 Cromwell's friends in Parliament passed an act forbidding any further negotiation with the King. It had come to light that while the King had been negotiating with Cromwell and Ireton, he had also been doing a deal with a group in Scotland known as Engagers. These people were so concerned by the influence of Independents that they felt it would be better to send an army into England to restore the King than to sit idly by while the English army gradually destroyed the Presbyterian interest in Parliament and the country. In return for their army, the King would have to accept the Presbyterian religion in England for a trial period of three years.

BEFORE DESCRIBING WHAT has come to be known as the second Civil War it is worth trying to assess the position occupied by Cromwell in early 1648. Even though some Presbyterians in Parliament may have felt that he had been working largely on behalf of the army, it was apparent that he had at least been trying to avoid a direct clash between themselves and the army. Also, he was not hostile to the Presbyterian religion as such; he merely objected to it being forced on Calvinists who wanted to worship in a different way. His position in Parliament was strengthened by the fact that the Presbyterian interest had been weakened by the events of the summer and by the expulsion of its eleven leading members, whilst his own backers remained firm. Furthermore, as he had taken a leading role in the events of 1647, his influence in Parliament was almost certainly stronger than it had been at the end of the Civil War.

In the army he had become almost as important as Fairfax himself. There had been no fighting and most of the action had been of a political nature in terms either of the army's dispute with Parliament, or of its relations with the King, or with the split between the generals and the Levellers. In the first two cases it was Cromwell and Ireton who led the way rather than Fairfax. In dealing with the Levellers it was Fairfax's concern for the discipline of the army that was decisive in controlling the unrest, but it was Cromwell and Ireton who were best able to join in the debates with the extremists, many of whose leaders such as Rainsborough and Harrisson had been his supporters in the old Eastern Association army. Indeed, the lack of support that he experienced at the end of the year from the extremists in the army arose from disappointment that he was not more sympathetic to the development of their ideas. The vehemence with which he expressed his advanced religious opinions may have blinded them to the fact that in social matters he was distinctly conservative.

When considering Cromwell's position in the army, a comparison with Fairfax has to be made. Fairfax shone in battle, where his retiring nature and long silences were as nothing when set against the admiration he received for his tactical brilliance, his shining example and his bravery. There can be little doubt that he was hugely respected throughout the army and by no one more than Cromwell. But Cromwell's arrival with the army in June 1647 added a certain excitement to life. Where Fairfax was withdrawn and often wracked by pain from his many wounds and gout, Cromwell was usually genial and vigorous. He enjoyed talking with the soldiers, and his friendliness, practical jokes and love of horses lifted the spirits of the men as he moved around the regiments. Of course he still had a quick temper and his utterances when engaged in serious discussion could be anything but genial. But in most of the main issues of the day it was Cromwell, informed by Ireton, rather than Fairfax who was making the running. His position was also strengthened by the gradual replacement of Presbyterians by Independents.

Ireton was the other person who rose to prominence in 1647. He had a deeper understanding of political theory and the constitution than

Cromwell and a far more logical mind. But he had little of Cromwell's magnetism. He was brilliant at formulating policies but less good at persuading people to accept them.

THE SECOND CIVIL WAR had little in common with the first. For one thing, it was short. The first of the fighting broke out in March 1648 and by the end of August it was all over bar some mopping up. Secondly, although there were marches and sieges and small battles, there was no set-piece battle to compare with Edgehill, Marston Moor or Naseby. The nearest thing to a formal battle was the series of actions spread over three days that occurred between Cromwell and the Scots in August, subsequently known as the battle of Preston.

The first signs of revolt arose in Canterbury, when crowds objected to new laws abolishing Christmas, but order was soon restored. Similar troubles arose in Suffolk and in London. A more serious situation rose in Wales on 22 February 1648, when Colonel Poyer, who commanded a regiment and who was also governor of Pembroke Castle, refused to hand over the castle to Colonel Fleming and disband his men without more money. Fairfax ordered Major General Laugharne, commanding the troops in Wales, to enforce the disbandment and sent Colonel Horton with his regiment of horse (formerly Butler's) together with three troops of Graves's regiment of horse, Lloyd's regiment of foot and eight companies of dragoons to help him. By this time it was early March but instead of following Fairfax's instructions Laugharne joined Poyer with his regiment and declared for the King. Soon the revolt spread throughout south Wales.

In April further trouble broke out in London when a large mob advanced on Parliament demanding release of the King and a settlement with him. The two regiments stationed in Whitehall to safeguard Parliament, commanded by Rich and Barkstead, dispersed the mob and reinforcements were sent to Tichborne's newly formed regiment in the Tower, bringing it up to a strength of over 1,000 men. Meanwhile further unrest was breaking out in Essex and Norfolk.

Not all of these uprisings represented spontaneous protest against heavy taxation and Puritan religious regulation. The Scots, who had been negotiating with the King, also tried to arrange for uprisings in Kent and in the Eastern Association to coincide with their intended invasion, and Royalists, including some who had fled to France in 1646, were stirring up revolt elsewhere in England. In Ireland the confederate leaders concluded an agreement with the Royalist Earl of Ormonde to secure the country for the King and send troops to assist his cause in England. At the end of April small groups of northern Royalists led by Sir Marmaduke Langdale seized the castles at Carlisle and Berwick.

Fairfax was now in a difficult position. Not only was he in the middle of a massive programme of reductions, but he was also under pressure from Parliament to put down the disturbances that were erupting in different parts of the country whilst taking steps to oppose the impending Scottish attack. Clearly the most immediate threat was from Wales, where there was an overt Royalist uprising. He therefore despatched Cromwell with his regiment of horse, three regiments of foot and two companies of dragoons to deal with the situation. Fairfax intended to go north himself to repel the Scots when the time came.

CROMWELL, MOVING FAST, arrived at Gloucester on 8 May, by which time his force had been supplemented by local forces so that he had 6,500 men with him. On the same day Horton was attacked near Cardiff by around 7,000 of Laugharne's Royalists anxious to dispose of him before Cromwell arrived; Fleming had already been killed by Poyer's men about ten days earlier. Surprisingly, Horton's regiments prevailed.

Cromwell now sent Colonel Ewer to attack the Royalist-held Chepstow Castle while he took the rest of his force towards the main centre of Royalist resistance at Pembroke Castle, which was manned by nearly 2,000 men. Ewer succeeded in taking Chepstow Castle by storm on 25 May, but Cromwell could only invest Pembroke Castle and try to starve it out until he could lay his hands on some cannon. His own artillery train, which was being brought by sea because of the state of the roads, was firmly aground in the Severn estuary. At the end of the month Tenby Castle fell to Horton, who then joined Cromwell at Pembroke, but Ewer's regiment was hurriedly returned to Fairfax.

MEANWHILE TROUBLE WAS mounting up for Fairfax in Kent, where bands of Royalists were taking control of one town after another. At the end of May the old Earl of Norwich became established as the Royalist leader, by which time he had in the county about 10,000 men. Fairfax gathered regiments from London and nearby areas to the tune of around 4,000 men and captured Maidstone. Many discouraged Royalists returned home, but Norwich managed to lead around 3,000 of them to Blackheath. Parliament was alarmed, but Skippon took control of London's defences and Norwich was obliged to get what men he could across the Thames into Essex, where other Royalists were gathering. Whalley shadowed him while Fairfax subdued remaining Royalist forces in Kent.

In Essex matters moved fast. On 2 June Fairfax sent three more regiments to join Whalley, but a Royalist colonel managed to raise 1,000 recruits. Norwich then met Sir Charles Lucas, who was the Royalist leader in Essex, at Chelmsford on 8 June and together they went to Colchester, which was held for the King by Lord Capel and Sir George Lisle. On 11 June Fairfax, having cleared Kent, crossed the Thames with most of his remaining regiments and immediately advanced on Colchester. Two days later he launched an attack. To the accompaniment of fierce fighting the Royalists withdrew behind the town walls and Fairfax realised that he had no option but to lay siege to Colchester and starve it out.

Another setback for Parliament occurred on 10 June when part of the fleet declared for the King and ten ships sailed for the United Provinces. Six weeks later, with the Prince of Wales as admiral and, of all people, Lord Willoughby of Parham as vice-admiral, they sailed back to the mouth of the Thames. Other prominent Royalists including Prince Rupert sailed with this fleet.

Although the Royalist strength in Colchester was no more than

4,000–5,000, it was a difficult place to seal off. In the end Fairfax was obliged to commit nearly 10,000 men to the siege and it was here that many of the famous commanders and regiments of the New Model Army were tied down until the end of the war. With Cromwell equally tied down outside Pembroke Castle, it was difficult to know how to handle the impending Scots invasion, especially as it was impossible to denude such key places as Gloucester and Oxford of their garrisons.

HAD THE SCOTS BEEN ABLE to co-ordinate their invasion with the Royalist uprisings in Wales, London, Kent and Essex, it is hard to see how the combined Royalist and Presbyterian cause could have failed. As it was, the New Model Army was hard pressed. In the north it was up to Lambert to do the best he could to ward off the threat. He quickly set to work to hinder the activities of Langdale's Royalists, who were gaining recruits by the day in the north-east, often men recently disbanded from Lambert's own army. He also had to rebuild his own army, which had been reduced to 3,000 men by these same disbandments. At this time he had three regiments of horse, and three regiments of foot, two of which were not yet ready for action. There were two further regiments of foot to defend Newcastle, but these could not be moved elsewhere.

Early in June a small number of Langdale's men gained entrance to Pontefract Castle by a ruse and captured it, which complicated Lambert's plans. On the credit side, he had received reinforcements from Fairfax in the form of Harrisson's regiment of horse, and after the fall of Chepstow Castle Cromwell had sent a regiment of foot and two troops of horse to reinforce him. Lambert had also received 1,500 men raised by Colonel Ashton in Lancashire. As soon as he could spare them, Fairfax sent his own regiment of foot and two troops from his regiment of horse, but they did not arrive until the beginning of July. By this time, therefore, Lambert had five regiments of horse, five regiments of foot and four extra troops of horse, not counting the Newcastle garrison and Ashton's Lancashire levies. Until the Scots crossed the border Lambert was active in opposing Royalist attempts to foster uprisings throughout the north, particularly in Northumberland, and it was his success in this field that provided a sound base for future operations.

The Scottish army, consisting of 3,000 horse and 6,000 foot but with no artillery train, finally crossed into England on 8 July, but it had little in common with the Covenanters' army of 1644. For one thing, it was led by the Duke of Hamilton, who despite having served with Gustavus Adolphus for a short time had little military understanding and was indecisive. His second-in-command was the Earl of Callander, who though more experienced, having served for some years in the United Provinces, was tactless and inflexible. Middleton, who had been with Waller for much of the Civil War, commanded the horse and the experienced Baillie, who had done well at Marston Moor, commanded the foot. But many influential people throughout Scotland such as the Marquess of Argyll, the Earl of Leven and David Leslie refused to support the Engagers, and the Kirk detested them. As a result the Scottish army was not well led, paid, or supplied. So much was this the case that the army had to move slowly and widely dispersed in order to live off the land. The locals were horrified by this mass of half-starved foreigners bringing with them lice, presbytery and enough women to settle in the area for good. The invasion quickly stifled any sympathy that there may have been for the Royalist cause in the north.

The Scots spent six days at Carlisle, during which time they were joined by Langdale with 3,000 men from Northumberland and Yorkshire. By 14 July Hamilton was at Penrith, where a further 1,000 horse and 4,000 foot reached him from Scotland. Lambert had taken up a position outside the town to delay his further advance, but in view of the disparity in their strengths he decided after a brief skirmish to withdraw south-east towards Appleby. He guessed that Hamilton would want to cross into Yorkshire at this point in order to link up with Langdale's men in Pontefract Castle. This was indeed the most favourable course for Hamilton to take, because there was more potential support for his cause in Yorkshire than in Lancashire and also because the Royalist fleet lying off the east coast would be well placed to support his advance and ease his supply problem. The Scottish Earl of Lauderdale was on his way to join the fleet in order to arrange for this to happen and, if possible, to get the Prince of Wales to lead the Engagers in Scotland. But by the time he arrived on 10 August it was already too late, as Hamilton was committed to the western route through Lancashire.

PEMBROKE CASTLE SURRENDERED on 11 July and Cromwell set off to take command of the troops opposing the Scots invasion. He left Pembroke with three regiments of foot and two companies of dragoons, having sent on his own regiment of horse in advance. By 5 August he had reached Leicester and three days later entered Doncaster. Here he waited for a few days for ammunition and some cannon to reach him from the arsenal at Hull. He also exchanged the recruits that he had picked up along the way for some of Lambert's more experienced soldiers who were containing the Royalists in Pontefract Castle.

On 17 July leading elements of the Scottish army advancing from Penrith bumped into Lambert's position at Appleby, thereby confirming him in his opinion that the Scots intended to cross into Yorkshire. After a brisk engagement in which Harrisson was wounded the Scots were driven off and Lambert made a further withdrawal to Barnard Castle, where he intended to make a stand. It was here on 27 July that Cromwell's regiment of horse reached him. A week later some Scottish horse arrived at Brough as though advancing on Barnard Castle but then turned south. At this point Lambert lost contact with them. As he was still unsure of Hamilton's intentions, he moved rapidly south to Knaresborough and then south-west to Otley. Here he would be well placed to intercept the Scots if they tried to move east from Kendal via Settle to Skipton and then either through Knaresborough to York, or through Otley to Pontefract. It was a sound move. Cromwell met Lambert on 13 August at Otley and took his forces under command.

Cromwell now had an army consisting of five regiments of horse and five of foot together with the equivalent of a further regiment of horse and the two weak regiments of foot brought by Colonel Ashton from Lancashire. Taking into account losses sustained over the past

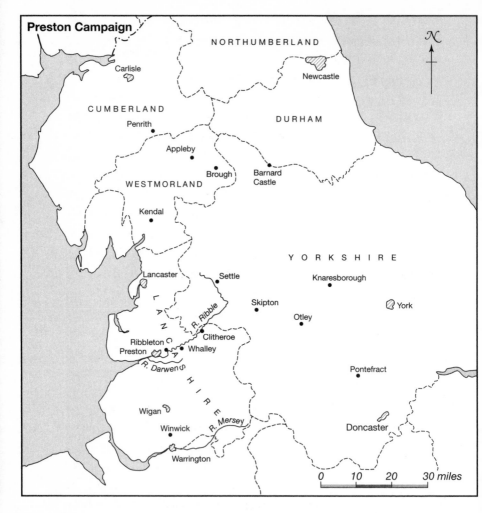

Preston Campaign

NORTHUMBERLAND

Carlisle

Newcastle

CUMBERLAND

DURHAM

Penrith

Appleby

Brough

Barnard
Castle

WESTMORLAND

Kendal

YORKSHIRE

Lancaster

Settle

Knaresborough

Skipton

York

Otley

R. Ribble

Ribbleton

Clitheroe

Preston

Whalley

R. Darwen

Pontefract

Wigan

Winwick

R. Mersey

Doncaster

Warrington

N

0   10   20   30 miles

three months' fighting and marching, he probably had around 9,000
men. His greatest weakness was however not men but intelligence.
Because Lambert had lost touch with the Scots he had no reliable information regarding their position or intentions; Lambert's estimate of
their strength at around 30,000 was also too high. But Cromwell would
undoubtedly have heard that their army was slow-moving and ineffi-
cient, and he also knew than Sir George Monro had crossed from Ulster
to Stranraer with the brigade that the King had sent to Ireland at the

time of the 1641 massacres. They only amounted to 1,200 horse and 2,100 foot but unlike most of Hamilton's army they were experienced and well trained.

Cromwell worked out that if the Scots had decided to stick to the western route, their leading troops might now be as far south as Warrington. In this case his safest course would be to move rapidly south in order to place himself where he could get between Hamilton and London, regardless of whether they went through Lancashire or Yorkshire. Meanwhile he could send out patrols to try and pinpoint Hamilton's real position. But this would take time and even if he did win a battle after blocking their path, he would only force them back towards Monro's brigade and Scotland so that many would be able to escape and fight another day. On the other hand, if he marched west he would almost certainly take them from the flank or get behind them, in which case they could hardly go on without turning to fight him. In view of his numerical weakness this was a gamble, but it is what he decided to do. It was a calculated risk based on his assessment of the uselessness of their army.

Having described what Cromwell decided to do in the light of the knowledge available to him, it is now worth looking at the situation from Hamilton's point of view. Working his way south from Penrith, he had got no further than Kendal by 8 August. Next day he got to Hornby, seven miles to the north-east of Lancaster, where he decided to wait for Monro. Soon Monro himself appeared to tell Hamilton that his men were now approaching. But Monro refused to have his men split up between Middleton and Baillie; so Hamilton formed a new force consisting of Monro's men and some Yorkshire levies, who he said were to stay in the rear of his army to act as a reserve.

On 13 August, while Hamilton was still at Hornby, Langdale, whose men were at Settle, visited him to tell him that Cromwell and Lambert had joined forces. Hamilton called a council of war to decide whether to cross into Yorkshire, crush Cromwell by sheer weight of numbers and move directly on London, or to continue south through Lancashire to join Byron, who was supposedly organising an uprising in north Wales and Cheshire. The council favoured the second course. The Scots would advance on Preston, and Langdale was told to bring his men along the right bank of the river Ribble to join them there.

On 16 August Hamilton's army was well spread out: his horse had pushed on beyond Preston to Wigan and his foot were approaching Preston. But Cromwell was closing in, having moved via Skipton and Clitheroe to Whalley, where Cromwell decided to move his army to the right bank of the Ribble to ensure that as few of Hamilton's men as possible could escape northwards after a battle. The crossing took place late on 16 August, most of the men spending the night at Stonyhurst to the north of the river. Next morning, 17 August 1648, the army moved towards Preston, probably along the line of the present road which runs through Hurst Green and Knowle Green to Longridge, where he was held up for a short time by Langdale's rearguard.

Langdale, with three regiments of foot and one of horse, turned to face Cromwell at Ribbleton just outside Preston, sending word to Hamilton to get some of his foot regiments, which were no more than three miles away, out to him as soon as he could. He deployed with his centre astride the road and with the rest of his force lining the lanes and hedges and ditches on either side of it. The position was strong and with one or two extra regiments might have held Cromwell for the rest of the day. Unfortunately for Langdale, Callander persuaded Hamilton that any troops sent would surely be lost and that he should concentrate on getting his foot across the Ribble and its tributary the Darwen by the bridges to the south of Preston, where they could be joined by the horse. Langdale should delay Cromwell for as long as possible to ensure that this happened.

Cromwell, who massively outnumbered Langdale, deployed five regiments of foot in his front line (Reade's, Deane's, Pride's, Bright's and Fairfax's[4]) with Ashton's two Lancashire regiments behind them in reserve. Close behind his front line regiments he held his own and Harrisson's regiments of horse. Because of the incessant rain the road itself and the fields and moorland on either side were little better than bogs. Cromwell described the road as 'a lane very deep and ill.'

The battle, which started at around 3.30 pm, swiftly became a slogging match with both sides fighting like tigers. To the right Cromwell sent two other regiments of horse (probably Twisleton's and Thornhaugh's newly raised regiment) to attack Langdale's horse, which was speedily routed, after which Cromwell sent these regiments to assist his hard-pressed foot regiments on the left. The left eventually had to be reinforced by the reserve regiments of foot as well. At one point Cromwell's and Harrisson's regiments of horse tried to charge down the road, although it was so deep in mud that they found great difficulty in doing so. At last by sheer weight of numbers Cromwell forced Langdale back, but it had taken around five hours. Most of Langdale's foot were either killed or taken prisoner. Some of his horse escaped to the north.

As soon as resistance ceased Cromwell's men fought their way into Preston and then south through the town towards the main bridge over the Ribble. By this time most of the Scots were across but Hamilton and his bodyguard, who had been watching Langdale's battle, were nearly cut off. Together with Langdale, who joined them at this time, they managed to swim their horses across the river near the flooded ford.

Soon afterwards Cromwell attacked the Scots who had been left to the north of the river to guard the approaches to the bridge and after a stiff fight killed or captured them. Determined to prevent the Scots, most of whom were now to the south of the Ribble, from escaping to the north, he sent half of one of Ashton's regiments and some dragoons to guard the bridge across the Ribble north of Whalley. By the time it got dark Cromwell had succeeded in forcing the bridge over the Ribble and then the smaller one over the Darwen, but his men were by now exhausted. He reckoned to have captured about 4,000 of the enemy and killed at least 1,000 more.

By the end of the day Hamilton had seen Langdale's force demolished but he still had nearly twice as many men as Cromwell. They were however dispirited, soaked by rain, and half starved as usual. He decided to move south towards Wigan during the night in order to become reunited with his regiments of horse. After that he felt that he would be ready to do battle with Cromwell. Unfortunately for him his ammunition wagons were stuck in the mud just to the south of the Darwen and the wagoners had made off with the horses, so that the men would have to make do with what they could carry in their powder flasks. A further disaster occurred when his foot regiments moved south in the darkness on one route and his horse moved north to join them on another, so that the two never met. Instead, early the next morning Middleton with the horse ran into three regiments of Cromwell's horse which were covering the move of his army across the Darwen. Middleton was immediately attacked and put to flight, Cromwell's horse following him for most of the fifteen miles to Wigan inflicting heavy losses all the way.

Cromwell left two regiments of foot and two troops of horse to hold Preston against Monro, should he decide to take a hand in the proceedings, and followed Hamilton with the rest of his army. He spent the night of 18 August near Wigan but Hamilton did not stop. Throughout the night of 18 August he pressed his soldiers on in an effort to reach Warrington ahead of Cromwell. He hoped to cross to the south of the river Mersey and defend the river line. But by now many of Hamilton's men had fallen out as they could march no further and the rest never reached Warrington. Instead they were brought to bay at Winwick, eight miles beyond Wigan, where they put up a commendable performance in a running fight during which Hamilton suffered further heavy casualties, around 1,000 being killed according to Cromwell's report. The survivors fell back towards Warrington.

As a result of this further defeat, on Callander's recommendation, Hamilton gave orders to Baillie to surrender what was left of the foot, while he himself went on with the horse, hoping to join Byron. But Byron's intended uprising never took place and Hamilton was hunted down by Lambert, who followed him with four regiments of horse and two of foot. Gradually Hamilton's force was rounded up by Lambert or by the local militia. Hamilton himself surrendered at Uttoxeter, Middleton was captured in Staffordshire and Langdale in Nottingham. Only the useless Callander got clean away to the Continent. By the end of the month Lambert had rejoined Cromwell, who was resting his long-suffering foot regiments, some of whom had marched from south Wales into Yorkshire, thence across the Pennines into Lancashire and finally as far south as Warrington.

NEWS OF THE SCOTS DEFEAT reached the Royalists in Colchester on 24 August and four days later the Earl of Norwich surrendered the town to Fairfax. To all intents and purposes, the second Civil War had come to an end. Cromwell, whose losses had been surprisingly light, still had work to do in the north. After a few days' rest he set off to find Monro. But Monro, who had declined to lead his force to rescue Hamilton after the debacle at Preston, was too far ahead. Marching across the country to Berwick, Monro entered Scotland, where he found a civil war in progress between the Engager government and an army raised by Leven, Leslie and the Earl of Eglington, who occupied Edinburgh and forced the Engagers back to Stirling. Both sides were anxious to avoid having an English army led by Cromwell in their midst.

On 18 September Cromwell reached Berwick and three days later crossed into Scotland. Next day he had met Argyll and offered him his assistance to the Covenanters in return for the restoration of Berwick and Carlisle, which were still occupied by the Scots. Lambert then took the horse on to Edinburgh as a threat to those still opposed to Argyll. Cromwell waited to receive the return of Berwick, after which he followed with the rest of the army. On 4 October he was officially welcomed into Edinburgh, where he remained until he was sure that Argyll's position was secure. During this time an agreement was reached which committed Argyll and the Engagers to disband their forces. Monro was to return forthwith to Ulster. Within the week Cromwell set off for Carlisle, leaving Lambert with three regiments of horse to ensure that the agreement was carried out. From Carlisle he moved to Pontefract, where he remained until the end of November supervising the siege.

CROMWELL'S FIRST CAMPAIGN as an independent commander had been a triumph. When he left Windsor in early May it was with orders to restore discipline amongst one or two regiments in Wales that refused to disband without more money. He then found himself involved in suppressing a small-scale Royalist uprising in the area which would have been simple enough had it not been for the lack of his artillery train. As it was, it took him two months to complete his task, by which time the bulk of the New Model Army was tied down by a series of dangerous uprisings near the capital. This obliged him to march the length of the country to repel a Scottish army that was more than twice the size of all the regiments that he could collect together. Undaunted by these odds, he moved straight into the attack and, within six days of joining Lambert, had totally destroyed the invading army in a series of engagements during which his own losses were very light. After that, he rapidly settled civil unrest in Scotland in such a way as to ensure that the country would for some time be unable to help the Royalist cause in England. By the middle of October he was back in Yorkshire ready for whatever further tasks might be given to him.

Of course his opponents were badly led, trained and supplied, and, having marched all the way from Scotland to Preston in pouring rain, were incapable of fighting effectively. But Cromwell's men had marched just as far in just as much rain and although some of his regiments were veterans of the New Model Army, others, particularly those raised by Lambert in the spring, had only been in existence for a few weeks. The real difference was the standard of leadership of Cromwell's officers, and in particular the operational experience and ability of Lambert and Cromwell himself.

Strategically it took Cromwell no time to realise that his best course was to make contact with the Scots at once and try to engage one part of their army after another, in order to offset his lack of numbers. Had he taken the option of getting between the Scots and London, it would have been difficult to prevent the enemy from closing up and deploying on a suitable piece of ground before fighting, thereby making the best of their great numerical superiority.

Tactically it was difficult for Cromwell to put his chosen course of action into effect because Lambert, who had done brilliantly in raising regiments and in suppressing Royalist uprisings throughout the north, had lost touch with the enemy at the critical moment. Thus when Cromwell arrived he had only the vaguest idea as to their whereabouts. But he would have heard about their shortcomings in terms of supply and discipline and he would have known that they must have been well spread out in order to live and move. When he did find out that there was enemy to his front, his decision to cross to the north of the Ribble in order to prevent most of Hamilton's army from escaping to the north was undoubtedly sound and bore witness to his determination and confidence.

He was also lucky to run into Langdale's tough and efficient force first, since by disposing of it, he got rid of his most dangerous opponents. He was equally lucky that Monro's experienced men had not been integrated into Hamilton's army by the time he arrived, as they too would have given it the backbone it lacked. But his luck reflected his boldness rather than blind chance.

When he did meet up with Langdale his success was due to his having concentrated an adequate superiority of numbers at the critical place and to his willingness to push his men straight into a slogging match in the mud. He also ensured that they kept on hammering away until most of his opponents were killed or wounded. After that, without giving his weary men any respite, he pushed them into Preston and captured the bridges, which enabled him to keep up the pressure on Hamilton's disorganised forces next day. He could not have foreseen that the Scottish horse and foot would pass each other in the night, thus preventing Hamilton from concentrating a sufficiently balanced army to oppose his further advance, but he certainly exploited the situation to the full. In short, although his operations may have lacked finesse, he was able to capitalise on the strength, training and fighting spirit of his regiments to rout his lumbering opponent. Cromwell, who had hitherto only acted as a subordinate commander, had shown beyond question that he was fully capable of successful independent command.

IT IS NOTICEABLE THAT from the moment that Cromwell met Lambert at Otley, he had no trouble in discovering God's mind in any of the military problems facing him. But once the campaign was over and he had sent back to Fairfax the regiments that he no longer needed, he spent much time trying to discern God's wishes for the future as he supervised the siege of Pontefract Castle, a task that Lambert could have done perfectly well on his own. And whilst he pondered, others acted.

The second Civil War had undoubtedly come as a shock to the New Model Army. Having weathered the first Civil War, none of them were keen to hazard their lives and suffer the hardships of a further campaign merely because a misguided Parliament had been incapable of dealing with a deceitful King. The first fruits of their resentment were felt by the defeated Royalists and Scots, who were treated with far less magnanimity than had been extended to those captured in the first Civil War. The Scots prisoners taken by Cromwell at Preston were sent as indentured labourers (virtual slaves) to Barbados, unless they could show that they had been forcibly conscripted into the Scots army. Hamilton himself was sent to London, where he was executed in the following year.

Meanwhile Parliament once more tried to reach an agreement with the King while the army was still away. In August the eleven members, excluded in deference to the army's wishes the previous year, were restored, and the Act pushed through by Cromwell's friends in January to prevent further treating with the King was repealed. Thereafter Parliament sent commissioners to the Isle of Wight to negotiate with the King, but by this time the army was getting restless, especially as its pay was increasingly in arrears. As the regiments concentrated around St Albans, Fairfax received requests from some of his officers to stop Parliament's talks with the King, but at first he did nothing. Ireton then prepared a lengthy paper setting out the position of those in the army who were no longer prepared to put up with the situation. It was discussed with Fairfax at a council of officers in early November. Ireton demanded, amongst other things, that the King be brought to justice, the monarchy abolished and Parliament reformed, but neither Fairfax nor a majority of the council was yet prepared to go that far. Instead, Fairfax contacted the King to offer him a further settlement, which was rejected.

At this, Fairfax and the council of officers agreed to Ireton's proposals, which were passed to Parliament on 20 November together with a demand for money with which to pay the men. Parliament prevaricated. On 1 December Fairfax sent Harrisson to take the King to Hurst Castle in Hampshire. Next day Fairfax occupied London and the eleven members hastily departed.

It was at this point that matters got beyond Fairfax's control. His own attempt to persuade Parliament to accept a moderate version of Ireton's proposal was turned down, whereupon Ireton, in conjunction with some of the Independents in Parliament, decided to act. On 6 December Colonel Pride went to Westminster with a detachment of soldiers and either arrested or sent away around 140 MPs with instructions not to return. This left 154 members, who would become known to history as the 'Rump'. The event became known as 'Pride's Purge', although it should more accurately be described as Ireton's Purge. Cromwell arrived back in London that same evening, having been recalled by Fairfax on 2 December. Cromwell maintained that 'he had not been acquainted with the design; yet since it was done he was glad of it'. Not everyone believed that he knew so little of his son-in-law's intentions.

Early in January 1649 the Rump, having disregarded objections from the Lords, set up a tribunal to try the King for betraying the trust reposed in him by the people. There were to be 150 commissioners to try him, of whom at least twenty had to be present. Cromwell, after much prayer and consideration, enthusiastically supported the arrangement. Like Fairfax, he was made one of the commissioners, but whereas Fairfax opposed the trial and refused to appear at it, Cromwell took a leading role both in appearing himself and in persuading others to do so. The High Court judges would have nothing to do with what was, to all intents and purposes, a kangaroo court; so a relatively unknown lawyer from Cheshire called John Bradshaw became president of the court. On 21 January the trial started. As the King refused either to plead or even to recognise the court, the proceedings were soon over. Cromwell was by now as determined as Ireton, Harrisson and the other hard-liners that the King should be killed, and he threw himself into the business of ensuring that enough of the other commissioners voted for a death sentence. In the course of doing this, his playful side asserted itself and he is reported as flicking ink at the assembled company as he bullied them into signing the death warrant.

On 30 January the King was executed. It was clearly judicial murder, but, as Cromwell said, it was 'cruel necessity'. The King was never going to agree to anything that cut across what he held to be the fundamental rights of the sovereign, and without doing so he could never reach an agreement with the Independents in the army and in Parliament. By killing him they exchanged a King whom they held safely in prison for one who was safely in France. Within a few weeks of his death, his son was proclaimed Charles II by the Scots and the Irish. There would soon be more work for the New Model Army.

7 · Ireland

Having struck off the head of the King, the Independents in Parliament, backed by an army from which most hostile influence had been expelled, had complete control of the country. Parliament instituted what it described as a Commonwealth and set up an executive in the form of a Council of State, the members of which were to be elected annually. For the first month Cromwell was President of the Council, after which Bradshaw took over. There were 41 members of the Council of State, of whom 31 were members of the Rump. They included Fairfax, who, though a Scottish peer since the recent death of his father, was also now a Member of Parliament. The monarchy was abolished. The House of Lords was also abolished, contrary to Cromwell's wishes. Some peers were elected to the Commons.

The removal of all restraints on the Commons, which in its new form was highly unrepresentative of the people, opened the way to a tyranny infinitely worse than anything practised by Charles I, who at least tried to govern in accordance with the laws and customs of the country. The army intended this state of affairs to last only for a few months until the Rump dissolved itself so that new elections on a greatly extended franchise could be held. But the Rump refused to dissolve. In the last year of his life Cromwell described the situation in the following words:

> This was the case of the people of England at that time, the Parliament assuming to itself the authority of the three estates that were before. It had so assumed that authority that if any man had come and said 'what rules do you judge by' it would have answered 'why we have none. We are supreme in legislature and judicature.'[1]

This new form of government was naturally objectionable to Royalists and Presbyterians within England, to say nothing of the extremists such as the Levellers and Fifth Monarchy men. Abroad, there was widespread objection to the killing of the King, particularly in Scotland and Ireland. The fact that his son had at once been proclaimed King in Scotland was a fair indication that there would at some stage be trouble from that quarter. But the Scots were wary of the English army after the recent campaign and were by no means ready to embark upon another one in order to restore their new king to the English throne. There were however two immediate tasks to be done.

The first concerned the depredations made by Royalist, French and Dutch privateers on English shipping. This problem had become more urgent since the Royalist fleet, which had returned to the United Provinces after the fall of Colchester, put to sea again in January 1649 under the command of Prince Rupert. Sailing to the south-west coast of Ireland, it set up a base at Kinsale from where it was well placed to cut across the sea routes of ships entering the English Channel. The second was the situation in Ireland, where the Royalist Marquess of Ormonde was attempting to expel Parliamentary influence from the country. The two were linked to the extent that Prince Rupert's fleet would be able to assist Ormonde unless Parliament's own navy was able to prevent it. Between them, Ormonde and Rupert represented a real and immediate threat to the Commonwealth interest and would have to be dealt with.

TO UNDERSTAND EVENTS in Ireland, it is necessary to go back in time. In the centuries following the original incursion into that country by the Norman Kings of England, a small area along the east coast, known as the Pale, was secured, settled and ruled directly from Dublin. But many Norman lords settled well beyond the Pale and virtually identified with the native Irish. These people were frequently at loggerheads with the authorities in Dublin, particularly after the Reformation. In Elizabeth's reign, Protestant adventurers from Devon set up settlements in the south of Ireland beyond the control of the Dublin authorities, slaughtering many of the native Irish in the process. In the reign of her successor, Ulster, in the north of the country, was settled by Protestant Scots, which caused the displacement of many native Irish families.

In the 1630s Strafford, while reforming the administrative, legal and legislative systems, greatly enlarged the army so that at the time he left the country in 1639 it consisted of around 8,000 well-found Irish troops led by properly trained officers drawn from the mainly Protestant Anglo-Norman families, commanded by Ormonde. Two years later, the uprising by the native Irish threw the country into turmoil, and it was at this time that the King sent Monro's brigade from Scotland to Ulster; a number of English regiments commanded by professionals such as George Monk were also sent.

The insurgents who carried out the uprising were for the most part directed by Catholic members of the Anglo-Irish gentry, except in Ulster where they followed Owen Roe O'Neill, a thoroughgoing Irishman and a first-class professional soldier.

The leaders of the various insurgent groups theoretically deferred to the President of the Confederate Catholics, Lord Mountgarret. In 1643 the King told Ormonde to broker a truce with Mountgarret. If this could be achieved the King would be able to get back the English regiments to help him in his war against Parliament, and he hoped to get hold of some of Ormonde's army as well if things settled down. In the longer term he even hoped that some Confederate soldiers might join him. A truce was agreed in 1643, and around 17,000 men of the English regiments returned to help the King. But the removal of the English troops and the fact that Ormonde was dealing with the insurgents made the Protestants nervous of a further Catholic uprising. So much was this the case that the Royalist commander in Munster, Lord Inchiquin, expelled all the Roman Catholics from Cork, seized the military supply dumps and declared for Parliament.

In 1646 the Confederate leadership refused to extend the truce, which further alarmed the Irish Protestants and those Roman Catholics loyal to the King. Ormonde, who was no longer strong enough to defend the Pale against possible Confederate attack, had nowhere to turn for help and reluctantly handed Dublin over to Parliament as the only authority capable of preserving the country from another massacre. Parliament put the Irish Colonel Michael Jones in charge. He was the son of an Irish bishop and had originally fought for the King in Ireland but later joined Parliament's forces in Wales in 1644. He took over from Ormonde seven regiments of foot and three of horse, and in 1648 Parliament sent a further six regiments of foot and three of horse to reinforce him. At this time it was the Confederates who were worried and they decided that only by throwing in their lot with the Royalists could they avoid being overrun by Puritans. Ormonde together with representatives of the Confederacy made their way to the court of the exiled Queen in France with an offer to raise an army to recover Ireland for the King. Inchiquin, who was worried by the direction that events were taking in England, again changed sides and rejoined Ormonde.

Ormonde returned to Ireland, reaching the headquarters of the Confederacy at Kilkenny one month after the battles round Preston and the fall of Colchester. His intention was to unite all those prepared to act together against Parliament. He speedily disbanded the Confederacy and formed a government made up of both Protestants and Roman Catholics, including some of the Confederate leaders. O'Neill remained neutral, as did a number of other local leaders in the far west of the country. On the other hand, Monro in the north became an ally. In January 1649 Prince Rupert's fleet arrived at Kinsale. Opposed to this array of Royalists, in February 1649, were Colonel Jones in Dublin and two other small Parliamentary forces: one in Londonderry commanded by Colonel Coote, and one in Ulster commanded by Colonel Monk. All were dependent on Parliament's small naval western squadron to keep open their links with England. Monk, who had returned to England in 1643 and been captured by Parliament, changed sides at the end of the war and was sent to Ireland.

IN JANUARY 1649 Parliament's first concern was to reorganise and enlarge the navy, so that it could support operations in Ireland, defend English shipping and expel Royalists from the Isles of Scilly and the Channel Islands. The Earl of Warwick was replaced as Lord High Admiral by an Admiralty Committee of the Council of State, which included both Cromwell and Ireton, although Ireton was not a member of the Council of State. Three army officers, Colonels Popham, Deane and Blake, were appointed as joint generals-at-sea to command the fleet. New ships were built and others bought. The Commonwealth navy grew rapidly and by the end of March ships were sailing west to deal with the immediate threat.

Parliament also decided to send an army into Ireland to destroy Ormonde's forces and gain control of the country. On 18 March 1649 it nominated Cromwell for the command. Cromwell was initially reluctant, but by the end of the month accepted and was appointed commander-in-chief and Lord Lieutenant in Ireland. At the same time Parliament appointed Fairfax captain-general of all the forces in England and Ireland, thus ensuring that Cromwell remained subordinate to him, although the extensive powers given to Cromwell in return for his acceptance of the command made this little more than a formality.

By early April considerable unrest was making itself felt in the army, partly because some of those selected for Ireland did not want to go, but mainly because of dissatisfaction felt by the Levellers at the political settlement reached after the death of the King. Firm action was taken against protesters both inside and outside the army. Later in the month a mutiny broke out in Whalley's regiment of horse, stationed in London. This was speedily suppressed by Fairfax and Cromwell, six men being condemned to death, one of whom was shot. Then in May Scrope's regiment of horse, selected for Ireland and stationed at Salisbury, mutinied. Most of the officers and some of the men fled to Fairfax while the remainder moved rapidly north to Wantage, being joined on the way by four troops of Ireton's regiment. The mutineers were soon reinforced by two troops of Harrisson's regiment, which brought the total up to 1,200. Fairfax swiftly got together three regiments of horse and some dragoons, and accompanied by Cromwell set off to quell the mutiny. By the night of 14 May the mutineers were resting near Burford when Fairfax, who had been covering 40 to 50 miles a day, caught up with them. He immediately sent in a small party commanded by Colonel Reynolds to attack them, achieving complete surprise: 400 prisoners and most of the horses were captured. By next morning the mutiny was over. A cornet and two corporals were executed and the rest of the mutineers were discharged from the army.

Despite a difference of opinion between Fairfax and Cromwell in the winter over the trial and execution of the King, they were now getting on well. After settling the mutiny they toured Hampshire and the Isle of Wight talking to regiments in an attempt to dissipate discontent and tighten discipline. Soon after their return to London they were entertained to a banquet in one of the Livery Halls during a day of thanksgiving for the restoration of order. England was settled and Cromwell could conclude his preparations for Ireland in peace.

MEANWHILE IN IRELAND Ormonde had opened his campaign, which was initially successful. In Ulster Enniskillen declared for the King and in May Ormonde's lieutenant general, the Earl of Castlehaven, captured Maryborough, 30 miles north of Kilkenny, which persuaded many of O'Neill's men to join Ormonde. Castlehaven, despite his Irish title, was a straightforward Englishman. Munro, who had been captured by Monk, escaped and resumed command of the Scots brigade in Ulster. Soon afterwards, in conjunction with Ormonde's forces in Connaught, he captured Sligo. As a result of these Royalist successes Monk abandoned Ulster and fortified himself in Dundalk and Drogheda at the northern edge of the Pale.

Although Parliament's position in Ireland had deteriorated greatly by June 1649, it had strengthened at sea. A new Irish squadron consisting of four powerful ships was guarding the approaches to Dublin, and a further squadron of ten ships under the generals-at-sea was blockading Rupert in Kinsale. Although Rupert had taken a number of prizes in the first six months of the year, money from which helped to maintain Charles II in France, he would not be able to help Ormonde in the face of Parliament's new-found naval strength.

By July Ormonde and Inchiquin were closing in on Dublin, but before getting there they heard that O'Neill had patched up a truce with Monk and was threatening their rear. Ormonde therefore despatched Inchiquin with 3,500 men to neutralise the threat. In this Inchiquin was successful, seizing Drogheda and Trim. He then moved his force in between Monk in Dundalk and O'Neill in Ulster. Monk, who had insufficient men to hold Dundalk, surrendered the town to Inchiquin and withdrew to England. But all of this took time and meanwhile Cromwell had despatched two regiments of foot and a quantity of cannon, powder and shot to Dublin, thereby greatly strengthening the defences.

CROMWELL'S PREPARATIONS for the forthcoming campaign left nothing to chance. First he was determined that his army should be backed by ample funds directly under his control. To this end he bullied Parliament unmercifully and also raised money from the city of London and from other benefactors. He even insisted on having a large private fund to be used for bribing Ormonde's officers to change their allegiance and for establishing a sound intelligence network. He started using the money in this way well before arriving in Ireland. Next, he gathered a large quantity of foodstuffs, such as wheat, oats, barley, peas, biscuits and cheese, which was sent to ports along the west coast for shipment to Ireland. This would ensure that his army could move fast without having to disperse in order to live off the land. Furthermore a well-paid and well-fed army would have less incentive to loot. He also collected together an impressive artillery train including some very heavy cannon and a large quantity of powder and shot. He had no intention of being left sitting outside fortified towns for weeks, as had happened at Pembroke Castle. Finally, the newly reorganised navy collected 130 ships of various sorts to transport his army to Ireland.

Cromwell left London on 10 July 1649 and made his way to Milford Haven. From the beginning of August he watched as the ships and men assembled, and while doing so heard the good news that Colonel Jones had won a considerable victory against Ormonde at Rathmines just outside Dublin on 2 August. This had come about after Ormonde moved his force in a wide sweep round the west of Dublin to a position about two miles south of the town in preparation for launching an attack. But Jones, realising the danger, silently marched his regiments out of the town east along the banks of the Liffey and then south-east along the shore of Dublin Bay before swinging inland into the flank of Ormonde's position in the early morning. His rapid and determined attack achieved complete surprise and Ormonde's unsuspecting army was thrown into confusion. Despite having no more than 6,000 men against Ormonde's much larger force, he put them to flight, inflicting heavy casualties on them. Furthermore he captured most of Ormonde's reserve of ammunition and a large amount of gold, valued at the time at £4,000.[2]

The effect of this victory, and the fact that Ormonde had again detached Inchiquin to Munster to guard the south coast against a possible landing by Cromwell, made it impossible for him to launch any further attack on Dublin itself. Cromwell was therefore able to disembark his army without interference on his arrival at the mouth of the Liffey on 15 August.

Including the two regiments sent to reinforce Jones earlier, Cromwell now had four regiments of horse and ten regiments of foot: six raised recently specifically for Ireland and four from the regular army. He also had a regiment of dragoons and his artillery train. In addition he took under command Jones's force which, when reorganised, produced three regiments of foot and two of horse. The strength of the army was about 12,500. Jones became his lieutenant general and second-in-command. Ireton, who was originally earmarked for this position, was made a major general.[3] (For details of the regiments in Cromwell's army at this time see Appendix A.)

Cromwell spent around two weeks in Dublin before setting off on his campaign. During this time he issued proclamations to the populace saying that his men would not loot and that anyone bringing in food for the army would be promptly paid. He also issued strict orders to his men to refrain from interfering with the local population. By these measures he reassured the local population and got a degree of support from them initially.

Although, even after Jones's victory at Rathmines, Ormonde's forces outnumbered Cromwell, they consisted of many different detachments commanded by men who were often antagonistic to each other and whose only bond was their dislike of the English Puritans. At the top end of the scale were a few regiments of English Royalists left over from the Civil War and the remains of the old Irish army that Ormonde used to command in Dublin, largely officered by Protestants. Some of the other detachments consisted of regularly organised regiments, but many of the rest were little better than guerrillas. The whole army was by this time spread over a large area from the Wicklow Hills south of Dublin, in a huge arc round the city, to the sea north of Drogheda. It was impossible to hold the force concentrated because it had to live off the land in the absence of proper logistic backing.

Cromwell, not wishing to become involved in the bogs and valleys of the Irish interior, decided first to capture Drogheda. This would open up the route into Ulster and remove an enemy strongpoint that would otherwise threaten his rear when he started on the next part of his campaign. He had already decided that after Drogheda he would move south along the coast to secure the main ports and towns between Dublin and Cork before ultimately moving inland.

Ormonde, anticipating an attack on Drogheda, replaced the governor with the formidable Sir Arthur Aston, a Roman Catholic who had fought for Gustavus Adolphus and who had been governor of Oxford for much of the Civil War. He then sent four undermanned regiments of English Royalists and two or three troops of horse to reinforce the garrison, together with two Irish regiments, bringing the total up to 3,100 men. He also ordered Inchiquin in Munster and his commanders in Ulster to close on him with whatever forces they could muster. But Aston was

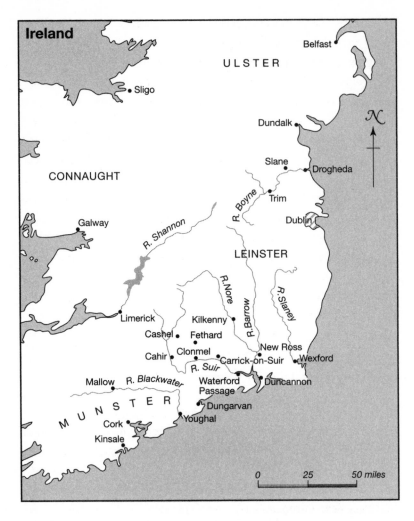

Ireland

ULSTER

Belfast

Sligo

CONNAUGHT

Dundalk

Slane

Drogheda

R. Boyne

Trim

R. Shannon

Dublin

Galway

LEINSTER

R. Nore

R. Barrow

R. Slaney

Limerick

Kilkenny

Cashel

Fethard

Clonmel

New Ross

Cahir

Carrick-on-Suir

Wexford

R. Suir

Mallow

R. Blackwater

Waterford
Passage

Duncannon

M U N S T E R

Dungarvan

Youghal

Cork

Kinsale

0   25   50 miles

short of powder and match and there was insufficient food, particularly
meat, to enable the town to withstand a long siege.

Despite these shortcomings, Drogheda was a hard nut to crack
because of its defences. This Norman-built town was in two parts separated by the river Boyne, which flowed from west to east through the
middle. Each part was surrounded by a stone wall twenty feet high and
up to six feet thick, and Aston added to the problem by digging fortifications at likely places both inside and outside the walls. The southern

defences were very strong, as the walls were set at the top of an embankment that was particularly steep on the eastern side. There was only one bridge across the Boyne linking the two parts of the town. There were three gates into the town to the south of the river and two more to the north. The next bridge across the river was at Slane some eight miles to the west, but the river could usually be forded at low tide about one mile away. At the end of August Ormonde with around 3,000 men was twenty miles away at Tecroghan a few miles north of Trim on the north side of the river.

Cromwell well knew that the key to a successful assault would be his heavy artillery. He had with him in Ireland 56 guns and he decided to take eleven siege cannon together with twelve pieces of field artillery to Drogheda. But as the siege guns needed a large number of draught animals to drag them, he arranged to send the whole lot by ship. This was admittedly a slight risk since Ormonde might attack him while he was on the move, but he correctly assessed that after Rathmines such a threat was unlikely to develop.

Cromwell assembled his troops outside Dublin on 31 August and headed north next day with eight regiments of foot, six of horse and some dragoons. He followed a route close to the coast in order to keep in touch with the ships carrying the artillery. Unfortunately bad weather delayed the ships, so that when he arrived outside Drogheda on 3 September he had to wait a further six days before the guns arrived. During this time Aston organised a number of sallies against Cromwell's outposts but had to desist when he found that his powder was running low. Ormonde did nothing to interfere with Cromwell's advance: his troops were too dispirited to risk even a skirmish, and a few of his horse even deserted to Parliament.

Aston's only hope was a drawn-out siege leading to casualties and disease amongst the attackers, who could be cut off from Dublin and harassed by Ormonde's superior numbers, but Cromwell had no intention of letting such a situation come about. By 10 September Cromwell had deployed his cannon in an arc from the east to the south of the town and on that day he summoned Aston to surrender. His message concluded with the words 'If this be refused you will have no cause to blame me.' Aston brusquely rejected the summons and Cromwell started to bombard the walls. His aim was to get into St Mary's churchyard at the south-east corner of the town. Once inside, his men would be covered by the town wall itself on two sides and by the wall of the churchyard on the other two sides. This would give him an opportunity to build up a force of foot and horse within this highly defensible enclave with which to break out into the town itself.

During the first night of the bombardment two small breaches appeared in the wall, one of which was near the gate leading to Duleek, roughly in the middle of the southern wall of the city, and the other in the corner by St Mary's church. Aston set about repairing the breaches as best he could and, realising the danger, sent men to build a three-line fortification to block anyone entering near the church. By the late afternoon of 11 September Cromwell considered that this breach was large enough and directed three regiments to assault it. The first assault was repulsed with the loss of its colonel. A second assault followed, which was also repulsed. Then Cromwell moved into the breach with some reserves, and soon his regiments had cleared the area round the church, capturing Aston's newly built defences at the same time. This was followed by a successful assault on the church itself, which provided a strongpoint capable of repelling the enemy's horse. Soon afterwards a regiment pushed through the other breach near the main gate.

There was now a period of consolidation while Cromwell's troops enlarged the two breaches and opened the gate to let in regiments of horse. As soon as this was done a general advance took place, which swept back the heavily outnumbered defenders. At the start of the attack Cromwell had given instructions that there should be no quarter, but there is evidence that some officers, intent on saving their men, offered to spare the lives of those that surrendered and then killed them once they were safely secured. The very fact that Cromwell only lost around 150 men, compared to the 2,800 members of the garrison killed, bears out this contention.[4]

Some of Cromwell's troops now moved to a fortified mound south of the Boyne called Mill Mount, where Aston had his headquarters. This was attacked and all the defenders killed, including Aston himself, who was said to have been clubbed to death with his own wooden leg and his body cut to pieces. Others moved rapidly to the bridge and prevented the defenders from raising it, which would have cut them off from the northern part of the town. They crossed over and moved through the streets, beating down what opposition remained. The last of the Royalists took refuge in two towers in the northern wall of the town and in the steeple of St Peter's church. Cromwell ordered the steeple to be set on fire, which caused these men to be burned. The others were all killed. Cromwell also ordered all Roman Catholic priests and friars to be killed, in addition to which a number of other civilians also died. A reliable estimate of casualties gives 2,800 of the garrison killed plus a further 700 civilians and clergy, although there is a considerable difference of opinion among historians as to whether there was any significant killing of civilians other than clergy.[5]

From a military point of view, Cromwell's handling of the campaign up to this point had been faultless. He had ensured that he had all that he needed to conduct the war and he had correctly assessed the need to capture Drogheda in order to open up a route into Ulster and to protect his rear before setting off to clear the south coast. His tactical handling of the storming of the town had also been first-rate, including his own participation in securing the breach after two failed attempts by his subordinates.

His determination to slaughter the garrison after Aston had refused his summons to surrender was just about consistent with the contemporary rules of war as practised on the Continent, although no such horror had been perpetrated during the Civil War in England. Despite the fact that Cromwell knew that most of the garrison consisted of Protestant English Royalists and many of the rest were respectable Irish Protestants or Catholics who had opposed the insurgents, he persisted in describing them all as 'barbarous wretches who have imbrued their hands in so much innocent blood'. He justified his conduct by saying that a slaughter at Drogheda would act as a deterrent to further resistance, thus saving life in the future. But this hardly excuses the 'knocking on the head of all their Friars', as Cromwell put it in a letter to the Speaker, nor does it excuse the loss of civilian life, which was contrary to the rules of war. The killing of prisoners that continued throughout the following day, well after the heat of the battle had subsided, was equally unattractive. If they were killed after being told that their lives would be spared, it was little better than murder. A particularly revolting example of this occurred three days after the battle when the Royalist Sir Edmund Verney, who was walking and talking with Cromwell himself, was taken aside by a person he thought an old friend and run through with a sword. The fact is that, for Puritans in general and for Cromwell in particular, war in Ireland was 'different'. His aim was to ensure that never again would the Irish be able to menace English settlers or England's interests.

CROMWELL NOW SENT Colonel Venables with two regiments of foot and two of horse to subdue Ulster and returned with the remainder of his army to Dublin for a few days of rest and refitting. On 23 September the army set out again. This time their target was Wexford, a port some 70 miles south of Dublin, long favoured by privateers preying on English shipping and the port through which Ormonde could most conveniently receive men or supplies provided by Royalists in France. Like Drogheda it was therefore a place of some strategic significance, and like Drogheda its defences were formidable. But there was one important difference in that the population had from the start been totally linked with the Roman Catholics of the Confederacy and, although now reluctantly allied to the Protestant Ormonde against the threat of Puritan England, had little liking for him or for his lieutenant general. This fact became significant when Ormonde appointed one of his officers, Lieutenant Colonel David Sinnott, to be the governor of Wexford a few days before Cromwell arrived outside the town.

Once more Cromwell moved his artillery together with extra supplies of food by sea, but this time he was not kept waiting by the navy, as Deane arrived off Wexford harbour three days ahead of him. Deane was however unable to disembark because of further storms. Wexford was situated on the south bank of the river Slaney, which meant that Cromwell would be more favourably placed to storm the town if he could get his army across the Slaney and attack from the south. The difficulty was that it would not be possible to land the guns and stores in this area until Rosslare Fort was captured, as it guarded the harbour from the south. Cromwell therefore sent his lieutenant general Jones with some dragoons to assess the situation. Fortunately, at his approach the fort was abandoned and its garrison retreated into Wexford itself, which enabled Cromwell to move his army and set up his cannon to the south of the town.

Cromwell had arrived outside Wexford with 8,000 men, which was scarcely enough to carry such a well-fortified town with a garrison of nearly 5,000 men. Nonetheless he immediately summoned Sinnott to surrender it. Many of the townspeople who knew what had happened at Drogheda were anxious that Sinnott should reach an agreement with Cromwell but he, hoping that Ormonde would be able to relieve Wexford, prevaricated. In fact Ormonde was approaching, but he was held off by a detachment under Jones.

At about this time news was received that two of Inchiquin's regiments had deserted to Parliament, handing over the port of Youghal on the south coast, 60 miles to the west. This indicated a weakening of Ormonde's position and Sinnott agreed to surrender, subject to receiving an assurance that Roman Catholics would be permitted to continue worshipping and that their priests would retain their customary privileges. This infuriated Cromwell who, worried by the incidence of sickness among his troops and concerned by the need to complete his task before the onset of the winter, was impatient of delay. On 11 October he started to bombard the defences.

Cromwell started by concentrating his fire on Wexford Castle, situated to the south of the town just outside the walls. But the ferocity of the bombardment so frightened the inhabitants of Wexford itself that some began to leave the town whilst others sent out their own representatives to Cromwell, independently of Sinnott, to broker a ceasefire. While this was going on, the castle surrendered and was immediately occupied by

Cromwell's men, who turned the heavy guns captured there onto the town. This caused panic among the defending garrison, who abandoned their positions and fled into the far side of the town. Without waiting for orders from Cromwell, who was still negotiating, several regiments launched an attack, and climbing over the walls unopposed, took possession of the town. A few of the defenders who made an attempt to defend themselves in the town centre were killed, and others trying to save themselves in boats drowned when their boats sank. Cromwell had given no orders for killing the garrison but his men carried on as they had done at Drogheda. Not only did they kill any soldiers that they could lay their hands on, but they also killed priests.

Although Cromwell did not order the killing, which he estimated resulted in the death of around 2,000 people, he did not blame his men, whom he saw as the instruments of God. Unlike Drogheda, both the garrison and the people of Wexford had been involved with the insurgents who had murdered Protestants in 1641, and Cromwell evidently felt that they deserved God's vengeance. It is also suggested that on entering the town the troops discovered that some Protestants there had been deliberately drowned and others starved to death, which inflamed tempers and lead to excessive violence.[6] From the point of view of the accepted rules of war this was a monstrous thing to have happened, but Wexford was taken with virtually no loss of life to Parliament and Cromwell could move on to the next stage of his campaign, having secured an excellent port containing much useful material such as iron, tallow and salt. He also captured 100 cannon and three well-armed warships.

CROMWELL'S NEXT OBJECTIVE was Waterford, 42 miles to the west and about six miles inland from the south coast on the banks of the river Suir. Four miles to the east of Waterford the Suir joins the river Burrow and the two rivers form a joint estuary running due south to the sea. The estuary was guarded from the open sea by two forts, one at Passage on the west bank held by Castlehaven and one at Duncannon on the east bank held by Colonel Wogan, formerly of the New Model Army.

Nine miles upstream from the junction on the east bank of the Burrow was the town of New Ross, situated where the road from Wexford crosses the Burrow on its way to Waterford, the second city of Ireland. Sir Lucas Taaffe, the governor of New Ross, and Ormonde with the remains of his army were encamped opposite the town on the west bank. The bridge had been destroyed to prevent it falling into Cromwell's hands.

Cromwell's army was by now reduced, by sickness and the need to garrison the various towns that he had occupied since leaving Dublin, to 5,600 men. Ormonde was however in an even worse position; and it is no exaggeration to say that large parts of his army were melting away. Also, as he got weaker, the unnatural coalition between the strongly Roman Catholic forces that had formerly belonged to the Confederacy and the towns that had supported them became less and less willing to co-operate with Ormonde and Inchiquin's Protestant-led forces.

As Cromwell left Wexford on 16 October, Inchiquin's governor of Cork handed the town over to representatives of Parliament. Soon afterwards the same thing happened at Kinsale after Prince Rupert sailed with his fleet to Portugal. Over the next few weeks Bandon and Timoleague also defected to Parliament. These developments were largely due to the machinations of Lord Broghil, a brother of the Earl of Cork, whom Cromwell had suborned from his allegiance to the King before leaving England. Cromwell made this man his master of the ordnance, and in this capacity he joined Cromwell at Wexford after the fall of the town. Accompanied by Colonel Phayre with half his regiment of foot, he moved by sea to Youghal. On arrival he raised a force of 1,500 foot and a troop of horse from his own estates and set off for Cork, where he met up with one of Inchiquin's colonels called Townsend. Together with two more of Inchiquin's colonels and Parliamentary sympathisers in the town, they expelled the governor, taking control in the name of Parliament. The other towns followed suit soon afterwards. Not only did these places fall into Cromwell's hands but an appreciable number of Inchiquin's men joined Cromwell's army at a time when he was in dire need of reinforcement.[7]

On 17 October Cromwell arrived outside New Ross, having

dispatched Jones to Duncannon with a view to capturing the fort there in order to open up the estuary.

Cromwell summoned Taaffe to surrender the town but received no reply for two days, during which he set up batteries of field artillery and started to bombard the walls. On 19 October Taaffe asked for terms and Cromwell, who had no desire to risk the losses of storming the town, permitted him to march out with his 1,000 men and the full honours of war. He was allowed to take all his arms and ammunition except for the cannon that had been in the town before the siege. Cromwell also guaranteed the safety of the civilian inhabitants, though refusing to permit celebration of the mass. This time, no one was massacred, either on purpose or by the unexpected intervention of the Almighty.

Cromwell stayed at New Ross for a month, during which time he rebuilt the bridge. More of his men became ill, as he did himself. Elsewhere in Ireland, matters proceeded well for Parliament, and by the middle of November the whole of Ulster was controlled by Venables and Coote. By this time Owen Roe O'Neill had died. Some of his men moved south to join Ormonde, who had withdrawn towards Kilkenny after the fall of New Ross, followed at a discreet distance by Ireton.

Jones's attempt to capture Duncannon was abandoned when Wogan ferried over some horse from Passage, thereby leading Jones to believe that he was stronger than he was.

On 17 November Cromwell, having received reinforcements that brought his army up to 7,000 men, moved west and three days later captured Carrick on Suir with its bridge over the river some twelve miles upstream of Waterford. This enabled him not only to cross to the south bank of the river but also to cut Waterford off from the west. Waterford had already refused to accept reinforcements offered by Castlehaven but soon afterwards accepted 1,300 of O'Neill's good Catholics, who passed into the town from the north. Once across the Suir Cromwell sent Jones to capture Passage, which he succeeded in doing by the end of the month.

On 2 December Cromwell decided to give up the idea of capturing Waterford. Despite the capture of Passage he could not get ships with his heavy artillery up the estuary past the fort at Duncannon, nor could he be supplied by sea. Furthermore he already had control of the south coast ports of Youghal, Cork and Kinsale, through which he could be supplied if he went further west. Incessant rain, malaria and 'the bloody flux', i.e. dysentery, was wearing down the army. He therefore moved via Dungarvan into winter quarters round Youghal. At this time his splendid lieutenant general, Michael Jones, died of the prevailing sickness. Cromwell spent the next few weeks visiting the recently acquired towns of Cork, Kinsale and Bandon.

BY THE END OF JANUARY 1650 Cromwell's army was rested and ready to take advantage of mild weather to move into the interior of Munster. His intention was to mop up a number of small garrisons before attempting to capture the three remaining major centres of opposition: Kilkenny on a tributary of the Barrow called the river Nore, and Clonmel and Waterford on the river Suir. When all of this was concluded it would be time to tackle Limerick, which controlled access to the Shannon basin. Ormonde had already shown his reluctance to challenge Cromwell in the open field and it would therefore be necessary for Cromwell to weaken his army bit by bit as he captured his bases and sources of supply. What Cromwell may not have realised was that as fast as he destroyed one Irish army, another would spring up. None of them would be particularly formidable, but it would take years rather than months for the country to settle down. In Ireland, it always does.

Cromwell's immediate plan was for Colonel Reynolds, with three regiments of horse and one of foot, to advance towards Kilkenny, crossing the Suir at Carrick to the east of Clonmel. Ireton would follow him with some reserve regiments and the artillery. Cromwell, with three regiments of horse and a weak regiment of foot, would swing west, crossing the river Blackwater at Mellow and the Suir three miles south of Cahir and thence towards Kilkenny. Broghil would remain behind to ensure that Inchiquin's men from Limerick could not interfere with the south coast ports, which were supplying the Parliamentary army.

Cromwell set off on 29 January and by 2 February was across the Suir. That day he summoned the garrison of Fethard, which surrendered on favourable terms. The nearby town of Cashel also surrendered. Thereafter Cromwell joined forces with Reynolds near Kilkenny. Reynolds was then left with a small force to mask Kilkenny while Cromwell moved around the area capturing a number of garrisons, culminating in the surrender of Cahir on 24 February.

Cromwell now sent word to Colonel Hewson, who had been left in command of Dublin, to march across country and join him outside Kilkenny with as many men as could be spared. Cromwell himself started to reduce the strong-points surrounding Kilkenny. At about this time his son Henry arrived from England at Youghal with further reinforcements. By 23 March Cromwell was ready to summon Kilkenny. But despite the fact that plague was ravaging the town, Butler, who was in command there, initially refused to surrender.

On 25 March Cromwell's artillery started to bombard the walls and Cromwell sent Colonel Ewer with 1,000 men across the river to attack Irishtown. This was in fact a diversion to cover an attack on Kilkenny itself, but despite the diversion the attack was beaten off. A second attack mounted later in the day was also beaten off. Cromwell then tried to mount a third attack, but the soldiers were having none of it and it failed to materialise. However by this time Butler asked for terms and was allowed to march out with his men. Cromwell now had control of Ormonde's capital, and he returned to Carrick to rest his men. It is estimated that up to this point in the campaign he had lost no more than 500 men in battle, although losses from disease were more extensive. Ormonde's losses must have been at least ten times as great.

From January 1650 Cromwell had been receiving unofficial suggestions that he should return to England and these were now reinforced by an official order that he should do so. Cromwell was however determined to take Clonmel before handing over his comand. The officer in command of the garrison was Hugh O'Neill, nephew of the recently dead Owen Roe O'Neill. He was a skilled and experienced soldier who had with him 1,500 foot and 100 horse from his late uncle's Ulster army, together with a few hundred men from Munster.

On 27 April Cromwell summoned O'Neill to surrender the town, which he naturally refused to do. Soon afterwards Cromwell was joined outside the walls by Broghil, whose force together with other reinforcements and deserters from Ormonde's army brought his strength up to nearly 14,000 men. Nonetheless as he erected his artillery batteries to the north-west of the town and gradually cut the garrison off from the outside world he was plagued by many sallies mounted by O'Neill which disrupted his arrangements and caused casualties to his men.

Inside the town O'Neill was busy reinforcing the massive walls with mounds of earth to deaden the effect of bombardment. He also built a second line of defences some way back. As a result of these measures it was not until 17 May that Cromwell succeeded in making a breach through which to assault the town. As his men poured through the breach O'Neill withdrew down a narrow lane to the next line of defence without offering any resistance. Eventually, when around 1,500 of Cromwell's men were through the breach, O'Neill launched a massive counter-attack. Few of the Parliamentary force inside the walls survived and O'Neill closed up the breach. Cromwell tried to organise a further attack but his foot regiments refused to carry out the assault. Cromwell accordingly dismounted two regiments of horse who succeeded in re-opening the breach, but a second full-scale assault failed. By now it was getting dark and Cromwell withdrew his whole force back to their original positions outside the town. He had lost between 1,500 and 2,000. In terms of losses it was the worst setback of his whole career.

During the night Cromwell received a delegation from the Mayor of Clonmel offering to surrender the town, providing that Cromwell guaranteed the lives of the occupants. This Cromwell agreed to do. What he did not realise was that O'Neill and his entire army had already escaped across the Suir to the south. He therefore got Clonmel, but O'Neill lived to reinforce Waterford and subsequently to carry out a long and skilful defence of Limerick.

CROMWELL'S TIME IN IRELAND came to an end on 29 May when he set off in a warship named *President Bradshaw* after the President of the Council of State. Ireton succeeded him as Lord Deputy and

Commander-in-Chief Ireland with Ludlow as his lieutenant general. By this time plague was sweeping through the country. The only sizeable force opposed to Parliament was the remains of Owen Roe O'Neill's army in Ulster, commanded by the Bishop of Clogher, and that did not last long, being soon destroyed by Coote and Venables. The bishop was captured and hanged and both his lieutenant general and major general were killed. In August 1650 Ireton took Waterford and went on to besiege Limerick, which he was unable to capture. At the end of the year Ormonde and Inchiquin left the country for the Continent. During 1651 new Irish armies formed, which caused Ireton to raise the siege of Limerick, but he returned there in the summer of 1651 and captured it at the end of October. But by this time he was worn out by the campaign, and he died the following month, his place being taken by Ludlow. The war continued sporadically until April 1653, when organised resistance finally ended. It was followed by what has come to be known as the Cromwellian Settlement.

The basic idea behind the settlement was, first, to reinstate settlers who had been dispossessed at the time of the massacres, and second, to hand over the 2¼ million acres of land in Ireland that Parliament had declared forfeit in 1642, to various speculators who had bought it. Before the campaign, soldiers whose pay was in arrears had been told by Cromwell that they too would be recompensed with Irish land. This was now becoming urgent, as there were around 30,000 soldiers in Ireland and the government was anxious to be relieved of the cost of maintaining them, especially as taxes raised in Ireland would only meet about one-fifth of the cost incurred. A third requirement of the settlement was to satisfy the people of England, and those in Ireland who had remained loyal to Parliament, that the rebels were being punished. Finally, all wanted to be sure that there would be no further trouble from the native Irish, and the Puritans in particular wanted to suppress Roman Catholicism.

The measures taken to achieve these various aims involved massive evictions and resettlement of the Irish. By 1656 two-thirds of all the land in Ireland was in the hands of new owners. Even those amongst the native Irish who were allowed under the settlement to keep a proportion of their land were often evicted and compensated in Connaught, where the quality of the land was lower. Over one-third of the total population of one and a half million who had been living in Ireland in 1641 had lost their lives from famine or disease or violence.

That the Cromwellian Settlement was draconian can not be denied, and since it was implemented by Cromwell's officers at a time when Cromwell was head of state in England, it is fairly named. But the campaign he personally fought between July 1649 and May 1650, with the exception of the killing at Drogheda and Wexford, was not particularly bloody. Indeed on nearly every occasion that he took a town the garrison were allowed to depart and the lives of the inhabitants were safeguarded. It is perhaps ironic that in the bloodbath at Drogheda, which is the event most frequently held against Cromwell by the Irish, most of the dead were either English Royalists or Irish Protestants fighting for the Royalists. At Wexford, as already mentioned, the killing was done contrary to Cromwell's intentions.

From a purely military point of view, Cromwell's campaign was very effective. During the nine months that he was in Ireland he succeeded in destroying the Royalist threat to England and he gained control of almost all of the country, although it took a further two years to mop up isolated pockets of Irish resistance. During the course of his campaign he fought no battles, because Ormonde and his general realised that they would undoubtedly lose a set-piece engagement. He successfully stormed a number of fortified towns, and obtained the surrender of others by demonstrating that further resistance would be useless. He was unsuccessful at Waterford, but by virtue of gaining control of the remaining Munster ports he was able to by-pass the place. His only major setback was at Clonmel, where he lost a large number of men, but even here he gained control of the town. The secret of his success was clearly the thoroughness of his preparation, particularly his logistic and financial arrangements, which enabled him to maintain his army in the field despite adverse weather conditions, famine and the twin scourges of dysentery and malaria.

Two particularly interesting aspects of the campaign, deserve attention. First, the use Cromwell made of sea power to move his artillery and to supply his army. The naval part of the campaign, which involved assembling enough shipping to blockade Prince Rupert in Kinsale and to defend his lines of communication, and at the same time to provide enough ships to move his artillery and stores, was impressive. The other interesting aspect was the trouble he took to subvert Royalist commanders into giving up important towns without a fight. He also frequently managed to suborn Protestant Irish soldiers from their allegiance to Ormonde or Inchiquin. Without this, he would have run out of men by the end of 1649. There was a down side, in that the men he so acquired were not of the same quality as the men of the New Model Army, nor even of the new regiments raised in England before the campaign. This fact became apparent on one or two occasion when even he in person could not get his men to attack after an initial setback. But when this happened he merely tried something else or accepted the situation, which is more easily managed during a siege than in the course of a battle in the open.

That Cromwell was able to identify the measures that he needed to take in order to ensure success is a tribute to his military skill. That he was able to take them arose at least in part from the strength of his political position after the execution of the King, since it was this that ensured that he got the necessary degree of priority when it came to allocating money and resources to his expedition. Certainly when he arrived back in England, he was treated as a conquering hero, receiving the thanks of the army, the city of London and of Parliament. He was also awarded an extra £2,500 per year for life and the rents of all properties formerly belonging to the King in Whitehall.

8 · Scotland

King Charles II, having realised that he was not going to resurrect his fortunes in Ireland, reached an agreement with the Scots in which he undertook to take the Covenant himself and impose the Presbyterian religion on England and Ireland should they succeed in restoring him to the English throne. He arrived in Scotland at the mouth of the Spey on 24 June and was taken to Dunfermline, where he was subjected to a hideous regime of religious indoctrination, complete with lengthy sermons several times a day. He was to all intents and purposes held prisoner by Argyll and the Kirk, who soon got rid of those of his friends who had accompanied him from the Continent; they even isolated him from Scottish Royalists.

The goodwill that Cromwell had forged between Argyll and the English Independents in the autumn of 1648 had not survived the execution of Charles I. On 20 June, a majority of the English Council of State decided that rather than wait for the Scots to invade England, the army should attack them at once. The advantage of this course of action was that the devastation of the countryside caused by the warring armies would be sustained by the Scots rather than the English. Parliament hoped that Fairfax as Lord General would command the operation with Cromwell as his second-in-command.

But Fairfax, though a member of the Council of State, was known to be reluctant to attack the Scots Covenanters with whom he had been allied during the Civil War, unless they first invaded England. The Council of State therefore sent a deputation consisting of Cromwell, Lambert, Harrisson and St John together with the veteran MP Bulstrode Whitelock, who like Fairfax had disassociated himself from the King's execution, to discover Fairfax's intentions. Fairfax, who had raised the New Model Army in April 1646 and commanded it ever since, was hugely respected, not only by the members of the delegation, but also throughout the country as a whole. For him to refuse to command the invasion of Scotland might seriously weaken the newly formed Commonwealth government. Although Cromwell must have known that he would become Lord General if Fairfax gave up, there is not the slightest doubt that he tried with all his might to persuade him to retain his command, as also naturally did Lambert, who had throughout been so closely attached to Fairfax. Harrisson too, although more closely attuned to Cromwell, did his best, but after two days, on 26 June, Fairfax resigned, giving ill health as his reason. The Act of Parliament appointing him Lord General was repealed and Cromwell was appointed commander-in-chief of all Parliament's forces in his place. On the same day Parliament declared war on Scotland.[1]

HAVING BECOME LORD GENERAL, Cromwell wasted no time. Fleetwood became lieutenant general of horse with Whalley as his commissary general. Lambert was made major general of foot with the additional responsibility for drawing up the order of battle. Major General Harrisson, with four regiments of horse and four of foot, was left in command in England as a whole, with Skippon to look after the capital. An expansion of the New Model Army to the tune of six more regiments of horse and ten more regiments of foot was authorised, which would have brought it up in time to a total of eighteen regiments of horse and 30 of foot.

On 28 June Cromwell left London with four regiments of horse and two of foot. Travelling via Leicester and York, he reached Newcastle within two weeks, picking up extra regiments on the way. Newcastle would be his base for operations until he could open up a new one in Scotland. By the time that he was ready to cross the border his army, now in excess of 16,000 men, consisted of eight regiments of horse and eight of foot most, of whom had operational experience and were well trained. Many of his old associates, such as Pride, Robert Lilburne, Okey, Berry, and Whalley's son-in-law Goffe, were now amongst his colonels. The long association of Cromwell with these key people was a great source of strength to the army. These zealots were in effect a 'band of brothers', not unlike Nelson's captains from a professional point of view, though very different in their characters and in their outlook on life.

In addition Cromwell brought with him an outsider in the form of Colonel George Monk, who would play an increasingly important part in his affairs over the coming years. Monk's experience, which included operations against Spain and France in the 1620s and the seven years that he spent in the United Provinces in the 1630s, would be useful. At Newcastle Cromwell formed a new regiment of foot for Monk, made up of five companies from the garrison of Newcastle and five from the garrison of Berwick. He also made Monk his acting lieutenant general of the ordnance in command of the artillery, which consisted of 50 large cannon in addition to the usual field pieces. In accordance with the system he had used so successfully in Ireland, most of the artillery would be moved by sea.

As in Ireland, Cromwell took great pains to ensure that his logistic and financial arrangements were in order. Realising that his line of supply from Newcastle might be cut, he arranged for all of his food supplies to be delivered by sea from England or from the United Provinces. In case the Scots proved capable of denying grazing lands to his horse, he arranged for 2,800 tons of oats and 10,700 tons of hay to be delivered by sea from the south of England or from Germany. For these purposes Cromwell assembled a fleet of 140 ships, which involved withdrawing warships from the blockade of Portugal: the blockade was so weakened that Prince Rupert was able to pass into the Mediterranean with the

Royalist fleet. A sum of £1,210,000 was also made available for the support of the campaign.[2]

Although the Council of State had visualised Cromwell invading Scotland with around 25,000 men, this would have involved too great a weakening of the army remaining in England, which might well have been needed to quell unrest or a further Royalist uprising. In order to further guard against these contingencies, an ordinance of 12 July was passed by Parliament authorising the raising of a militia for home defence. It was also agreed that Cromwell would receive reinforcements of a further 8,500 men as they could be made available. In the event it was as well that Cromwell did not have a larger army with him in the early stages of his campaign, because, despite his care of his logistic arrangements, they proved scarcely adequate. Nonetheless the Scottish army greatly outnumbered his own.

While finalising his arrangements for the campaign Cromwell did not overlook the business of softening up the enemy. As he had done in Dublin at the start of his Irish campaign, he issued a declaration to the people of Scotland designed to reassure them that they had nothing to fear from his army. A second declaration, addressed to the godly, was designed to persuade them that he was at one with them on most matters and only wished to rescue them from their error of consorting with such an ungodly person as King Charles II. He also tried to make light of the differences between godly Presbyterians and godly Independents. In addition, he wrote privately and secretly to a number of important people in an attempt to subvert their loyalty to the King in the hope of finding one or two like Lord Broghil in Ireland who might be of assistance to him. Having completed his preparations, Cromwell crossed the border at Berwick on 22 July and advanced into Scotland.

AT THIS JUNCTURE it is worth examining the geographical factors relevant to the way in which the campaign developed. A span of 30 miles should be kept in mind. The small fishing port of Dunbar is just under 30 miles (about 25 miles) north-west of Berwick. Edinburgh is 30 miles west of Dunbar. Roughly speaking, Stirling is 30 miles west-

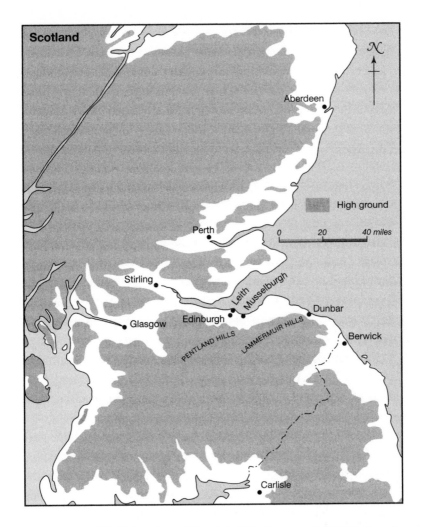

north-west of Edinburgh and Perth is 30 miles north of Edinburgh. Thirty miles is the distance that an army could cover in two days if unopposed, although this would be pressing it a bit: perhaps two and a half days would be more realistic.

In terms of ground, there is a narrow coastal strip between the mountains and the sea running all the way from Berwick to Dunbar and then on to Edinburgh. Between Edinburgh and Stirling and between Stirling and Perth and thence north-east to Aberdeen, there are wider strips of agricultural land between the various ranges of mountains. Within the mountains themselves as in the Pentland Hills to the south of Edinburgh and the Lammermuir Hills to the south of Dunbar, the land is inhospitable and provides poor grazing for horses. Roads and tracks are few and ill defined.

Cromwell's ultimate aim was to ensure that Scotland could never again threaten the security of the Commonwealth government in England. To that end he would need to defeat the King's forces and install a friendly Scottish government backed by an English garrison. As it was already well on in the campaigning season, he must have realised that he might be unable to complete such an ambitious programme in 1650. Should he be unable to do so, he would at least need to capture a major port and hold an area large enough to support his army until he could resume operations in 1651. The fact that he had established his first base in Newcastle and was entering Scotland at Berwick made it obvious to the Scots that his immediate objective was Edinburgh and its port of Leith.

The commander of the Scottish army was the seasoned professional David Leslie, who had fought so effectively beside Cromwell at Marston Moor. He was a far more formidable opponent than either the late Duke of Hamilton or the Marquess of Ormonde and he had a sizeable and ever-growing army at his disposal. But he had some massive difficulties with which to contend. In the first place, his army had been hastily raised in a series of forced levies, so that many of his men were operationally inexperienced and untrained. Worse still was the fact that the General Assembly of the Kirk insisted on purging the army of most of its non-Presbyterians and former Cavaliers, which quickly disposed of a good proportion of those with previous military experience. Even the King was soon sent away from the army in case his somewhat relaxed attitude to religion should rub off on the rank and file. The Scottish Kirk made the English Independents appear broad-minded. Leslie was also handicapped by logistic shortcomings, which restricted his ability to manoeuvre.

Leslie's plan of campaign took account of the strengths and weaknesses of his situation. First he did his best to remove all food supplies from the land through which Cromwell's army would be moving. Able-bodied men not already called up withdrew into the hills with their flocks, so that Cromwell's advancing army found only women, old men and children. Next Leslie drew up his men to cover Edinburgh and Leith, behind rapidly constructed fortifications which ran from the Pentland Hills in the south to the Firth of Forth in the north. He had no desire to engage Cromwell's highly trained regiments in battle, despite his numerical superiority. His immediate objective was to prevent Cromwell reaching Edinburgh and Leith until the onset of the autumnal rains and gales forced him to withdraw into England. Providing he could avoid a battle, there seemed to be a good chance of him doing so.

BY 28 JULY CROMWELL had occupied Dunbar, where there was a small all-weather port. Immediately ships started to arrive and unload supplies, although more slowly than planned. Soon afterwards Scottish irregulars cut Cromwell's lines of communication with Berwick, so that shortages started to make themselves felt in the army. By this time Lambert and Whalley with the advance guard had reached Musselburgh and made contact with an enemy detachment, which was quickly overrun. On 29 July the main body of the army arrived and deployed facing Leslie's fortifications. They were now within five miles of Leith, which was bombarded from the sea by four of Cromwell's warships.

At this point the heavens opened. Throughout the night the men faced the enemy, who wisely refused to come out into the open. Next morning, soaked and hungry, Cromwell moved them back towards the shelter of Musselburgh where stores could be landed from the ships over the beach. In the course of the withdrawal Lambert was wounded and captured for a short while, until rescued by Whalley. During the following night Leslie sent a strong body of horse to beat up the army where they were sheltering from the storm. In this they were initially successful, although eventually driven off with the loss of two senior officers and around 45 men killed, with a further 80 taken prisoner. But the English had also suffered casualties and on 6 August Cromwell withdrew the whole force to Dunbar.

Cromwell's first attempt to bounce Leslie into fighting a battle had failed. He now set about building up his supplies and preparing his men for a more carefully planned advance. This preparation included a heavy dose of sermons and prayer, which doubtless refuelled their fighting spirits. But Cromwell was not content with refreshing his own men spiritually. He also wrote to Leslie and the General Assembly of the Kirk, accusing them of intolerance and referring to their association with the King as a covenant with death and hell.

These courtesies completed and with stores fully replenished, the army set out again for Musselburgh, where they arrived on 12 August. By this time Cromwell had discovered that Leslie's large army was running short of food and forage despite the fact that it could draw on the fertile country between Edinburgh, Glasgow and Stirling. Cromwell therefore decided that if he could move his army in an arc round the south of Edinburgh so as to cut Leslie off from these sources of supply, Leslie would be bound to come out from behind his fortifications and give battle.

On 13 August Cromwell set off to occupy a position near the village of Colinton on the northern edge of the Pentland Hills from where he would threaten the roads to Queensferry and Stirling. By 17 August most of Cromwell's force was drawn up facing Leslie. But Leslie, working on interior lines, swiftly occupied an unassailable position between two lakes at Corstorphine just to the south of the road to Queensferry. Despite pressure from his hungry army to attack, backed by urging from representatives of the Kirk, he doggedly refused to do so.

Cromwell now moved further west in an attempt to cut off Leslie's links with Stirling, but Leslie again moved to block him, taking up a strong position behind boggy ground, a deep ditch and in an area of small fields divided by strong banks near Gogar Park. The English deployed for battle but after an exchange of fire by the artillery Cromwell realised that an attack was out of the question. Meanwhile the rain continued, supplies failed and the English were ravaged by sickness. Soon Cromwell decided to withdraw once more to Musselburgh, which he reached, having been harried unmercifully by the Scots, who made a determined attempt to cut his line of retreat. That the English escaped at all was partly due to the storm, which hampered the efforts of the Scots, and partly due to Monk's field artillery skilfully placed on the high ground covering the retreat.

In a letter to the Council of State written on 30 August Cromwell credited God with saving the army, no mention being made of the artillery.[3] On the same day the council of war decided to withdraw once more to Dunbar, fortify the town, build up stores of food and ammunition and provide accommodation for the sick. It was felt that such activities might well provoke Leslie into attacking them. Acting on this decision the army withdrew, arriving at Dunbar on 1 September.

By this time as a result of sickness, desertion and battle casualties the army had been reduced to 3,500 horse and 7,000 foot camped in and around Dunbar in the mud and rain. Many of the officers and men felt that the important question was not whether Leslie could be persuaded to attack, but whether the army could be got back to England in any semblance of order. But although Cromwell himself was uncertain as to the way things were likely to develop and although he realised that the navy would be unable to support the army through such a small port as Dunbar indefinitely, he was not yet considering abandoning the campaign. In a letter to Hazlerigg at Newcastle written on 2 September asking for reinforcements to be prepared he described himself as being comfortable in spirit and having much hope in the Lord. Furthermore his senior officers were fully behind him and the discipline of the army was unimpaired.

By this time Leslie, who had been shadowing Cromwell in the Lammermuir Hills as the English army retreated along the coast from Musselburgh, had occupied a position about one and a half miles south of Dunbar and 500 feet above it on Doon Hill. His 6,000 horse and 16,000 foot were spread out in a line from north-east to south-west in the conventional manner with the foot in the centre and the horse on the flanks. A strong detachment was also sent to block the road to Berwick at a defile near the village of Cockburnspath, about eight miles from Dunbar, in case Cromwell tried to get his foot out by sea and send his horse out by land. But although the Scots heavily outnumbered the English they were considerably more uncomfortable, since the rain and the howling wind on top of Doon Hill were even worse than they were around Dunbar.

An important feature of the terrain was a stream, much swollen by the recent rains, known as Brock's Burn, which ran through a steep and narrow wooded valley some 40 feet deep, along the front of the Scottish position. This obstacle protected the Scottish position, but it made it impossible for the Scots to attack the English unless they were prepared to come down from the hill.

In the event it was the Scots who broke the impasse. Representatives of the Kirk, quoting inspiring but irrelevant passages from the Old Testament, urged Leslie to attack. Soldiers battered by the wind and the rain made known their desire to leave Doon Hill. Leslie, unsettled by these pressures, gave orders for the army to move down to the coastal strip in preparation for an attack. Believing that Cromwell had started to evacuate some of his troops by sea, he felt that at last the Scots were strong enough to take him on in open fight. By the evening of 2 September the Scottish army had deployed with most of the horse on the right of the line astride the road to Berwick, while the foot were drawn up on the lower grassy slopes of Doon Hill. The remainder of the horse was on the left. Although Brock's Burn still ran between the contestants, the gorge through which it flowed, at these lower levels, was no longer steep enough or narrow enough to make it an effective barrier except on the left of Leslie's line. This fact explains why Leslie had moved so much of his horse to his right, they being necessary to watch the many places where the English could cross the burn in this area. Meanwhile the English had drawn up on the other side of the burn facing the Scots, expecting to be attacked next day.

Throughout 2 September while both sides were moving into position Lambert was intently watching the Scottish deployment. Soon after 4 pm he rode out with Cromwell to take a final look at Leslie's layout; and they both simultaneously thought that they detected two fatal weaknesses in the Scottish position. The first was that the bulk of the Scottish horse on the right had spread too far towards the sea, as a result of which there were gaps between their squadrons that made them vulnerable to attack. The second was that the left of Leslie's line was so cramped up against Brock's Burn and its gorge that they would be unable to come to the assistance of his right wing. This situation had come about because Leslie had deployed his army ready to attack and was not thinking about defence, being convinced that Cromwell was in no state to take offensive action.

Cromwell now decided to send for Monk, who was not only an officer of long experience, but also an acknowledged authority on tactics. On his arrival Monk confirmed the weaknesses detected by Lambert and Cromwell and urged them to attack before the Scots could do so. Soon afterwards Cromwell held a mounted council of war in sight of the Scottish position, which later moved into a building. Despite what they had seen, some of the colonels were in favour of evacuating as much of the foot as possible by sea and leaving the horse to cut its way out to Berwick. At this point Lambert stood up and tried to persuade the council that an attack would be safer and stood a chance of being completely successful. Cromwell backed him and an assault was agreed.

Cromwell's plan in outline was that Fleetwood and Lambert on the left should attack the Scottish right wing with six regiments of horse while Monk with four regiments of foot, less a few companies, would cross the burn and attack the Scottish centre. Okey with his regiment of dragoons and Overton's regiment of foot would mount a feint on the Scottish left to prevent them from trying to relieve their centre or right. Cromwell himself with one regiment of horse and a brigade of three regiments of foot commanded by Pride would be in reserve. All would depend on the ability of the English to re-deploy from their present positions under cover of darkness without the Scots realising that they were about to be assaulted. The attack itself, which relied on surprise, was to be launched before dawn.

Fortune favoured the bold. Throughout the early part of the night when the army had to re-deploy there was wind and rain, which masked the movement of the men from the Scots. Later the sky cleared and the

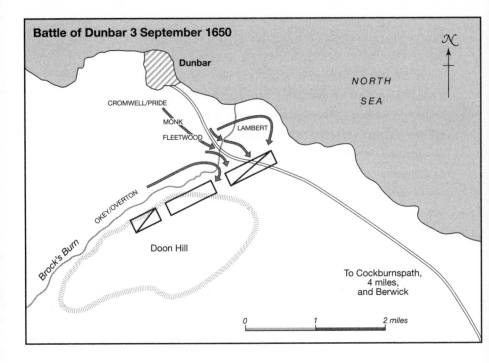

Battle of Dunbar 3 September 1650

Dunbar

CROMWELL/PRIDE

MONK

FLEETWOOD

LAMBERT

OKEY/OVERTON

Brock's Burn

Doon Hill

NORTH SEA

To Cockburnspath, 4 miles, and Berwick

0   1   2 miles

N

moon shone out, so that that most difficult of operations, the night attack, was made easier to control. During the night Cromwell, who put these favourable arrangements down to the personal intervention of the Almighty, moved around on a small horse as used by the dragoons. The tension of the occasion caused him to bite his lip so vigorously that it bled, although apparently unnoticed by him.

Meanwhile the Scots, although they remained drawn up for battle, had no idea that an attack was imminent and slept on the ground in their ranks. In some cases their officers withdrew into what cover they could find, such as sheds or barns at some distance from their men, and the major general of foot even gave permission for the musketeers to extinguish their matches.

It is always difficult to know in any detail how a battle developed, especially one fought largely in the dark. At the time all that matters is the result, which forms the basis for future action. Over the ensuing months and years eyewitness accounts are collected together and reconciled, so that ultimately a general consensus is reached, although it is inevitably vulnerable to reanalysis. This is particularly so with regard to the battle of Dunbar because the outcome was so extraordinary.

During the re-deployment Lambert took three regiments of horse in a wide sweep almost to the sea, where they crossed Brock's Burn and advanced up to the ford on the Dunbar to Berwick road. A strong body of Scots guarded this ford and it was here that the first serious fighting took place at around 5 am. As Lambert charged the Scots, the rest of the horse and Monk's brigade of foot crossed the burn in the general area of the ford. This meant that a large number of English regiments were concentrated against the Scottish right wing, which soon began to crumble. The English thus had their backs to the sea and were facing up towards Doon Hill; their horse on the left of their foot, which was spread out with its right flank along the burn.

Despite being taken in the flank and caught largely by surprise, the Scots fought fiercely, and at times elements of both the English foot and horse were forced to give way. Cromwell, watching intently, pushed his reserve across the burn at just the right moment, probably into gaps that were appearing in the Scottish line as it moved to meet the English attacking its right flank. At 6 am the rising sun came up over the horizon and Cromwell saw that the battle was going well. 'Now let God arise and let his enemies be scattered' he roared: he might well have added the rest of the first verse of Psalm 68 but he is not recorded as having done so. As the Scottish right collapsed, their horse started to stream back across Doon Hill, which freed much of the English horse to turn in on the Scottish foot. Some of the remaining English horse pursued the Scots to ensure that they did not return to the fray. Others came behind those Scottish regiments that had originally formed the left of the Scottish line up against Brock's Burn and who were being occupied by Okey's and Overton's detachment. Here also the Scots horse gave way, being driven into the rear of those facing the main English assault, thus adding to the confusion.

By 7 am the battle was over. According to one not entirely reliable story Cromwell was now euphoric, laughing uncontrollably as if drunk.[4]

The Scots had lost 3,000 killed and around 10,000 prisoners. Amazingly, no more than 40 of the English had been killed, some authorities putting the loss as low as twenty. It was an astonishing result brought about partly by the discipline and fighting spirit of Cromwell's soaked and disease-ridden soldiers and partly by the masterly way in which he brought superior numbers to bear against first one part of the Scots army and then the next.

IT IS SOMETIMES SAID that Cromwell had been outmanoeuvred by Leslie, that he was on the point of ordering a dangerous and humiliating retreat and was only saved by the idiocy of the Scottish clergy who forced Leslie to abandon his impregnable position and fight at a grave disadvantage. This is far from being the case. It is true that Leslie had frustrated Cromwell's first two attempts to bring him to battle and that he had occupied a strong position on Doon Hill. But by early September Leslie's men were half-starved and could not have stayed in this exposed position for much longer because of the lack of an effective supply system and adequate cover. Leslie's options were either to leave Doon Hill and attack, or to leave it and retreat. Pressure from the clergy and from his own officers may have influenced him to adopt the first option, but in any case it seemed a good bet.

By contrast Cromwell had some shelter for his men around Dunbar and could in the short term be supplied by the fleet. He was thus in a position to take advantage of any opportunity that Leslie might offer, while Leslie's options were being steadily eroded by the circumstances in which he found himself. Although some of Cromwell's officers may have felt that all was lost, he and his senior officers were far from despair. It was a measure of Cromwell's tactical ability that he was able to seize his opportunity when it came, forestall Leslie's attack and lead his men to victory. At Dunbar Cromwell proved himself a tactician of the first order in a way that he had never done before.

After the battle the English horse pursued the Scots for a good distance. It is said that before doing so they halted to sing Psalm 117, which would have delayed them no longer than it takes to tighten a girth.

Next day Lambert took seven regiments of horse and one of foot to occupy Edinburgh, which surrendered to him without further ado. Only the Castle held out until the end of the year. Cromwell arrived with the rest of the army three days later, having secured the port of Leith. Meanwhile Leslie retired rapidly on Stirling, concentrating his remaining men on holding the line of the river Forth, with particular reference to the bridge over the river at Stirling itself. Cromwell now had the port he needed and good shelter for his men and he was able to control most of the fertile lowland area between Edinburgh and Glasgow, thus giving his army access to supplies other than those brought in by sea. He had beaten and scattered Leslie's army and reduced its strength by over a half. The war was not yet finished, but the uncertain situation that had prevailed a few days earlier had been transformed as if by magic.

Cromwell gave his army one week to rest in Edinburgh. Then, leaving Colonel Lilburne and four regiments of foot in the capital, he set off to attempt Stirling before the winter put a stop to the campaign. Four days later he was outside Stirling, hoping that the garrison would surrender. This did not occur; a council of war decided that it was not worth assaulting the town, since even if captured it would be difficult to hold throughout the winter. Furthermore, as the town was on the right bank of the river, it would still be necessary to mount a further operation to capture the bridge giving access to the Highlands.

Instead the army withdrew to Linlithgow, about half-way between Stirling and Edinburgh. Cromwell then set about consolidating his position by fortifying Linlithgow and clearing his land lines of communication with England. Lambert and Monk were given the task of opening up the route to Berwick, along the east coast. Whalley, despite the fact that he had been slightly wounded in the recent battle, was to secure the road to Carlisle. Cromwell had already asked for reinforcements to be sent to restore the strength of his army.

For the rest of 1650 the English contented themselves with consolidating the position south of the river Forth. This involved clearing out a group of extreme Covenanters who had established themselves to the south of the river Clyde and bringing about the surrender of Edinburgh

Castle, which took place on 24 December after four days of bombardment by heavy guns brought in by the navy through Leith. It was also necessary to mop up some Scottish strong-points that had become isolated after the battle of Dunbar.

WHILST ALL THIS WAS going on, the Scots decided that they could no longer afford to exclude former Engagers and Royalists from their councils or their army. In January 1651 Charles II was crowned at Scone. Soon afterwards the new Duke of Hamilton, whose brother had been executed after the defeat of the Engagers in 1648, joined Argyll on the Council. The King, now largely freed from his bondage to the Kirk, set about building a new army. It is reported that in the early months of 1651 he was immensely energetic in raising troops. Gradually a new Royal army emerged which by June consisted of 16,000 foot and 6,000 horse directed by an astonishing array of generals. The King himself was commander-in-chief with the old Earl of Leven as his Lord General, although it was accepted that the lieutenant general, David Leslie, would exercise effective command. Nominally in command of regiments made up of former English Royalists was the King's close friend the Duke of Buckingham with the Presbyterian Edward Massey, who had distinguished himself as the Parliamentary commander in Gloucester in 1643, as his major general. Having been excluded from the New Model Army and ejected from the Long Parliament in Pride's Purge, Massey disliked Independents. Middleton commanded the horse.

During February a number of organisational changes took place on the English side. To start with, Fleetwood returned to London to join the Council of State and to take over command of the army in the south of England. Harrisson, also a member of the Council of State, was moved to the north-west to take charge of that area together with the west midlands, Hazlerigg at Newcastle remaining in charge of the north-east. Monk became governor of Edinburgh and was confirmed in the post that he had held since the previous July, that is to say lieutenant general of the ordnance. Meanwhile Cromwell, returning from an abortive attempt to occupy Fife to the north of the Firth of Forth, succumbed to exposure and a bad attack of dysentery and Lambert took over temporarily as commander of the army in Scotland. Cromwell gradually recovered but had relapses in April and May; so it was not until early June 1651 that he was ready to resume active command of the army. Lambert stood in for Fleetwood as second-in-command and on 6 May Deane was moved from his position in the fleet to become the major general.[5]

During this long period of comparative inactivity the morale of the army suffered and there were a number of cases of drunkenness and desertion. On the other hand its strength increased because of the arrival of reinforcements, so that by the middle of June it numbered around 21,000 men consisting of ten regiments of horse, fifteen regiments of foot and two of dragoons. In July Harrisson arrived in Edinburgh to confer with Cromwell regarding future operations. He then returned to England while Cromwell concentrated the army around Queensferry. From there Cromwell conducted a number of raids towards Stirling, establishing his headquarters at Torwood five miles south-south-west of Stirling. But these moves were essentially a diversion under cover of which Lambert transported 4,000 men in flat-bottom boats across the Firth of Forth to Inverkeithing. Cromwell, who had foreseen the likelihood of wanting to cross the Firth of Forth, had ordered these boats to be built at Newcastle before he entered Scotland the previous year.

The effect of Lambert's move was that Leslie despatched a large detachment under his major general of foot, Holborne, to deal with the incursion, which Cromwell was quick to observe. Cromwell's reaction was to advance with the main body of his force towards Stirling, whereupon Leslie sent orders to Holborne to return. As they turned about, Lambert, taking advantage of the confusion, attacked Holborne with devastating results. 2,000 Scots were killed and 1,400 were taken prisoner.[6] English losses were in single figures. Leaving eight regiments to watch Stirling, Cromwell brought the rest of the army back to Queensferry and took them across the river to join Lambert. Together they advanced on Perth, capturing it on 2 August.

The Scots lines of communication with the Highlands and with the

fertile plain running north-west from Perth to Aberdeen were now effectively cut. The main Scots army would have to abandon the strong
position it now occupied, either to attack Cromwell's superior force at
Perth, or to attack the eight regiments that Cromwell had left to watch
Stirling. If they adopted the second alternative the whole of Cromwell's
army would be closing in on them from behind. Neither of these alternatives was particularly attractive. There was one other alternative, which
was to take the unguarded road to Carlisle and then to invade England
in the hope that such a move would spark off so many Royalist
uprisings that the forces left to defend the realm would be swamped.

Contrary to the advice of David Leslie, who advocated a direct confrontation with Cromwell, King Charles decided to adopt the third
course. From the King's point of view all now depended on getting into
England and sparking off Royalist uprisings as quickly as possible, and
he set off with 3,500 horse and 7,500 foot. His army consisted of a
strange mixture of English and Scots, Highlanders and Lowlanders,
Covenanters and Engagers. There was plenty of scope for disagreement
from top to bottom. Buckingham disputed Leslie's right to command
once the army reached England, and the Duke of Hamilton generally
regarded Leslie as being too cautious. Leslie considered that the army
would not fight and Hamilton regarded the whole invasion as 'a des-
perate venture at which people were laughing';[7] the old Earl of Leven
wisely stayed in Scotland with Argyll.

IT IS CLEAR THAT CROMWELL and Harrison had foreseen a Scottish
invasion of England. Harrisson, who was at the time east of the
Pennines, moved west via Ripon and Skipton in order to delay the
advancing Scots. From Cromwell's point of view he needed to concentrate enough men to confront the King before English Royalists could
intervene: once the King was defeated, other Royalist uprisings could
be put down without difficulty.

Fleetwood and the Council of State equally understood this, since
elaborate measures were swiftly put into effect. While Cromwell brought
his army down from Scotland, Fairfax came out of retirement and with

2,500 militiamen secured Yorkshire and the all-important installations at Hull. Militia assembled at four other points to secure respectively East Anglia, London, the Welsh borders and the midlands. Further measures taken under the auspices of the Council of State included the mobilising of the London trained bands, 15,000 strong, the dispatch of ships to watch ports in France and the Spanish Netherlands, and the imposition of martial law in Lancashire, Cheshire, Shropshire and north Wales.

As soon as the Scots set off for England, Cromwell sent Lambert with 4,000 men to follow them and harry their communications. He left Monk with four regiments of horse and three of foot, some 5,500 men in all, to subdue Scotland. Cromwell himself, with nine regiments of foot and two of horse amounting to 10,000 men, travelled via Kelso towards Durham. Had he followed the Scots and Lambert he would have found the country bereft of supplies, which could in any case be more easily collected from counties such as Yorkshire and Nottinghamshire than from the poorer counties in the west. The eastern route was also more accessible to his ships.

The Scots crossed the border on 6 August, reaching Penrith on 8 August. Lambert reached Penrith the next day but instead of staying behind the Scots he turned east with most of his men, leaving Robert Lilburne to shadow the invaders. On 13 August Lambert met up with Harrisson, who had with him 3,000 horse and dragoons and three regiments of foot. They met a few miles north-east of Bolton and together moved rapidly to the bridge over the river Mersey at Warrington in the path of the Scottish army. Here they met the Cheshire and Staffordshire militia, which brought their combined force to between 12,000 and 13,000, slightly outnumbering the Scottish army, which had been steadily losing men from desertion ever since crossing the border. They then set about destroying the bridge to impede the Scots' advance, but while they were doing so the Scots, led by the King in person, arrived and attacked them.

It was no part of the overall plan for Lambert to bring on a battle with the Scots. Had he been successful the Scots would have retreated back into their own country and a further campaign would have been needed to dislodge them. But the Scots might well have been success-ful, since the country was unsuitable for the deployment of the horse regiments which made up two-thirds of Lambert's force. In this case there would have been little between the King and London except for militia, as Cromwell was still many miles away. Lambert therefore withdrew, letting the King move on to Worcester, where he arrived on 22 August.

Cromwell, who had marched via Durham, Catterick, Ripon, Chester-field and Coventry, now met up with Lambert and Harrisson at Warwick, bringing the combined force up to 22,000. It was a triumph of organi-sation and hard marching. Cromwell's contingent had covered the 300 miles from Edinburgh in three weeks at the astonishing rate of twenty miles a day. On 22 August the Council of State, having already ordered the fortifying of Gloucester, Ludlow, Hereford and Bristol, ceased co-ordinating measures to deal with the Scots invasion and passed all authority to Cromwell.

Meanwhile the King must have been disappointed by the response of English Royalists to his arrival. There were two reasons for their reluc-tance. First, although they objected to the commonwealth government, they objected to a greater extent to having a Scots army in the country. Second, they were conscious of the disaster that had overtaken the Scottish army in 1648 and of the fate of those Royalists who had risen for the King on that occasion. They therefore mainly stayed at home, except for the Earl of Derby, who brought 250 of his retainers from the Isle of Man. The King met the Earl on 16 August near the bridge at Warrington and asked him to go north into that part of Lancashire where his influ-ence was greatest and try and raise support for the cause. In this he had some success, raising 1,500 men. But a few days later he and his recruits were attacked and put to flight by Lilburne, whom Lambert had left to harass the rear of the Scottish army.

The King did not intend to stay long in Worcester, believing that his best course was to push on towards London. But his men were worn out by marching. They needed to rest and repair their equipment. But within a few days a move towards the south-east became impossible, because Cromwell had closed up sufficiently to threaten the flank of such a march and had secured the crossing over the Avon at Evesham. A move to the south was ruled out when Massey was refused entry to Gloucester, the city that he had defended so valiantly during the Civil War. A move to the west was equally impossible because Shrewsbury declined to receive the King's forces. Even a retreat to the north would have been perilous with Cromwell's vast army no more than 25 miles away. The Scots would have to fight at Worcester.

The King therefore set about defending the town against attack by restoring the walls and repairing a fort just outside the south-east corner of the city wall called Fort Royal. The path from the walls to the fort was also enclosed on either side by strong fortifications. In addition he sent parties to break down the bridges over the Teme at Bransford and Powick and the bridges over the Severn at Upton ten miles downstream of Worcester, and Bewdley fifteen miles upstream of Worcester. He also managed to recruit around 2,000 men, which went some way towards replacing recent losses from desertion, bringing his numbers back to around 12,000 men.

By 27 August Cromwell's army had edged closer to Worcester, its headquarters being at Evesham. Here Cromwell was joined by Fleetwood, who had been busy mobilising the militia in the midlands and in counties further south. Many of these detachments joined Cromwell over the next few days, as also did three of the new foot regiments recently raised for the New Model Army.

Next day Lambert was sent with some horse and dragoons to secure a bridgehead over the river Severn at Upton. On arrival he found the bridge badly damaged and the position held by a Royalist outpost, but in a sharp engagement in which Massey was wounded he drove out the opposition. Later Fleetwood arrived with a large force of horse and foot, and Lambert rejoined Cromwell and Harrisson. Soon afterwards the main part of the army moved to the high ground immediately to the east of Worcester, Cromwell's headquarters being in the village of Spetchley. By 2 September 1651 the situation was as follows: Fleetwood with 11,000 men was at Upton on Severn, where he mended the bridge.

Lilburne with a smaller detachment secured the bridge at Bewdley, where he was reinforced soon afterwards by some troops of militia horse sent by Fleetwood. Cromwell with the rest of the army was on the east bank of the river. Although he had been obliged to leave his heavy artillery in Scotland, he had brought with him his field guns, and both he and Lambert had been supplied with further artillery pieces by the Council of State during their march south.

The King, with most of the foot and three weak regiments of horse, was in Worcester itself, a walled city to the east of the river which had one gate leading to a bridge across the river at its north-west corner. There were three further gates: Fore Gate in the north wall, St Martin's Gate in the east wall and Sidbury Gate in the south-east corner, now covered by Fort Royal. Outside the walls to the north of the city on the east bank was David Leslie with the bulk of the Scottish horse, consisting of three detachments; one commanded by Hamilton and Buckingham, one by Middleton and one by a Dutchman called Druschke. Outside the city to the west, covering the junction of the Teme and the Severn and the site of the demolished Powick Bridge were three bodies of foot commanded by Major General Montgomery. He had one regiment of foot covering Powick Bridge, four regiments of foot covering the rest of the Teme up to its junction with the Severn, and four regiments of foot and three of horse in reserve.[8] The King was short of artillery support, having brought with him no more than sixteen very light cannon, good for nothing more than giving covering fire for an assault. There were also some heavier guns left by the Parliamentary garrison but some of these were probably spiked, that is to say, rendered unusable.

THE BATTLE OF WORCESTER was neither a regular seventeenth century battle in which both sides drew up with the foot in the centre and the horse on each flank, nor a conventional storming of a walled city, although it contained elements of both. Cromwell, with his massive superiority in numbers, was anxious to avoid the casualties likely to be suffered by a storm, but at the same time he wanted to be sure of completely destroying the King's army so as to put a final stop to all resistance

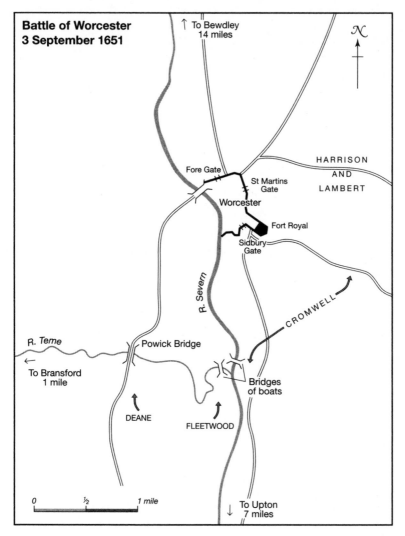

**Battle of Worcester
3 September 1651**

To Bewdley
14 miles

N

HARRISON
AND
LAMBERT

Fore Gate

St Martins
Gate

Worcester

Fort Royal

Sidbury
Gate

R. Severn

CROMWELL

R. *Teme*

Powick Bridge

To Bransford
1 mile

Bridges
of boats

DEANE

FLEETWOOD

0   ½   1 mile

To Upton
7 miles

throughout the British Isles. His chosen method for doing this, which he put to his council of war on 31 August, was to entice one part of the King's army after another into the open and swamp each in turn with vastly superior force. In order to achieve this plan he needed to be able to cross from one bank to the other of both the Severn and the Teme in close proximity to Worcester itself. For this purpose he ordered twenty large boats to be prepared at Upton which could be towed up the river and put in position as two pontoon bridges. One of these would be placed over the Severn just upstream of its junction with the Teme, and one across the Teme just upstream of its junction with the Severn. A ford above Powick Bridge would provide a further crossing until the bridge itself could be repaired. Cromwell's concept for the battle was both practical and original, but installing the bridges in the face of Scottish opposition would be a hazardous affair.

Early in the morning of 3 September Fleetwood moved north from Upton, having divided his force into a left and right wing. The right wing, which he commanded himself, consisted of four regiments of foot. Movement was slow because the men had to keep pace with the boats that were being towed up the Severn. For this reason they did not reach the line of the Teme until after 1 pm. On arrival Fleetwood pushed a 'forlorn hope' across the Teme in small boats to seize a bridgehead, behind which he established the pontoon bridge. He then secured enough of the bank of the Severn to get the larger bridge in place over that river. Despite great difficulty, both of these bridges were erected within half an hour of the sites being secured. The left wing, which was commanded by Deane, consisted of three regiments of foot and one of horse. With this force he crossed by the ford above Powick Bridge, after first dispersing a Royalist rearguard which was in the churchyard to the south of the bridge. A further detachment of horse and dragoons was sent to secure the bridge at Bransford.

Both wings were resisted vigorously by the Scottish foot, which retreated by bounds from hedge to hedge. And despite Fleetwood's overall superiority it began to look as if he would be unable to get enough men across the Teme to take on the foot regiments opposing him. The struggle could be seen by the King, who was watching from the tower of Worcester Cathedral, and by Cromwell, watching from the high ground to the east of Worcester. The King himself took some horse from Worcester out through the gate and over the bridge to support the foot regiment opposing the crossing above Powick Bridge. At about the same time Cromwell led his reserve consisting of two regiments of horse and four of foot, from the east of the Severn over the bridge of boats, and attacked the flank of the Scottish foot opposing Fleetwood's pontoon bridge over the Teme. After a hard fight the Scots gave way, thus jeopardising the position of the Scottish regiments opposing the crossing above Powick Bridge. The King with his horse returned to Worcester. Faced by the combined force of Cromwell and Fleetwood, the Royalist position west of the river gradually collapsed and the survivors of this part of the battle withdrew into Worcester.

While from the tower of the cathedral the King watched the gradual disintegration of his position to the west of the river, he decided that an attack on that part of Cromwell's army left on the hill to the east of the river stood a chance of success. Personally leading his troops out of Sidbury Gate and supported by a further detachment out of St Martin's Gate, he stormed up the hill under cover of fire from Fort Royal. He was joined in the attack by Middleton and by the three very weak regiments of horse under Hamilton and Buckingham, but at this time Leslie with the rest of the Scottish horse did not stir. This attack must have been launched at about 3.45 pm.

The Parliamentary force being attacked consisted of three regiments of foot and six regiments of horse of the New Model Army reinforced by eight militia regiments, making a total of perhaps 13,000 men, commanded by Lambert and Harrisson. The foot occupied positions behind hastily prepared barricades of wood and soil. The ensuing battle went on for about two hours, with the Royalists making some initial gains. Eventually Cromwell led his two regiments of horse back across the bridge of boats and joined the fray, and the Royalists were once more pushed back into the walled city, where considerable confusion resulted from the heavy concentration of men in a confined space. By this time many had been killed and wounded, including the Duke of Hamilton. Leslie, who had failed to support the attack when he might have made a useful contribution, now appeared, riding here and there to little effect, before withdrawing once more to his position to the north of the city.

The final stages of the battle began with three regiments of the Essex militia attacking Fort Royal. By sheer weight of numbers they fought their way over the outer fortifications and took control of the fort itself, at which point they turned the Royalist guns back on the defenders within the city. Soon, as darkness fell, regiments of the New Model army got inside the walls, where chaos reigned. For a time the King with his own regiment of horse fought on in the streets, but most of the foot regiments decided that the game was up. Some escaped northwards but many more were killed or captured, the prisoners being locked in the cathedral for the night. Harrisson, assisted by Whalley, was put in charge of the pursuit.

At some point the King left the city with a bodyguard of horse and disappeared. The excitement of his wanderings, culminating in his escape by sea to France, is illuminated by many stories of courageous and devoted loyalty. The gallantry and determination displayed by the King during the battle is less well known.

IT IS DIFFICULT TO KNOW how many Royalists were killed during the fighting and how many were killed afterwards by Cromwell's men scouring the countryside. Other fugitives died at the hands of local people who had been infuriated by the looting of the Scots as they marched to Worcester. It would seem that about 2,500 were killed and about 6,500 taken prisoner.

The few that straggled back to Scotland would have found little comfort, because by the time that they got there, Monk had established complete control of the country having occupied Stirling on 14 August. Having lost both Stirling and Perth, the Committee of Estates and the General Assembly met together at a village fifteen miles north-west of Dundee, where they were surprised and captured by a party of horse sent by Monk. This one action disposed of most of the Scottish leaders in Church and state, including the Earl of Leven. On 1 September Monk took Dundee by storm. Thereafter he established garrisons in Ayr and Leith in the Lowlands and in Perth, Inverlochy and Inverness in the Highlands. Soon afterwards the Council of State imposed a Declaration of Union with Scotland, abolishing its independent institutions and bringing its legal system into line with England.[9] From then until the Restoration in 1660, Scotland was governed from London. Leslie and the old Earl of Leven were incarcerated in the Tower with Middleton and Massey, both of whom escaped. Leven was released to please Queen Christina of Sweden in 1653, but Leslie remained in custody until the Restoration.

CASUALTIES IN CROMWELL's army were surprisingly low, considering the length and intensity of the fighting. The total killed did not exceed 200, which fully justified his concept for the battle, particularly his desire to avoid carrying out an attack on the city until he had effectively destroyed the King's army. Having made a thoroughly good if unconventional plan, he carried it out with faultless efficiency, committing his reserve at the right moment and then withdrawing it for further use when the situation required it. Certainly he had a vast preponderance of numbers, thanks mainly to his own strategic planning, but the King also had a strong position and troops who proved capable of great feats of courageous resistance, contrary to Leslie's forecast that they would not fight. Cromwell's total victory on the day was due largely to his tactical skill and his ability to control his widely spread forces. Of course great credit is due to the fighting qualities of his men and the ability of his experienced subordinate commanders to work together as a team. No more perfect instrument of military power than the New Model Army, as it was on 3 September 1651, has ever fought on English soil. Cromwell arrived back in London on 12 September to a well-deserved hero's welcome. Although he remained Lord General, his days as an operational commander were over.

9 · Epilogue and Assessment

Cromwell died exactly seven years after the battle of Worcester. For the first year and a half he contented himself with carrying out his duties as Lord General and by fulfilling his role as a member of the Council of State. Then in April 1653 he took some soldiers down to the Palace of Westminster and turned out the Rump. For the remainder of his life he governed the country.

He was now in a position to consummate his ambition of leading the English into the paths of godliness. Unfortunately the majority of his countrymen did not want to embrace his brand of godliness, which might not have mattered had he been content to coerce them into religious conformity. But, to start with at least, he wanted to do it by consent, which caused him to set up a nominated 'Parliament of Saints', soon dissolved. It was followed by two more Parliaments, each of which had to be dismissed because in various ways it was undermining the army. This was something Cromwell could not permit, because in the last resort only the army could secure the Independents, who underpinned his rule. Eventually he was forced back onto ruling through the army, dividing the country up into eleven major generals' commands. An advantage of this system was that the taxes that he needed to maintain the army and to support his foreign policy were collected promptly. And

Cromwell wrung more money out of the long-suffering people of England than any previous monarch had succeeded in doing.

By the time Cromwell died, the people of England were longing for relief from the heavy taxation and extraordinary laws abolishing all sorts of activities, from the celebration of Christmas to horse racing, including football, dancing round the maypole, and going to the play. Adultery carried the death penalty. Within nine months of his death the whole republican edifice collapsed. Thanks largely to General Monk the survivors of the Long Parliament were recalled and the King was invited to return and 'enjoy his own again'. His arrival in the kingdom was accompanied by great rejoicing: godliness was on the way out.

For most of the next 200 years Cromwell's reputation was attacked by republicans, who saw his seizure of supreme power in 1653 as having destroyed the Commonwealth. It was attacked by almost everyone else on the grounds that he had been influential in overturning the country's accepted constitutional arrangements, which had evolved over the centuries. But in the first half of the nineteenth century certain liberal elements turned all this round and presented him as a purveyor of freedom and even as the founder of our democratic institutions. Considering the record of events between 1646 and 1658, they must have had some difficulty in getting this line accepted, but they evidently succeeded to some extent, because in 1899[1] his statue was placed outside the very Parliament that he as Lord General had forcibly sent packing.

Fortunately it is no part of this book's purpose to examine Cromwell's performance as head of state. It is with some relief therefore that further examination of his activities after the battle of Worcester can be abandoned and attention concentrated on an assessment of his performance as a military commander. Only one thing remains to be said about him as the ruler of the country, and that is that the overwhelming power that he then possessed, together with the forcefulness of his personality, still colours the way in which his military exploits are regarded. Whether he ruled as a hero or as a massive destructive force, people have difficulty in visualising his military exploits as being conducted on any lesser scale. It is for this reason that he is sometimes credited with an unnatural insight into the way in which armies operate, at a time when he was still learning how to handle a troop of horse. Although as late as the end of the first Civil War in 1646 he had no experience of commanding an army in the field, there are still people who regard him as the chief military opponent of Charles I. They seem to ignore the fact that it was Essex, Waller, Manchester and Fairfax who commanded Parliament's armies and not by any stretch of the imagination Oliver Cromwell. In attempting to assess him as a military commander it is worth bearing this in mind.

IN THE SEVENTEENTH CENTURY a commander often had to raise, train and sometimes even equip his army before he could use it. This applied to all Parliament's armies between 1642 and the formation of the New Model Army in April 1645. When in 1643 Cromwell raised his regiment of horse, known to history as the Ironsides, his contribution became important because of the care with which he selected his officers, the degree of discipline that he enforced, and the intensity of training that he gave to his regiment. On becoming Manchester's lieutenant general in 1644 he was able to extend his influence to all the regiments of horse in the Eastern Association army. And throughout these two years he underpinned their discipline and training by selecting officers and men who broadly shared his religious views, thereby producing a very close-knit body of horsemen. Of course at this time it was only Cromwell's regiments of horse that embodied the idea of the close-knit, well-disciplined group sharing a common brand of religion. Manchester's foot regiments, though well led and trained by Crawford, were by no means a tightly knit group since some were commanded and influenced by men who shared Crawford's Presbyterian outlook, whilst others were being deliberately taken in another direction by colonels encouraged by Cromwell.

In 1645 it was Fairfax, not Cromwell, who formed the New Model Army from elements of all Parliament's old armies, and he was determined to avoid religious strife within his force. Realising that, contrary to Parliament's official position, Independents were likely to be more assertive than Presbyterians, he selected them at the expense of the Presbyterian and Scottish influence. When Cromwell arrived to be his second-in-command it became certain that the spirit of Cromwell's former regiments of horse would spread throughout the army on the wings of the Independents, although it would take several years to do so. Thereafter, right up to the Restoration in 1660, the cohesiveness of the New Model Army, based on strict discipline, good training and the Calvinism of the Independents, held fast. Any officer placed in command of a part of it, whether Cromwell himself, or Ireton, or Lambert, or Monk, would be able to rely on a basic core of trained and disciplined troops. Fairfax raised the New Model Army, and its victories in 1645 and 1646 were his own. But by 1648 its spirit was Cromwell's, and it remains one of Cromwell's chief claims to fame that he should have inspired such an effective and formidable force.

HIS OTHER MAIN CLAIM to fame is of course his success as a wartime commander. In order to assess this it is necessary to consider Cromwell's personal qualifications for command, after which his performance can be analysed.

Without doubt, the first qualification that a commander needs is knowledge of the job. This involves accumulating and retaining basic facts and being in a position to exploit them by clear thinking and accurate expression. At the start of the Civil War in 1642 the 43-year-old Cromwell had no military understanding in terms either of experience or of study. He was therefore obliged to pick it up as he went along. In collecting the necessary knowledge Cromwell was fortunate in working with professionals from whom he could learn, such as Crawford, Meldrum and Thomas Fairfax. And although Manchester was no professional, he knew as a *grand seigneur* how to extract the sinews of war from an area, thereby ensuring sound administrative backing for his army. The lessons that Cromwell learnt from Manchester stood him in good stead in Ireland and Scotland.

A major difficulty arises when considering whether Cromwell had the ability to think clearly on military matters. Because in his letters and speeches he often describes himself as waiting on God to show him the solution to a particular problem, it would be easy to think that he was indecisive, or slow to make up his mind. But in practice he usually acted in plenty of time. Like everyone else, he added up the pros and cons of a situation in an attempt to determine the best course of action and during this time, being totally devoid of vanity, he was fully prepared to gather the views of others. The only difference was that when the solution presented itself to him, he put it down to God. This not only saved him from wondering whether he had reached the right decision, but it also gave him the confidence to feel that those reaching a different conclusion were wrong. When it came to expressing himself militarily, in marked contrast to some of his political utterances, he was not only clear and accurate but also persuasive and sometimes inspiring. By the end of the first Civil War, after four years, continuous operational service, Cromwell had amassed enough basic knowledge and experience to command an army in the field.

But the collection of knowledge combined with an ability to think and express oneself clearly is not the only quality needed by a commander. He also needs vast amounts of physical energy so that he can push himself and his followers to the very limits of their endurance when there is anything to be gained from it, and he needs mental energy so as to keep turning things over in his mind. Cromwell certainly had the will for this, but he started his military career at an advanced age and was always older than most of the commanders with whom he was working. For example, he was nine years older than Monk, twelve years older than Crawford, thirteen years older than Thomas Fairfax, nineteen years older than Fleetwood and twenty years older than Lambert. Furthermore, in his early life he had been subject to fits of depression, and neither his age nor his depression provided an ideal background for campaigning in the middle of the seventeenth century when dysentery, malaria and plague added to the debilitating effects of exposure to the elements. But Cromwell was upheld by the feeling that he rode with God and that God would look after him. As a result he managed to keep going at a terrific rate for two or three months at a time, after which he needed to recuperate. On balance, Cromwell was not ideally suited either physically or temperamentally to the operational command of an army, but by sheer force of character he was able to carry it off.

Another quality that a commander needs is courage, so that he can put himself in the best place to see what is going on and control events. He also needs it to encourage his troops by his example. Cromwell's form of courage was for the most part of the practical variety. He was invariably well placed to carry out his function, although he was not always in front of the front rank as, let us say, Gustavus Adolphus would have been. On the other hand, if an attack looked like flagging he would lead in the reserve in person and fight with them until the situation was restored. On one occasion, in the initial charge at Marston Moor when he received a slight wound, his courage was questioned. But it seems certain that it was the work of a mischief-maker who objected either to Cromwell's religious leanings or to the fact that he was receiving excessive credit for his part in the battle. Overall, it is clear that Cromwell showed steady courage throughout his military career through many encounters with the enemy and that in this department he was in every way fully qualified as a military commander in the various ranks in which he served.

As a brave and energetic man who had built up a detailed knowledge of a commander's job during the first Civil War, and as one whose confidence was underpinned by his belief that God was with him at every turn, Cromwell deserved, and got, the support of his officers and men when he started to exercise command in his own right during the second Civil War.

PLANNING INVOLVES RELATING the resources available – or capable of being made available – to the achievement of a particular aim. In making an operational plan, the first thing is to collect as much information as possible about the enemy, the terrain, and the condition and location of one's own troops. The next thing is to see what additional resources can be made available and how. It should then be possible to work out two or three different ways of combining these resources together for the achievement of the aim. In doing so, account needs to be taken of such things as the best way to take advantage of ground, the grouping of units, including the proportion to be held in reserve, and the timing of moves. Clearly the business of being able to provide food, powder and shot at the time and place required, is important and often determines the rest. When two or more possible courses have been identified, all that remains is to chose one of the alternatives which can then be elaborated into a plan.

Every campaign starts with an opening plan followed by a number of subsidiary plans, some of which may be battle plans. To take Cromwell's campaign in 1648 as an example, he first needed a plan to assemble his force and move it to Wales, taking under command Parliamentary regiments allocated to him on the way; in other words, it was largely a matter of movement and logistics. He then needed plans for the reduction of Royalist strongholds, which involved collecting information about the enemy and making decisions as to which of his regiments should attack Tenby and which should besiege Pembroke. Another movement and logistic plan was needed to move his force north to repel the Scots, taking Lambert's regiments under his command as he came up with them. He then had to find out as much as he could about the Scottish advance to decide on his overall plan for dealing with it, and finally he needed a number of battle plans as he overtook and engaged the various parts of their force.

Throughout the three campaigns that he fought as an independent commander, Cromwell's strategic arrangements were particularly notable for the extent to which he foresaw his future requirements and for the way he set about obtaining the resources he needed. The prominent use that he made of the Parliamentary navy to supply his armies and to move his heavy artillery was also unusual. He avoided the delays caused by regiments foraging locally for their sustenance by moving supplies in wagons if he could not supply them by sea. His greatest success in strategic terms was the concentration outside Worcester of forces from Edinburgh, the north of England, and the midlands and the south. The speed with which this was accomplished was astonishing and was responsible for bottling the Scots up so that they could neither advance nor retire in safety. It stands comparison with Napoleon's concentration at Ulm in 1805. Some of the credit belongs to Fleetwood and the Council of State, who were managing affairs in the midlands and south of England while Cromwell was marching south from Scotland.

Cromwell's tactical plans were often extremely daring, as for example his decision to come in on the flank of Hamilton's advance and his attack on Leslie at Dunbar. From a tactical point of view he consistently tried to squash one bit of his opponent's army after another by concentrating superior force against it. Even when much stronger, he seldom sought to attack his enemy's whole force at once, as had been the custom in the first Civil War in battles such as Edgehill or Naseby. A good reason for this was that maximum casualties to the enemy came about when a body of troops, whether horse or foot, broke. As soon as they turned tail, they had no defence against their pursuers and could be ridden down and killed with little risk. By overwhelming one part of the enemy's force after the other, he was often able to defeat them with disproportionately small number of casualties to his own men. This system worked well at Preston and Dunbar. It also worked at Worcester because by securing a crossing point over the river Severn he was able to reinforce his troops on the western side until the enemy were beaten there, before returning to the eastern bank to take part in the fighting on that side of the river. In each case, success depended on the enemy having laid out his own forces in such a way that one part could not come to the rescue of the threatened part before the damage was done.

On balance, his plans for capturing fortified towns were more conventional. He did however make good use of what would now be termed psychological warfare. This took the form of offering favourable terms for rapid surrender, with the alternative of annihilation should he be put to the trouble and expense of a storm. His conduct after the capture of Basing House and Drogheda ensured that no one took this threat lightly.

ALTHOUGH A COMMANDER's plans are important, the real test lies in implementing them. In this respect he needs to push his plan through in the face of the many difficulties that are bound to arise, but he also has to accept that he may have to change them if new developments require him to do so. A commander often comes under pressure to change his plans when things seem to be going wrong, in which case he has to judge whether to stick to his guns or try to achieve his aim in a different way. Reaching the right conclusion requires great strength of will and sound judgement, because he has not only to overcome the enemy but also to carry his own side with him. In the seventeenth century, commanders usually held a council of war before the start of each new phase of an operation in which they listened to the views of their subordinates. Cromwell had taken part in many such councils when Fairfax was commanding and must have noticed that although Fairfax listened carefully to what was being said, he sometimes acted against the views of the majority. By comparison, Cromwell always tried to get his council to back him, even going to the extent of getting someone else to put forward his view so that he could appear to be supporting them rather than putting up the idea himself. But once a decision was taken, he was very determined to see it through.

In battle Cromwell usually let his subordinate commanders get on with their appointed tasks without getting too closely involved himself. But he kept a close eye on events in order to commit his reserve at the right moment in the right place. At that point he might march with them to ensure that they went to the right place, or if they were already there, he might put himself at their head for a short time to ensure that they were making the most of their opportunity. But he would disengage himself as soon as possible in order to return to where he could control the battle as a whole. In all of this he was greatly assisted by the fact that his immediate subordinates were competent men with plenty of battle experience. Because of this, Cromwell was able to anticipate the methods used by commanders such as Marlborough or Wellington rather than adopt the ways of the great men of his day such as Condé, Gustavus Adolphus or Prince Rupert. Fairfax, who commanded the New Model Army before it was as well established and trained as it was during Cromwell's campaigns, was always in the thick of his battles and was frequently wounded. Cromwell suited his method of command precisely to the situation in which he found himself, which was greatly to his credit.

The suggestion that in his whole military career he never suffered a reverse is a bit far-fetched. For example, Cromwell's failure at the second battle of Newbury did as much to prevent Parliament from winning that battle as his charge at Marston Moor prevented it from losing that one. But in the three campaigns in which he commanded the army, he never suffered defeat in a battle. He certainly had setbacks, such as the initial repulse of his force at Clonmel, but they did not affect the outcome of any campaign. Furthermore, in each of his campaigns, he started by being considerably outnumbered by his opponent. On the other hand neither the Duke of Hamilton nor the Marquess of Ormonde was even remotely competent as a soldier. Leslie was a different matter, but after Dunbar his influence in the Scottish army declined so that by the time of the invasion of England he was being largely ignored.

In Ireland and in Scotland, Cromwell's biggest problem was keeping his army supplied and healthy, and in these matters his foresight combined with his political influence proved adequate to the task. In all his military activities from 1649 onwards his political position as an influential member of the Council of State proved invaluable when it came to financing his campaigns.

IT IS DIFFICULT TO COMPARE Cromwell with the great captains of history. For one thing he never fought as the commander of an army against a really high-class enemy commander. Nor did he ever have to plan or execute a campaign with an ally. On the other hand, when in command he planned his campaigns and fought his battles in ways that could hardly have been more effective. In all three of his campaigns the aims were totally and triumphantly achieved. In addition, he did it all with a minimum expenditure of his men's lives.

To this must be added what was possibly his greatest achievement: the infusing of the New Model Army with his spirit, thus making it the superb instrument of military might that it became, so that any competent commander could use it to good purpose. And although the New Model Army was largely disbanded at the Restoration, the principles of discipline, training and sound logistic backing were adopted by Charles II's small standing army and have survived to the present day. Before Cromwell, armies were raised for a specific purpose, used and disbanded with nothing to show for their existence. Since Cromwell, although regiments have been raised and disbanded, there has been a thread of continuity running through the army as a whole. In the same way that Blake is regarded as the father of the Royal Navy, so should Cromwell be regarded as the father of the British army.

Appendix

Regiments of horse and foot in Ireland, 5 August 1649

Regular regiments of horse
Ireton's
Horton's (formerly Butler's)
Reynolds's (raised in Kent in 1648)

Regular regiments of foot
Hewson's (formerly Pickering's)
Ewer's (formerly Hammond's)
Deane's (formerly Rainsborough's)
Cooke's (formerly Tichborne's Tower guards)

Regiments of horse raised in England for Ireland in 1649
Cromwell's regiment of twelve troops, which became two regiments during the campaign

Regiments of foot raised in England for Ireland in 1649
Venables's
Tothill's (intended for Londonderry)
Huncks's
Ireton's
Stubber's
Phayre's (intended for Munster)

Regiments of horse formed from the reorganisation of Jones's army:
Jones's
Coote's.

Regiments of foot formed from the reorganisation of Jones's Army:
Fenwick's
Castle's (taken by Slade when Castle killed at Drogheda)
Moore's.

Notes to the text

Foreword

1   JOHN CHILDS, *Warfare in the Seventeenth Century* (Cassell, 2001), p. 120.

Chapter 1

1   JOHN MORRILL (ed.), *Oliver Cromwell and the English Revolution* (Longman, 1990), pp. 25-33. This passage, written by Morrill himself, gives a more detailed account of these events, showing how Cromwell's reputation and material interests were affected.

2   HUGH TREVOR-ROPER, *Catholics, Anglicans and Puritans* (Fontana, 1989), p. 44 and fn.

3   SIR PHILIP WARWICK, *Memoirs of the Reign of King Charles I* (London, 1813), p. 273.

4   C.V.WEDGWOOD, *The King's Peace* (Collins, 1978), pp.130-2

Chapter 2

1   JOHN CRUSO, *Militarie Instructions for the Cavallrie* (1632), reprinted with notes and commentary by P. Young, (Kineton, The Roundwood Press, 1972).

2   SIR CHARLES FIRTH, *Oliver Cromwell and the Rule of the Puritans* (Oxford University Press) reprinted 1968, pp. 82-3.

3   PETER YOUNG, *Edgehill 1642* (Kineton, The Roundwood Press, 1967), pp. 319-20

4   JOHN BUCHAN, *Oliver Cromwell* (Hodder and Stoughton, 1934), p.158.

Chapter 3

1 SIR PHILIP WARWICK, *Memoirs of the Reign of King Charles I* (London, 1813), p. 278

2 For a discussion of this matter see FRANK KITSON, *Prince Rupert, Portrait of a Soldier* (Constable, 1994), pp. 115-116.

3 All three of the letter extracts in this paragraph are taken from PETER GAUNT, *Oliver Cromwell* (Blackwell, 1997), pp. 49-51, quoting PUBLIC RECORD OFFICE E 179/83/398; W.C.ABBOTT (ed.), *The writing and Speeches of Oliver Cromwell* (reprint 4 vols, Oxford, 1988), vol. 1 pp. 258-9.

4 LAURENCE SPRING, *The Regiments of the Eastern Association* (Stuart Press, 1998).

Chapter 4

1 JOHN GILLINGHAM, *Cromwell, Portrait of a Soldier* (Weidenfeld and Nicolson, 1976), pp. 64–5.

2 J.S.A. ADAMSON, in John Morrill (ed.), *Oliver Cromwell and the English Revolution* (Longman, 1990), pp. 58–9.

3 C.H. FIRTH, *Cromwell's Army* (Methuen, 1962), pp. 26-30.

4 JOHN WILLCOCK, *Life of Sir Henry Vane the Younger* (Saint Catherine Press, 1913), pp. 138–40.

5 PETER WENHAM, *The Great and Close Siege of York* (Kineton, The Roundwood Press 1970), p. 36.

6 PETER YOUNG, *Marston Moor 1644* (Kineton, The Roundwood Press 1970), p. 91.

7 The layout of both the allied and Royalist armies given in this and subsequent paragraphs is very much as given in YOUNG, *Marston Moor* pp. 94–9 (Royalists) and 101–6 (Allies).

8 YOUNG, *Marston Moor* pp. 240–5, reproducing Sir Thomas Fairfax 'A Short Memorial of the Northern Actions during the War there' and originally printed in *Stuart Tracts (1603-1693)* (Westminster, 1903).

9 YOUNG, *Marston Moor* p. 128 (Westminster) quoting *Memoirs of Denzil Lord Holles, 1699*, p. 16.

10 SIR CHARLES FIRTH, *Oliver Cromwell and the Rule of the Puritans* (Oxford University Press, 1968 reprint), p. 108.

11 JOHN KENYON, *The Civil Wars of England* (Weidenfeld and Nicolson, 1988), p. 115

12 EDWAD HYDE, EARL OF CLARENDON, *History of the Great Rebellion* ed. Roger Lockyer, (Oxford University Press for Folio Society, 1967), p. 242.

13 LAURENCE SPRING, in *The Campaigns of Sir William Waller's Southern Association* (Stuart Press, 1997) p.48 suggests that the attack did not go in until 4.40 pm, by which time the sun had already set.

Chapter 5

1 For a more detailed and scholarly account of these manoeuvres see the chapter by JOHN ADAMSON, 'Oliver Cromwell in the Long Parliament', in John Morrill (ed.), *Oliver Cromwell and the English Revolution* (Longman, 1990), pp. 62-3.

2 JOHN GILLINGHAM, *Cromwell – Portrait of a Soldier* (Weidenfeld and Nicolson, 1976), p. 80.

3 Ibid, p. 81.

4 The layout of the two armies as given here is mainly taken from PETER YOUNG, *Naseby 1645* (Century Publishing, 1985), chapters 13 and 14.

5 For a discussion of this contentious point see FRANK KITSON, *Prince Rupert, Portrait of a Soldier* (Constable, 1994), p. 243 .

6 There is a difference of opinion among historians as to the exact site of this action based on the possibility that the Long Sutton to Langport road might have crossed the Rhyne Wagg some hundreds of yards further to the north. MARTYN BENNETT, in *Travellers Guide to the Battlefields of the English Civil War* (Webb and Bower, 1990), p. 163 places it even further to the north, where the road from Somerton to Langport crosses the Rhyne Wagg.

Chapter 6

1 IAN GENTLES, *The New Model Army* (Blackwell, 1992), p. 88.

2 SIR CHARLES FIRTH, *The Regimental History of Cromwell's Army* (Clarendon Press, 1940), vol 1, p. xx.

3 GENTLES, *New Model Army* pp. 231-4.

4 Ibid., p. 261.

Chapter 7

1 Quoted by SIR CHARLES FIRTH, *Oliver Cromwell and the Rule of the Puritans in England* (Oxford University Press, 1968 reprint), p. 229.

2 D. M. R. ESSON, *The Curse of Cromwell* (Leo Cooper, 1971), p. 87.

3 SIR CHARLES FIRTH, *The Regimental History of Cromwell's Army* (Clarendon Press, 1940) p. xxii.

4 TOM REILLY, *Cromwell, an Honourable Enemy* (Phoenix Press, 2000), pp. 69–72

5 GENTLES, *The New Model Army* (Blackwell, 1992) p. 361.

6 ESSON, *The Curse of Cromwell* p. 121.

7. GENTLES, *The New Model Army* p. 368.

Chapter 8

1   MAURICE ASHLEY, *Cromwell's Generals* (Jonathan Cape, 1954), pp. 23–4.

2   IAN GENTLES, *The New Model Army* (Blackwell, 1992), p. 388.

3   ASHLEY, *Cromwell's Generals*, p. 34.

4   GENTLES, *The New Model Army,* p. 397, quoting JOHN AUBREY, *Miscellanies upon Various Subjects* (Ottridge, 1784), pp. 160–1.

5   ASHLEY, *Cromwell's Generals*, p. 49.

6   GENTLES, *The New Model Army* p. 403.

7   MALCOLM ATKIN, *Cromwell's Crowning Mercy* (Sutton Publishing, 1998), pp. 12, 15, 17.

8   Ibid., pp. 171–3 gives details on which this deployment is based.

9   Ibid. p. 151.

Chapter 9

1   BLAIR WORDEN, *Roundhead Reputations* (Allen Lane The Penguin Press, 2001), p. 296. Chapters 8, 9 and 10 of this book trace in some detail the ways in which Cromwell's reputation has fluctuated over the years.

Index

Grey of Groby, Lord 48, 55–9
Grey of Warke, Lord 48, 52, 59

Hamilton, Duke of 150–1, 153–4, 155–6, 223
Hampden, John 17, 30, 43, 52
Harrisson, Thomas 109, 188, 202, 203, 204, 205, 211, 212
Hazlerigg , Sir Arthur 71, 100, 202
Hereford 125–6
Hertford, Marquess of 49
Holles, Denzil 69, 91, 141
Hopton, Sir Ralph (1596–1652) 60–61, 105
Hull, siege of, 1643 65, 66
Huntingdon 20, 52

Inchiquin, Lord 166, 169, 171, 184
Ireland 28–9, 164–7, 168–9, **172**, 183–4
    the Cromwellian Settlement 12, 184–5
    Cromwell's campaign 12, 169–83, 185–6, 223
    Cromwell's forces, 1649 227
    King tries to arrange truce 46
    and the second Civil War 147, 152–3
Ireton, Henry 50, 109, 112, 141–2, 145–6
    demands abolition of the monarchy 160–61
    in Ireland 181, 183–4
    at Naseby 116, 120

James VI and I, King of Scots and King of England and Ireland (1566–1625) 18
Jones, Colonel Michael 166, 170, 176, 181

Kent 148
Kilkenny, siege of, 1650 181–2
King's Lynn 52, 65

Lambert, Colonel 84, 188, 218
    Scottish campaign 193, 197, 199, 203, 205–6
    the second Civil War 149–50, 151, 158, 158–9
    at Worcester 207, 211
Langdale, Sir Marmaduke 147

Langport, battle of, 1645 127–9, **128**
Laud, William, Archbishop of Canterbury (1573–1645) 23, 25, 26
Leicester, siege of, 1645 111–2, 125
Leslie, Major General David 77, 83, 88, 91, 150, 212, 213, 223
    and Cromwell's Scottish campaign 192–3, 194, 196, 197, 200, 201, 202, 203, 204
    at Worcester 208, 211
Levellers, the 139, 142, 145, 167
Leven, Earl of 77, 150, 202, 204, 212–3
    at Marston Moor 81, 86, 87, 91
Lincoln 77, 92, 94
Lincolnshire 48, 52, 54, 64, 67, 76, 77
Lindsey, Earl of 34
Linlithgow 201
logistics 36, 219–20
London 44, 46, 141, 146
London trained bands 32, 44, 205
Long Parliament 26–30
Lostwithiel 93
Lowestoft 52
Lucas, Sir Charles 10, 42
Lumsden, Major General Sir James 77, 83, 88, 91
Lyme Regis 93

Manchester, Edward Montague, 2nd Earl of (1602–71) 9, 59–60, 63, 64, 66, 71, 216, 217
    Cromwell's criticism of 103–4
    failure to follow up second Newbury 100, 101
    falls out with Cromwell 94–5
    at Lincoln 92, 94
    at Marston Moor 80, 81, 83, 86, 87
    reorganises Eastern Association administrative system 73
    at second Newbury 95, 96, 98, 99, 100
    at York 76, 77, 78
Marston Moor, battle of, 1644 11, 80–92, **83**, 101, 219, 223
Massey, Edward 139, 202, 207, 212–3
Maurice, Prince 10, 93, 96–8, 100, 105, 110

DATE DUE
